THE GOSPEL ACCORDING TO DANIEL

A CHRIST-CENTERED APPROACH

BRYAN CHAPELL

BakerBooks

a division of Baker Publishing Group
Grand Rapids, Michigan

© 2014 by Bryan Chapell

Published by Baker Books
a division of Baker Publishing Group
P.O. Box 6287, Grand Rapids, MI 49516-6287
www.bakerbooks.com

Printed in the United States of America

Library of Congress Cataloging-in-Publication Data is on file at the Library of Congress, Washington, DC.

ISBN 978-0-8010-1611-0 (pbk.)

14   15   16   17   18   19   20   7   6   5   4   3   2   1

To the faithful people of Grace Presbyterian Church whose love of Scripture, the grace of the gospel, and my family provides constant encouragement and great joy in serving the One who comes in glory on the clouds of heaven to receive an everlasting kingdom for all peoples, nations, and languages.

Contents

Introduction

I f I were writing a regular introduction to the book of Daniel, I would inform readers that Daniel records the events and visions of his life more than five hundred years before the birth of Christ. I would add that Daniel and his people are in captive exile in Babylon at the time of his writing. Israel's wayward idolatries have led to this discipline from God that is also preparation for the nation's greater fruitfulness in the future. Finally, I would give some detail of the successive rulers under whom Daniel served and the successive kingdoms Daniel prophesied during his long years of captivity. These are important facts, and they can be researched at greater depth in any good study Bible or commentary.[1] But rehearsing these facts is not my purpose in writing this book.

My passion and privilege for the past three decades have been to help others see the presence of the gospel throughout Scripture. My contention has been that Christ's grace does not wait until the last chapters of Matthew to make its appearance but rather is the dawning light increasing throughout Scripture toward the day of the Savior. Jesus contends the same when, after his resurrection, he speaks to disciples on the road to Emmaus and "beginning with Moses and all the Prophets, he interpreted to them in all the Scriptures the things concerning himself" (Luke 24:27).

Of course, key questions for us are: (1) How do all the Scriptures bear witness to Christ? and (2) Why is this important?

How All the Scriptures Bear Witness to Christ

Christ-centered exposition of Scripture should not require us to reveal Jesus by some mysterious magic of allegory or typology. Rather, solid exposition should identify how every text functions in furthering our understanding of who Christ is, what the Father sent him to do, and why. The goal is not to make Jesus magically appear in every detail of Hebrew history or prophecy but rather to show where every text stands in relation to the ultimate revelation of the person and/or work of Christ. To do this we must discern the message of grace unfolding throughout Scripture, of which Jesus is the culmination.

Our goal as expounders of God's Word—to state it again—is not to force every text to mention Jesus, but to show how every text furthers our understanding of God's grace, of which Christ Jesus is the ultimate revelation. In many and varied ways the Lord shows us that he provides what humanity cannot provide for itself, including what he spiritually requires. As he provides food for the hungry, rest for the weary, strength for the weak, faithfulness for the unfaithful, and a blessed future for those with a sinful past, we gain more and more understanding of the merciful nature of our God. Both the dawning and the full light of grace prepare and enable the people of God to understand who Jesus is, what he does, and the honor due him.

Keeping Sight of the Witness of Grace

This Christ-centered approach to discerning the gospel in all Scripture becomes important when we read Daniel's accounts because his amazing little book has so much else to capture our attention. Daniel combines classic stories of epic heroism with spectacular revelations of the power of God to orchestrate future events for his ultimate glory. As a consequence, we may not see the gospel truths of Daniel if we fall into two common but errant approaches to the book: making Daniel the object of our hero worship or making Daniel the subject of our debates.

Avoiding Hero Worship

We are tempted to make Daniel the object of our worship in the first half of the book, which is largely a biography of his life. Daniel's courage and faithfulness in a land of cruelty and captivity can easily tempt us to make him the primary hero of the text. In doing so we neglect Daniel's own message: God is the hero. God saves a sinful and weak people; he preserves young men from impurity and old men from lions; he answers prayer and interprets dreams; he exalts the humble and humbles the proud; he vindicates the faithful and vanquishes the profane; he rescues covenant-forsaking people by returning them to the land of the covenant; and he promises a glorious future to those with a sinful past. Daniel acts on the grace God repeatedly provides, but God is always the One who first provides the opportunity, resources, and rescue needed for Daniel's faithfulness. If we reverse the order and make God's grace dependent on Daniel's goodness, then we forsake the gospel message that Daniel is telling and produce the hero worship of adventure tales rather than the divine worship of the gospel according to Daniel.

Maintaining Redemptive Focus

The second half of the book contains prophetic content that can make us susceptible to a second interpretive error: making Daniel primarily the subject of our debates about eschatology (the end time). The book of Daniel contains some of the most amazing and detailed prophesies in all of Scripture. Centuries and millennia in advance, Daniel predicts events as momentous as the succession of vast empires and relates details as precise as the symptoms of a disease that will slay a future king. Daniel also speaks about the future of the people of God in visions that are hard to understand and that relate to some events still future to us.

These are incredibly important prophesies, but we can become so stressed and combative about the interpretation of particular aspects that we neglect the prophet's central message: God will rescue his people from the miseries of their sin by the work of the Messiah. The righteous will be vindicated, evil will be destroyed, and the covenant blessings will prevail because Jesus will reign. All this occurs *not* because humans control their fate or deserve God's redemption but because the God of grace uses his sovereign power to maintain his covenant promises forever. This gospel according to Daniel should give us courage against our foes, hope in our distress, and perseverance in our trials—if we will not let every prophetic mystery derail us from the main message of prevailing grace.

Why the Witness to Grace Is So Important

To Keep the Message Christian

Why should we take care to maintain focus on the gospel of grace in our interpretations of Daniel? The first reason is to keep our messages Christian. We are not Jews, Muslims, or Hindus whose followers may believe our status with God is determined by our performance. We believe that Christ's finished work is our only hope. To make Daniel simply an example of one who fulfills God's moral imperatives and thus earns his blessing is essentially an unchristian message. Apart from God's justifying, enabling, and preserving grace, no human can do what God requires to be done. Jesus said, "Apart from me you can do nothing" (John 15:5). Interpretations of Daniel devoid of the enabling grace of Christ—even in its Old Testament forms of unmerited divine provision—implicitly deny the necessity of Christ.

A key question that we must ask ourselves at the end of every exposition of Scripture is, "Would my message have been acceptable in a synagogue or mosque?" Was our core message only "Be as good as this biblical hero," or "Be better than other people," or, at least, "Be better than you were last week"? If any of these are the primary message we take from Daniel, then we inevitably leave people with the understanding that their status before God depends on their performance. That message is inevitable in virtually every other faith, but cannot represent the Christianity of the Bible.

To Provide the Power of Grace

The power of grace to stimulate love for God is the ultimate reason we preach redemptive interpretations of Scripture. Sermons marked by consistent adulation of the mercy of God continually fill the Christian heart with more cause to love God. This love becomes the *primary* motivation for Christian obedience as hearts in which the Spirit dwells respond with love for their Savior. This is why the apostle Paul could say the grace of God actually is "training us to renounce ungodliness and worldly passions, and to live self-controlled, upright, and godly lives in the present age" (Titus 2:11–12).

Our teaching and preaching should be designed to fuel a preeminent love for God that makes doing his will the believer's greatest joy (2 Cor. 5:9), knowing that this joy is the strength for fulfilling our responsibilities (Neh. 8:10). The great Protestant Reformers reminded us that the task of those who teach and preach the Bible is not to harangue or guilt parishioners into "slavish duty" but rather to fill them up with "a childlike love" for God by extolling the wonders of his grace (Westminster Confession of Faith, XX.i). Consistent proclamation of motivating and enabling grace drives despair, pride, and disobedience from the Christian life. Despair dies when we know our failures are not greater than the grace of God. Pride has no place when we know our performance is not the basis of his love for us. Disobedience departs when our greatest desire is to walk with the Savior who loved us and gave himself for us.

Thus, emphasizing the grace of all the Scriptures is not simply an interpretive scheme required by the Bible's overarching themes; it is regular exposure of the heart of God to ignite love for him in the heart of believers. We preach grace in order to fan into flame zeal for our Savior. Our informational goals remain in place (we need to teach people what to believe and what to do), but relational and spiritual goals remain primary. We never neglect expounding the gospel truths that pervade Scripture in order to fill the hearts of believers with love for God that drives out love for the world. For without love for the world, its temptations and disappointments have no power. We simply are not tempted to do what we have no desire to do or to despair over what we do not hold most dear. Grace leads to godliness. That is why it is so important to find and flesh out the gospel of grace in the book of Daniel.

If we are able to discern that the prophet's heroism is really a gift of God, and if we come to see that Daniel's prophecies are really a means of encouraging us to not be overwhelmed by the discouragements of a broken world—because God is unrelentingly working his redemption plan for his wayward people—then we will have discerned the good news of the gospel Daniel wanted us to know, even if we still have a few questions about his prophesies.

1

The Undefiled

—— DANIEL 1 ——

In recent years much of my time has been spent helping different generations of church leaders understand each other. An older generation came
of age during a time of a perceived Christian consensus in our nation. The
goal of many of those believers was to encourage the "moral majority" to
become active enough politically to control the institutions of our society. A
following generation matured in a time when Christian young people could
only perceive themselves as a minority in a pluralistic culture, and its leaders
have not sought to obtain control so much as credibility. For these younger
leaders the pressing question is, "How do we make Christianity credible to a
society that wants nothing to do with the faith of our fathers?" The Bible, with
great prior wisdom, prepares for the questions of such a younger generation
with the historical accounts of Daniel and his friends. They are young people
forced by a Babylonian invasion to leave their culture of majority faith and,
as captives, live their faith as a minority in a culture whose majority follows
a pagan pluralism. For Daniel to make the historic faith of Israel credible in
such a culture is an immense challenge that contains timely instruction for
us. How will he and his young friends be faithful among the faithless? The
answer is in living their convictions with undefiled courage such as we find in
the first chapter of Daniel:

In the third year of the reign of Jehoiakim king of Judah, Nebuchadnezzar king of Babylon came to Jerusalem and besieged it. And the Lord gave Jehoiakim king of Judah into his hand, with some of the vessels of the house of God. And he brought them to the land of Shinar, to the house of his god, and placed the vessels in the treasury of his god. Then the king commanded Ashpenaz, his chief eunuch, to bring some of the people of Israel, both of the royal family and of the nobility, youths without blemish, of good appearance and skillful in all wisdom, endowed with knowledge, understanding learning, and competent to stand in the king's palace, and to teach them the literature and language of the Chaldeans. The king assigned them a daily portion of the food that the king ate, and of the wine that he drank. They were to be educated for three years, and at the end of that time they were to stand before the king. Among these were Daniel, Hananiah, Mishael, and Azariah of the tribe of Judah. And the chief of the eunuchs gave them names: Daniel he called Belteshazzar, Hananiah he called Shadrach, Mishael he called Meshach, and Azariah he called Abednego.

But Daniel resolved that he would not defile himself with the king's food, or with the wine that he drank. Therefore he asked the chief of the eunuchs to allow him not to defile himself. And God gave Daniel favor and compassion in the sight of the chief of the eunuchs, and the chief of the eunuchs said to Daniel, "I fear my lord the king, who assigned your food and your drink; for why should he see that you were in worse condition than the youths who are of your own age? So you would endanger my head with the king." Then Daniel said to the steward whom the chief of the eunuchs had assigned over Daniel, Hananiah, Mishael, and Azariah, "Test your servants for ten days; let us be given vegetables to eat and water to drink. Then let our appearance and the appearance of the youths who eat the king's food be observed by you, and deal with your servants according to what you see." So he listened to them in this matter, and tested them for ten days. At the end of ten days it was seen that they were better in appearance and fatter in flesh than all the youths who ate the king's food. So the steward took away their food and the wine they were to drink, and gave them vegetables.

As for these four youths, God gave them learning and skill in all literature and wisdom, and Daniel had understanding in all visions and dreams. At the end of the time, when the king had commanded that they should be brought in, the chief of the eunuchs brought them in before Nebuchadnezzar. And the king spoke with them, and among all of them none was found like Daniel, Hananiah, Mishael, and Azariah. Therefore they stood before the king. And in every matter of wisdom and understanding about which the king inquired of them, he found them ten times better than all the magicians and enchanters that were in all his kingdom. And Daniel was there until the first year of King Cyrus. (Dan. 1:1–21)

Almost three decades after several people were killed because someone put cyanide in Tylenol bottles to blackmail the manufacturer, newspaper headlines announced that police might be closing in on the culprit. The story of the deadly contamination is a distant memory to most of us now, but when I was in seminary it was an immediate concern to a student friend of mine and his wife. She worked as a quality control inspector at a pharmaceutical company in order to support the family. One day, through mistaken procedures, a major order of syringes was contaminated and would not pass inspection. When the wife of my friend reported the contamination to her boss, he quickly computed the costs of reproducing the order and made a "cost-effective" decision: ship the order. He ordered her to sign the inspection clearance despite the contamination. She refused.

Because of government regulations, she was the only one that could sign the clearance. So the syringes did not ship that day. The next day, a Friday, the wife got a visit from the company president. He said that he would give her the weekend to think it over, but if the forms were not signed on Monday, her job would be in jeopardy.

In fact, much more than her job was in jeopardy. Because the wife's job was this couple's only means of support, the husband's education and ministry future were also in jeopardy. All their hopes, dreams, and family plans of many years could be shattered as a result of a choice to be made over the next two days. For this young couple, all the high-minded doctrine they had been receiving in seminary about God's attributes, power, and provision boiled down to one very concrete decision. Could they afford to remain undefiled from the contamination the world was urging them to approve? Was the witness of holiness worth what it would cost?

This couple's predicament was not unique to them, of course. In all ages God's people are pressured to pollute the purity of their dedication to God. The pressures come from an array of sources: bosses, finances, competitors, friends, relatives, and congregations, as well as our own desires for success and significance. This couple faced such pressures. You have faced them. Daniel and his friends faced them. These pressures face anyone who seeks to live an undefiled life in a world of sin. That is why the Bible, in order to help us face these pressures, speaks so plainly about the risks, reasons, and rewards of holiness.

The Risks of Holiness

The account of Daniel and his friends makes it clear that there are risks to holiness. The Bible is practical enough to tell us to play "heads-up baseball." Get prepared. Pay attention. You cannot do what your position in the culture requires if you do not know what is likely to come your way. And what is likely to come your way as a faithful believer is risk.

What Are the Risks?

The facts of Daniel's life are simple enough. He was a prisoner of war in Babylon. He had come from a noble family. But Babylon's conquest, deportation, and captivity of the people of Judah apparently dimmed any hope of power or honor that Daniel might have had. Although his future once looked bright, it now lay in dark shadows. Then came an unexpected ray of hope: King Nebuchadnezzar of Babylon wanted some young Israelites trained for government service, probably for the purpose of managing fellow captives. As a result, Daniel and other promising Jewish slaves began training for positions of honor and power. They faced the possibility of going from being the king's slaves to being in the king's governing service. All Daniel and his friends needed to do was to go along, accept the privileges offered, and then the future that had looked so bleak would be bright again. And, of course, Daniel needed to keep his head down to keep his head on. To question the king's decisions not only would jeopardize Daniel's future but, in pagan Babylon, also would jeopardize his life (1:10).

But Daniel *did* question. For reasons that are not entirely clear, Daniel believed he would defile himself if he took the meat and drink that were offered to him. It is possible that the food had been included in some practice of idolatry, but it is also possible that accepting the fine fare simply seemed wrong to Daniel in light of the suffering of the rest of Israel. At any rate, the Bible says, "Daniel resolved that he would not defile himself with the king's food, or with the wine that he drank. Therefore he asked the chief of the eunuchs to allow him not to defile himself" (1:8).

Some idea of the risk involved in such a request is made apparent in the response of the chief of the guards: "I fear my lord the king, who assigned your food and your drink; for why should he see that you were in worse condition than the youths who are of your own age? So you would endanger my head with the king" (1:10). Translation in plain English: "The king will chop my head off if I don't keep you—his prize captives—in good shape." Daniel responded, "OK, give us vegetables and water for ten days and see if we look any worse than the others" (1:12–13, paraphrase). Then the guard whom God had already caused to favor Daniel (1:9) agreed to this "vegan diet."

These facts are so familiar to us and so bathed in the aura of Sunday-school story time that we may no longer be able to connect with their reality. I cannot help but relate them to the accounts of John McCain in the 2008 presidential campaign. Regardless of political affiliation, everyone acknowledged that he was a true war hero. We should remember why. He was the son of a high-ranking naval officer, but he graduated fifth from the bottom of his class at the Naval Academy. The future looked bleak for such a graduate, so he took the risk and volunteered for combat duty as a Navy pilot in the Vietnam War. On his twenty-third mission, he was shot down. In the crash, he broke both arms and a leg. He was then captured and put in a primitive prison where his wounds could not properly heal. When his captors discovered the identity of his father—and that McCain was military "royalty"—they offered him the opportunity to be released, but only if he made certain compromises. They said, "You'll get out of this hell, out of this pain, out of this disgrace, if you will just testify to our gracious handling of you." McCain refused to defile himself by betraying his country and fellow prisoners with such a lie. As a consequence, he spent five and a half years in prison with over half in solitary confinement, and with his wounds not only improperly treated but used as a means to torture him. John McCain's experience reminds us that, in the real world, doing the right thing is no guarantee of good results.

Why Mention the Risks?

Decisions not to defile—to be faithful and act righteously—really can involve terrible risk. Why state this again? Because when we are removed from the pressures, we may find it easy to say that we would not struggle to risk security and success to maintain faithfulness to our nation or to our God. But it is not that easy! And the Lord cares enough about us to put this clear message in Scripture: holiness is risky business. If we do not know this or will not face such hard realities, then we are not ready for the battles that are surely in our path.

It does not take real war conditions to be in a real war for holiness. If you were being asked to sign a clearance form for contaminated products and the decision determined the future of your career and family plans, would the choice really be easy? The wife of my friend did refuse to sign the forms for the contaminated syringes. And she was fired.

We should never minimize the risks of holiness. The Bible does not. We should not pretend that living for the Lord is always painless, easy, or fun—for then we are abandoning and abusing those who have suffered for their stand for God and his holiness. Whenever we pretend that holiness is easy, we isolate and undermine those who must take a stand in this world. And a time will come when every believer must make such a stand. Our society may praise idealism, but it rarely tolerates living those ideals. And the problems are not just in our dealings with others. We, too, have personal idolatries that can jeopardize holiness and produce defilement. Some of the idols we are prone to serve include success, security, position, pleasure, or just being admired. They may not sound sinister, but to sacrifice holiness to obtain them is just as defiling as the food that Nebuchadnezzar offered to Daniel and his friends. University students are often tempted by moral compromise and dishonesty in academics or finances because those are pressures common in college. Young parents may be tempted by feelings of being trapped or victimized by the degree of care their children need. The drive to succeed can tempt those in business to act without integrity or compassion. All of these pressures are normal and should be expected in the pursuit of holiness; if we do not know this or do not acknowledge it, then we will not be prepared for the challenges that are sure to come.

Recent events in Haiti reminded me that in his teens my son contracted a parasite on a mission trip to that impoverished nation. The parasite triggered Crohn's disease—a chronic and incurable illness. There was risk in his witness; there always is. The risks may be very different for different persons. The risks may not be to health but to income, seniority, or position. But regardless of the difference in the *nature* of the risks, we help each other by acknowledging that risk is *normal* for believers. As my daughter began seminary recently and took a job at a computing firm to pay the bills, her coworkers encouraged her to lie to meet her employer's requirements. What was so telling about this to me was that when I went to seminary thirty years earlier, coworkers at my outside job also encouraged me to lie about quotas that I had to meet. For both of us, the decision to dedicate our lives to the Lord seemed to bring some of the greatest temptations to betray him.

Of course, the experiences of my daughter and me are not unique. We should acknowledge that, whether because of the products they make or the practices they approve, many Christians feel compromised every day in the workplace. Confusion about what to do, fear of consequences, and lack of faith in God's provision inhibit their holiness, but nothing is more crippling than the sense of being alone: "It's just me; no one else has these struggles. God makes their lives easy, but he's forgotten me." Others need our confession that we also face challenges in order to maintain their bravery.

There is a fellowship of risk that enfolds all who strive for holiness. We will each be more willing to stand for the Lord and less prone to fall into discouragement when we are aware of the risks we share with faithful believers, like seminarians before us, missionaries before us, business leaders before us, Daniels before us—and a Savior before us. Do not forget where the story of Daniel leads. From these captive people will come generations of suffering people who will be relieved by a suffering Savior. We should expect nothing else. The world that opposes the things of God will oppose those who seek to live for him. That is part of the story. We just have to remember that it is not the end of the story.

The Reasons for Holiness

If there are such risks to holiness, then we need to know why the Lord allows them. Why not simply make the work of the faithful easy?

Preparation

The first reason that God allows us to face such risks is that they are preparation for spiritual battles that always lie ahead. Starting with this first chapter, the book of Daniel goes from one thrilling adventure to the next. A quick scan of the next five chapters will reveal more encounters with death-dealing kings, nightmare visions, a giant idol of gold, a foray into a fiery furnace, a king turned into a wild animal, and a prophet thrown to the lions. Adventure movie directors should love this material. Each trial leads to a new and greater challenge. And that's just the point. Contamination continues to threaten lives kept pure for God. Each initial choice of holiness is preparation for later battles.

Our tendency when facing today's battles is to wonder why God is abandoning us to such difficulty. Instead, Daniel helps us to understand that the Lord is not *abandoning* but *preparing* us for greater work in the future. Only weeks after assuming responsibilities at the first church I pastored full-time after seminary, I discovered that one of my officers was living with a woman not his wife. Other officers and many families in the church had their livelihoods entangled with a company well known for its ethical and moral transgressions. Generational antipathies divided other families, and some of our spiritually mature leaders, on whose help I was depending, unexpectedly died. More than once I wondered if the Lord had put me to work and then gone on vacation. One day I was strengthened when I overheard a godly woman in our church speculate with another, "I wonder what the Lord is preparing Bryan to do that requires him to go through so much testing?"

That comment was scary in that it made me wonder what lay ahead that could be worse than these circumstances. But the comment also helped me to think that the trials were not purposeless. The Lord was *preparing*, not *abandoning*. And since that period, there has never been a time in my ministry without challenge: sometimes relational, sometimes financial, sometimes denominational. I spoke to our seminary board recently about a major challenge on the horizon, but I reminded them that they had supported me years previous in a similar set of events. The Lord had not only brought us through the past but was then preparing us for the present.

If you don't think that way—that present trial is preparing for future purposes, that God is giving you experience and strength by testing your mettle—then present trials will overwhelm you. I have mentioned often to students my experience of being in line at my own seminary graduation. I looked down the line of my graduating friends and recognized that every single one of us had been through a major life trial during seminary. Suddenly I realized that Satan had been doing whatever he could to stop us. If such opposition is all we see, then discouragement will destroy us. But if we are able to see that the Lord is also preparing his servants—never allowing more than we can stand but stretching, molding, and strengthening us for greater work in his kingdom—then we can face today's battle with the resolution and hope that the Lord intends. That is how it was for Daniel and his friends, too. Today's battles were preparation for tomorrow's. The Lord was preparing them to be his instruments. If I had not had trials in seminary, I would not have been ready for those in the local church; if I had not had trials in the local church, I would not have been ready for those in the denomination; if I had not had those in the denomination, I would not be ready to serve the wider church today.

Protection

The perspective that present trials are preparation for tomorrow's battles underscores another reason that the Lord allows the pressures of defilement: protection. By being prepared, we are being protected from the consequences of our enemy's victories. Daniel will face greater battles than this test of his diet. He will have greater responsibilities than whether to eat vegetables or sweets. As a consequence of committing to serve the Lord with integrity, Daniel was without defilement (1:8). The biblical term for "defile," used without a negative term attached to it, means "to redeem." However, in this negative mode, the word includes the notion of desecration. The implication is that Daniel wished to be spiritually protected from the taint of sin. His desire for holiness kept his heart close to God. As a result, Daniel not only grew in the knowledge of Babylonian literature and learning, but he also had understanding of visions and dreams from God (1:17). The understanding that Daniel had of God's ways indicates that his holiness helped preserve a closeness with the Lord—a fellowship of Daniel's spirit with the Spirit of God—so that he could face Satan's assaults with wisdom and courage. Prepared by the lesser battles of this day, Daniel will also be protected in the greater battles of tomorrow.

During my summers as a college student I worked for a major road construction company in western Tennessee. As an assistant to one of the supervisors, I earned excellent pay. That was important because the university I attended was very expensive and neither I nor my family had the money to pay for my education. Besides, jobs were hard to come by, so it was vital to my future that I hold this one.

One morning my supervisor told me I was doing such a good job for him and the company that he was going to give me a special privilege. He owned a hunting lodge in a nearby county, and he wanted me to spend a day or two there enjoying the outdoors. I thanked him for the offer but explained I needed every day of work I could get for college expenses and could not afford the time off.

"Don't worry about that," he said. "You just do a little painting and repairing at my cabin while you're there, and I'll keep you on the payroll."

I was off like a shot. By that evening I was at the cabin savoring a meal of fresh, fried catfish and looking forward to another day of little work and lots of fun. Then the telephone rang. It was my father calling. When he arrived home from work that evening, my mother had explained where I was and under what arrangements.

"What are you doing collecting company pay for private work?" my dad asked.

Well, I had not quite thought of it that way. I did not want to think of it that way. "Dad," I said, "I can't go back to my boss now and tell him what he asked me to do is unethical. He may get offended, and I may lose this job. How am I going to get through school if I don't have this job?"

Dad replied, "I know you need this job to prepare for what you want to do. I also know what you need to prepare for life, and this is not it."

I went home. I knew he was right. And, as time has lengthened since the situation, I have understood even more how right he was. My father accurately saw that careless ethics early in life could lead to greater compromises and worse consequences. If the deceit, however slight it seemed, had worked that time, what kind of precedent would it have established in my life? Would I have looked back at some point on a successful career and said, "See how beneficial it was for me to be unethical at that point?" If so, what decisions might I have been tempted to make at difficult moments in that career? In what greater dangers might I have placed myself by believing that past compromise helped me? My father's insistence on non-defilement was preparation for life *and* protection from greater wrong down the road.

One reason the careless defilement of holy commitments cannot be permitted is that it only leads to further harm. Defilement distances God's people from his protections. If we do not practice holiness today, his standards do not protect us tomorrow. The consequences of sin are pleasant only for a season (Heb. 11:25), but then the result is great hurt. God loves us enough to protect us from this future hurt by calling us to present holiness. The trial is never without purpose. God protects us from greater harm by giving us the opportunities to learn how to depend on him now, so that the later trials and temptations do not overwhelm us. This is why we need to make sure we have present commitment to holiness. Because of pressures and difficulties, you and I may be tempted to say, "I will serve the Lord better . . . later." My response to that is, "No, you will not! And neither will I." Whether our present trials are personal, private, moral, financial, or familial, if we are not preparing for tomorrow's battles with holiness today, we will not be spiritually strong enough to stand for the Lord later. Today's trials are the training ground for tomorrow's battlefield. The time to be undefiled is now. Later is too late.

The Rewards of Holiness

Welfare

The preparation and protection afforded by Daniel's holiness indicate that God's commands for purity are neither arbitrary nor capricious. The Bible's call to holiness reflects our God's desire for us not to walk away from the goodness he wants to provide in our lives—goodness that accompanies holiness. There are rewards of holiness evident in Daniel's life that we need to understand. The first is his personal welfare.

God made provision for his goodness to be evident in the lives of Daniel and his friends by protecting their welfare. Apparently the vegetables and water were good for them. "At the end of the ten days it was seen that they were better in appearance and fatter in flesh than all the youths who ate the king's food" (1:15). We do not know if this means a clear adolescent complexion or a strong muscular build, but it means something like that. God preserved their health. God also preserved their lives, so that a capricious king did not deem them unfit for his service and lop off their heads. God kept Daniel and his friends safe. From the little note at the end of the chapter we know that Daniel was preserved through intrigue and empire transitions until Cyrus was made king over Babylon, seventy or more years later (1:20–21).

More than that, God overwhelmingly blessed Daniel and his friends with spiritual gifts: they were made ten times wiser than all of Nebuchadnezzar's wise men, and Daniel also had understanding of dreams and visions. Daniel's protection of his relationship with the Lord was rewarded with a special closeness and communication that allowed him to understand the things of God. This is a very simple reminder that if we are responsible for leadership among God's people (as pastors, lay leaders, or parents), our wisdom is inevitably tied to our piety. God gives understanding and usefulness to those who are faithful to him. Piety and spiritual discernment are inseparable.

God is more than capable of protecting us, and one of the rewards of our holiness is the preservation of our welfare. God did not abandon my seminary friend's wife, who was forced to leave her job at the pharmaceutical company. Because she would not sign the clearance forms for the contaminated syringes, the order was not delivered to the customer on time. Officials of that company investigated the delay and discovered how this woman had protected them from the contaminated syringes, even at the cost of her own job. The company for which the syringes were intended was so appreciative that they hired her and increased her pay. She finished putting her husband through seminary, and the family rejoices to this day in that expression of God's special protection.

I experienced something similar with my road-crew supervisor. When I followed my father's advice and told my boss I could not do private work for company pay, he simply said, "OK," and did not fire me.

God is more than able to provide for the welfare of those who stand for him. But now you and I have a problem, don't we? These "success stories," whether of characters biblical or contemporary, turned out so nice and neat. But life does not always come packaged with so pretty a ribbon tied around it. God is always able, but is he always willing to rescue the holy from earthly trials?

In fact, this gift of Daniel's welfare is not wrapped nearly as nicely as it may at first appear. Yes, Daniel is preserved for now, but he is also in captivity now. He will remain a captive his entire life, until he is over ninety years old. He will see his people enslaved for many decades. He will see them forced to bow to pagan gods. He will never again see his homeland. And the visions and prophecies God will grant him include predictions of the suffering of his people for many generations to come. So in what way can we speak of God *really* preserving the welfare of Daniel and his people with any sort of honest reflection of the greater context of the prophet's life?

The first way is by being reminded that there is a greater reality. This life is not the end of all things, nor is it the bulk of our existence. We are beings whose spiritual welfare is being prepared and protected beyond the confines of our earthly existence. Some of us may not receive the tangible rewards of holiness till we are in heaven with the Lord. Yet God "rewards those who seek him" (Heb. 11:6). The rewards of holiness are guaranteed, but they are not always immediate, discernible, or even present in this life. The question we face—the matter of faith we are being challenged to consider—is whether the eternal rewards are real enough to weigh against earthly risk. That is what the life of Daniel is really meant to confirm: that God is able and willing to provide what is best for his people for eternity.

Witness

The other reward of Daniel's holiness is witness. Daniel's stand for holiness clearly had an effect on others. When Daniel stood his ground, he did not stand alone. In near focus are his three friends: Shadrach, Meshach, and Abednego. The simple message is that our holiness serves as a witness to those near us. By our holiness we demonstrate our trust in and loyalty to our Lord. But more than those close to Daniel are affected by his witness; Daniel himself was blessed. Of great reward to him, and to any who stand for their Lord, is knowledge that by our faithfulness to God in hard situations we are participating in the proclamation of our Lord's gracious nature. By standing for God in the face of risk, we declare that possessing and declaring the grace of God are more precious to us than anything this life can offer or deny.

We are meant to see Daniel's life not as a guarantee of uninterrupted glee but as a token of the irrepressible grace of God. Why are Daniel's people in captivity? The simple answer is because they have sinned. They have turned from the God of their forefathers, warped their worship of him, and compromised with his enemies. They deserve none of his attention, much less his mercy. And yet, *by the earthly blessings* of the life of Daniel, we and they are made to understand that God is still present among his people. He is still helping Daniel. God's covenant faithfulness has not left them. He is still providing for them. They have been faithless, but he remains faithful (see 2 Tim. 2:13). He has provided a witness from among the nobility (perhaps the royalty) of Israel—the nation through whom he promised a Redeemer for the nations of the earth. And when that witness and his companions honor God, the Lord shows his presence by his supernatural activity. The display of God's power in Daniel's preservation, and the continuation of his promises exhibited in the prophecies he gives to Daniel, proved our Lord's abiding care. Amid the present and future suffering of God's wayward people, Daniel's life is really a lens by which God shows that divine love is real, his covenant is unending, and his promises are more sure than anything this earth can offer. Though we may walk away from him, he will not walk away from us. Even if we fail to live as Daniel did in this account, God perseveres in his love as demonstrated through Daniel's life.

In response to Daniel's holiness—his decision to remain undefiled—God provides for Daniel's immediate welfare. But, more importantly for him and for us, through Daniel's holiness God provides a witness of the reality and perpetuity of the spiritual truths that are eternally important.

If Daniel would risk position, privilege, and life itself for a pure relationship with his God, then that must be quite a relationship and that must be quite a God. His stand for his God *amid earthly deprivations* is a witness to the incomparable blessings of the grace of his God. By his willingness to risk everything for his God, Daniel shows how precious is a relationship with God.

There are not always tangible benefits nor only negligible damages as a result of holiness. But this life is only a moment in God's time (Ps. 39:4–5; 90). Our immediate concerns are almost nothing compared to the immensity and beauty of the plan God has for our souls. The rewards of holiness may only be tasted in the present, but we will definitely feast upon them in eternity (John 14:2; Rev. 21:4). God safeguards the personal and spiritual welfare of his own with a view to what provides for their ultimate good and the good of the lives they touch (2 Tim. 4:6–8, 16–18).

These eternal truths do not deny that Daniel's earthly circumstances remained dire in many ways. Yet God safeguarded and guided Daniel so that even the worst-seeming disasters became instruments of God's grace for him and others. A holy person is a powerful tool in God's hands even in times of trial—or especially in times of trial—for his or her witness to our souls, our families, and the nations.

We should remember that there are two groups of people not mentioned in the chapter, but definitely in view, who are affected by the witness of Daniel. The first group is the people of Israel. We know from the later prophecies of Daniel that the people of Israel will go through many generations of heartache. They will often wonder, "Is God faithful? Does he care? Can he protect?" The life of Daniel stood as a continuing witness to them that, though the present may be difficult, God's promises are greater and he is faithful.

God also intends for another group of people to know this: us! We also are witnesses to God's faithfulness through the experience of Daniel. By preserving a person named Daniel, God was preserving a nation called Israel in order to send a Savior named Jesus to save persons like us and ten thousand times ten thousand more of the same. Daniel's willingness to risk everything to make that redeeming God powerfully known expresses how great and precious is the incomparable grace of God toward those who will trust in him.

When our son's trip to Haiti resulted in the infection that triggered Crohn's disease, we worried and wept and wondered if we had been right to let him go. We were blessed to have a Christian doctor who had an eternal perspective about such questions and trials. He said to Jordan, "No regrets. You were in the service of the King, and God will use this as he knows is best." That was an amazing thought for a young man graduating from high school and facing a lifetime of chronic illness. The Lord can use us as tools of his glory, even in the hard things—and especially in the hard things—to clarify for the world the really important things of eternity.

In our family album is a picture of my son a few years later on another mission trip to hurricane-ravaged Honduras. Next to him are his brother and his sister, who also said, "This disaster is an opportunity for the gospel. We know the risks, but we also know the eternal rewards of a holy purpose. Our circumstances may involve suffering here, but living with holy priorities through such pain will make more evident the weight of the eternal promises we say are so much more real and precious." So in our album are more pictures of our son, Jordan, digging foundations for homes, leading impoverished children in song, and leading a Bible study in Spanish.

In one of those pictures a little girl with a red bow in her hair leans over Jordan's New Testament to see what he is reading. She lingered after the other children had gone and, with Jordan's witness, claimed Jesus as her Savior. Eternity will be different because a young man in our day, like a young Daniel centuries ago, took risks for the sake of honoring his God. He took those risks for a reason, knowing that such witness can bear witness to the greatness of God's grace and the greater rewards of his eternal care. For those who know the grace of their God, there really is no greater reward than to know we have been used by him as witnesses to secure the eternal welfare of others. While we may be looking for some great plan to transform culture, God still calls us never to forget the power of simple piety. The way that we make a difference even as a minority in a culture turned from our God is to honor him with holy lives dedicated to witnessing his grace. As we pursue holiness, our spiritual welfare and witness are God's delight—as well as our greatest reward.

2

When the Bottom Falls Out

— DANIEL 2 —

The second chapter of Daniel displays the provision of the Lord. Here God is just as honest as he was in chapter one, where the risks of holiness were plainly revealed. There, without sugarcoating or fancy coloring, God plainly said that holiness carries risks. In this next chapter, God not only prepares us to expect some trauma when holiness is pursued, but he also teaches us how to handle difficulty when it comes. God will not leave us helpless. In this slice of Daniel's life, God gives us the weapons we need to stand for him, when our holiness comes under assault:

In the second year of the reign of Nebuchadnezzar, Nebuchadnezzar had dreams; his spirit was troubled, and his sleep left him. Then the king commanded that the magicians, the enchanters, the sorcerers, and the Chaldeans be summoned to tell the king his dreams. So they came in and stood before the king. And the king said to them, "I had a dream, and my spirit is troubled to know the dream." Then the Chaldeans said to the king in Aramaic, "O king, live forever! Tell your servants the dream, and we will show the interpretation." The king answered and said to the Chaldeans, "The word from me is firm: if you do not make known to me the dream and its interpretation, you shall be torn limb from limb, and your houses shall be laid in ruins. But if you show the dream and its interpretation, you shall receive from me gifts and rewards and great honor. Therefore show me the dream and its interpretation." They answered a second time and said, "Let the king tell his servants the dream, and we will show its interpretation." The king answered and said, "I know with certainty that you are trying to gain time, because you see that the word from me is firm—if you do not make the dream known to me, there is but one sentence for you. You have agreed to speak lying and corrupt words before me till the times change. Therefore tell me the dream, and I shall know that you can show me its interpretation." The Chaldeans answered the king and said, "There is not a man on earth who can meet the king's demand, for no great and powerful king has asked such a thing of any magician or enchanter or Chaldean. The thing that the king asks is difficult, and no one can show it to the king except the gods, whose dwelling is not with flesh."

Because of this the king was angry and very furious, and commanded that all the wise men of Babylon be destroyed. So the decree went out, and the wise men were about to be killed; and they sought Daniel and his companions, to kill them. Then Daniel replied with prudence and discretion to Arioch, the captain of the king's guard, who had gone out to kill the wise men of Babylon. He declared to Arioch, the king's captain, "Why is the decree of the king so urgent?" Then Arioch made the matter known to Daniel. And Daniel went in and requested the king to appoint him a time, that he might show the interpretation to the king.

Then Daniel went to his house and made the matter known to Hananiah, Mishael, and Azariah, his companions, and told them to seek mercy from the God of heaven concerning this mystery, so that Daniel and his companions might not be destroyed with the rest of the wise men of Babylon. Then the mystery was revealed to Daniel in a vision of the night. Then Daniel blessed the God of heaven. Daniel answered and said:

"Blessed be the name of God forever
    and ever,
    to whom belong wisdom and
        might.
He changes times and seasons;
    he removes kings and sets up
        kings;
he gives wisdom to the wise
    and knowledge to those who have
        understanding;
he reveals deep and hidden things;
    he knows what is in the darkness,
    and the light dwells with him.
To you, O God of my fathers,
    I give thanks and praise,
for you have given me wisdom and
        might,
    and have now made known to me
        what we asked of you,
    for you have made known to us
        the king's matter."

Therefore Daniel went in to Arioch, whom the king had appointed to destroy the wise men of Babylon. He went and said thus to him: "Do not destroy the wise men of Babylon; bring me in before the king, and I will show the king the interpretation."

Then Arioch brought in Daniel before the king in haste and said thus to him: "I have found among the exiles from Judah a man who will make known to the king the interpretation." The king declared to Daniel, whose name was Belteshazzar, "Are you able to make known to me the dream that I have seen and its interpretation?" Daniel answered the king and said, "No wise men, enchanters, magicians, or astrologers can show to the king the mystery that the king has asked, but there is a God in heaven who reveals mysteries, and he has made known to King Nebuchadnezzar what will be in the latter days. Your dream and the visions of your head as you lay in bed are these: To you, O king, as you lay in bed came thoughts of what would be after this, and he who reveals mysteries made known to you what is to be. But as for me, this mystery has been revealed to me, not because of any wisdom that I have more than all the living, but in order that the interpretation may be made known to the king, and that you may know the thoughts of your mind.

"You saw, O king, and behold, a great image. This image, mighty and of exceeding brightness, stood before you, and its appearance was frightening. The head of this image was of fine gold, its chest and arms of silver, its middle and thighs of bronze, its legs of iron, its feet partly of iron and partly of clay. As you looked, a stone was cut out by no human hand, and it struck the image on its feet of iron and clay, and broke them in pieces. Then the iron, the clay, the bronze, the silver, and the gold, all together were broken in pieces, and became like the chaff of the summer threshing floors; and the wind carried them away, so that not a trace of them could be found. But the stone that struck the image became a great mountain and filled the whole earth.

"This was the dream. Now we will tell the king its interpretation. You, O king, the king of kings, to whom the God of heaven has given the kingdom, the power, and the might, and the glory, and into whose hand he has given, wherever they dwell, the children of man, the beasts of the field, and the birds of the heavens, making you rule over them all—you are the head of gold. Another kingdom inferior to you shall arise after you, and yet a third kingdom of bronze, which shall rule over all the earth. And there shall be a fourth kingdom, strong as iron, because iron breaks to pieces and shatters all things. And like iron that crushes, it shall break and crush all these. And as you saw the feet and toes, partly of potter's clay and partly of iron, it shall be a divided kingdom, but some of the firmness of iron shall be in it, just as you saw iron mixed with the soft clay. And as the toes of the feet were partly iron and partly clay, so the kingdom shall be partly strong and partly brittle. As you saw the iron mixed with soft clay, so they will mix with one another in marriage, but they will not hold together, just as iron does not mix with clay. And in the days of those kings the God of heaven will set up a kingdom that shall never be destroyed, nor shall the kingdom be left to another people. It shall break in pieces all these kingdoms and bring them to an end, and it shall stand forever, just as you saw that a stone was cut from a mountain by no human hand, and that it broke in pieces the iron, the bronze, the clay, the silver, and the gold. A great God has made known to the king what shall be after this. The dream is certain, and its interpretation sure."

Then King Nebuchadnezzar fell upon his face and paid homage to Daniel, and commanded that an offering and incense be offered up to him. The king answered and said to Daniel, "Truly, your God is God of gods and Lord of kings, and a revealer of mysteries, for you have been able to reveal this mystery." Then the king gave Daniel high honors and many great gifts, and made him ruler over the whole province of Babylon and chief prefect over all the wise men of Babylon. Daniel made a request of the king, and he appointed Shadrach, Meshach, and Abednego over the affairs of the province of Babylon. But Daniel remained at the king's court. (Dan. 2:1–49)

I remember the events that led her to tears. My wife, Kathy, had just come home from a weekly grocery trip. She came into the house holding the lip of a full grocery sack in one hand, balancing a crying baby on the other arm, and urging forward two tired and grouchy preschool sons. Just as she squeezed through the back door and swung around the kitchen counter, the side of the paper grocery sack ripped. The sack and everything in it crashed to the floor, including a large, economy-size bottle of liquid dish soap. When the soap bottle hit the linoleum, the lid sprang off. The honey-like innards glugged out, and the mess spread across the kitchen floor.

Kathy told me what happened next. She put the crying baby (still crying) into her highchair. She told the two boys to jump over the pool of soap. Then she also leapt across the puddle to grab a roll of paper towels. But as she got on her knees to sop up the soap, she heard a strange hissing sound coming from the grocery sack. Despite its torn lip, the sack was sitting half upright on the floor where it had crashed. Kathy looked inside to see what was hissing.

A two-liter strawberry soda bottle had ruptured inside the dropped bag. The hissing sound was soda escaping from the bottle and rapidly filling the bottom of the paper sack. Kathy grabbed the bottle and the few groceries remaining in the grocery sack and threw them into the sink. Then slowly, ever so carefully, she lifted the paper sack with its pool of soda and inched toward the sink. She almost made it. But then the bottom fell out. As a consequence, carbonated strawberry soda and liquid detergent began to swirl together around her feet. The result? Strawberry suds! The kids loved it, but not Mom—not even a little bit.

What do you do when the bottom falls out? If it is a full grocery sack, the remedy is plain enough. You shed a few tears and get out the mop. But what do you do when the bottom falls out of your life—your career, your family's security, your health? What do you do when things just go horribly wrong? Though we don't like to think about it, we all know the unthinkable can happen. Believers are not insulated from life's crises; the bottom can fall out for us, too (John 17:15). We live in a fallen world and, like everyone else, may face crippling disappointments and disasters never anticipated (Matt. 6:34):

- A teenage boy enters a hospital in respiratory distress. The doctor suspects the problem is drug related. But the boy's Christian parents can't believe it; they've never known their son to consume anything stronger than soft drinks. The doctor turns out to be right.

- A state school board official, a lay leader in his church, is arrested for shoplifting a bottle of wine. The police report says he took the bottle into the restroom where he finished it off. How could he make such a foolish choice? Later reports tell of job pressures, personal medical problems, family tensions, and a daughter's recently diagnosed brain tumor. The hidden wine binge was just a desperate attempt to escape it all for a while.

- A seven-year-old girl is diagnosed as having leukemia. Her father, a believer, has just been laid off from his job. The medical benefits are gone. The nightmare is just beginning.
- A wonderful church elder, one of our dearest friends, watches helplessly for a year and a half as his only daughter's marriage disintegrates. Then he loses his job. And then his daughter is killed in an accident caused by a drunk driver.

All are real events. All involve real Christians. All remind us that the events of the second chapter of Daniel have a lot to do with today's realities. That's because the bottom fell out of Daniel's life, just as it did for all the people mentioned above.

Not everything was rosy in Daniel's life—the first chapter of his biography makes that clear. Although he had been born into Israel's nobility, a cruel and idolatrous despot had overrun Daniel's homeland and taken him captive. Still, events had been on the upswing of late. Because of his background and gifts, Daniel won an appointment to train for the king's service. At the end of that training he was judged to be superior to all his peers and even ten times wiser than the wise men of Babylon (1:20). So Daniel entered the king's service.

We do not know the exact position given to Daniel, but the term used to describe his duties ("stood before," 1:19) is the same used to describe Joseph's duties when he became a governor for Pharaoh ("entered the . . . service," Gen. 41:46). With God's help, and without compromising his faithfulness, the young Jewish captive had risen above his circumstances. Everything was going great. Everything was looking up. Everything was working out. Then the bottom fell out.

The king had a dream. The dream troubled the king; in fact, it scared him. So he called in his wise men to find out what the dream meant.

"Tell us the dream, O king, and we shall interpret it for you," his enchanters and sorcerers said.

"Not a chance," the king replied. "If you're as wise and all-knowing as you claim, you tell me what my dream is. Then, when you tell me what it means, I'll know if you really have any insight."

Of course, these counselors could not tell the king what his dream was. Their failure and excuses so angered the king that he ordered all the wise men of the kingdom killed. Don't forget, Daniel was a wise man, too. In fact, he was the wisest (1:20). As a result, the commander of the king's guard went looking for Daniel. In one hand this officer held a sword, and in the other, an order for Daniel's execution (2:12–13). By any reasonable assessment, the bottom had just fallen out for Daniel. After much suffering, Daniel had clawed back to some semblance of a decent life and in one sword stroke it would all be over.

In Daniel's response to this collapse of his circumstances, we learn what faithfulness to God looks like when the bottom falls out. What should we do when the bottom falls out? We want to cry in grief, or to yell in anger, or simply to collapse. All those responses are understandable. But Daniel demonstrated responses to his crisis that can help us engage our Lord's help when the bottom falls out of a believer's world. Daniel's first spiritual response to his crisis appears in verses 17 and 18: "Then Daniel went to his house and made the matter known to Hananiah, Mishael, and Azariah, his companions, and told them to seek mercy from the God of heaven concerning this mystery, so that Daniel and his companions might not be destroyed with the rest of the wise men of Babylon."

The simple message of these verses is this: when the bottom fell out, Daniel fell to his knees.

The Response of Prayer

The Priority of Prayer

Daniel responded to crisis with prayer. He secured extra time from the king, but the extra time was not to devise an escape plan (2:14–16). Daniel immediately gathered those who loved the Lord and urged fervent prayer (2:17–18).

Perhaps it does not strike you as significant that Daniel's first response to crisis was prayer. We tend to think of Daniel as a faith giant, one of those "Bible people" who is supposed to pray. We should remember, though, that if anyone had a reason to skip prayer—or pursue any number of other first responses—it was Daniel.

The Alternatives to Prayer

Daniel had alternatives to prayer that could seem more practical and productive. First, since he was ten times wiser than the wisest of Babylon, Daniel could have used his extra time to figure out some solution to his predicament. Smart people apply their minds to the problem when a crisis comes, and Daniel had no shortage of mental ability (1:20; 2:23).

In addition to his intelligence, Daniel had power (2:23). After all, he was in the king's service and apparently already had some governing authority (1:19). Surely Daniel could apply the savvy he had learned from managing the politics of the king's court to this crisis. As a young man, Daniel had already learned to speak with "prudence and discretion" to royal authorities (2:14). Surely he could finagle for some more time, call in a few favors, twist a few arms, and work the angles. Perhaps those aware of the situation expected him to wangle something from his experience and resources, but instead he sought the help of his God.

Daniel had the same options that we have in a crisis. He could have resorted to his intelligence, his power, or his resources, but instead he turned to his God. Daniel chose prayer as his first response. Despite my theological credentials and ministry pursuits, this is a lesson I find that I have to learn over and over.

The Lessons of Prayer

When I was pursuing graduate studies at a secular institution, I discovered how unpopular and dangerous Christian commitments can be. In my research, I used an analytical method that reveals much about the way our minds assimilate information. Earlier researchers developed this approach on the assumption that all truth claims are relative and subjective—without any basis for determining right and wrong. But I began to use the method to show how objective truths can be known and shared. As a Christian, I understood that the core of our faith is jeopardized if we allow secular presuppositions to rule out the possibility of shared truth. However, when my "philosophical position" became known at the university, a professor on my examining committee told others that he would block my graduation.

I was devastated. Thousands of hours of study, thousands of dollars of tuition, hundreds of pages of writing, many years of schooling and career planning, dreams for which my family had dearly sacrificed—all were about to unravel. I couldn't sleep. I couldn't eat. I could hardly talk to my wife, Kathy, about how bad our situation was. This really was the bottom falling out for us!

So I got busy. I called my faculty adviser. I made an appointment with the department chairman. I began taking steps to get different persons assigned to my examining committee. I explained my problem to sympathetic teachers. I alerted my future employer that my credentials were in jeopardy. I redoubled my efforts to produce unassailable arguments and reexamined my dissertation for any possible weakness in wording or logic that could be used against me.

What was missing in all this frenetic activity? Prayer. My prayers were not absent because I made a decision to exclude prayer. I did not cross prayer off my list of important things to do. I always intended to get to it. Prayer just didn't make it to the top of my "to do" list. I was applying all my energies to making sure that I handled this crisis. My focus was on what I needed to do to work out the best solution, grab the reins, and take charge. Bryan Chapell needed to find the experts, the allies, the path, and the means to fix his problem.

Not until I was several days down my path of personal solution did it hit me that I had not really prayed. Yes, I had whispered a few silent "help me's." But I had not fallen to my knees in concentrated, humble, dependent prayer. I had not gathered those who love me and love the Lord to pray as Daniel did with his friends (2:18). I realize now that we often reveal how serious we are about prayer by involving others in our praying. Thankfully, the Lord did ultimately convict me of my need to pray—and finally Kathy and I prayed together.

The problem did *not* immediately go away. Up until the day I defended my research before the examining committee, we knew my degree was in jeopardy. Because I had not changed in my conviction that we can communicate real truth, I stood in opposition to the perspective of most of my professors. Yet, as aware as I was of the potential problems my beliefs could cause, I was still surprised by the very first question.

The highest-ranking professor in the department has the privilege of asking the first question in such an exam. This was his question: "How can you use this methodology that assumes the relativity of truth and at the same time have a commitment to particular truths?"

I gulped, thinking inside, "So much for a nice, easy start." Then, as my stomach knotted with the knowledge that I was probably torpedoing my future, I explained that the research method I was using revealed much about how our minds function. I said that I was not undermining the value of the method nor the results derived from it. I simply did not agree that one had to presuppose the relativity of truth to use this research tool.

Then something completely unexpected happened. The questioner, the senior professor in the department, simply said, "OK." I could hardly believe my ears. The other committee members could hardly believe theirs either, and their wide eyes showed it. The ranking professor had just declared that my response was "OK"! Now any other professor who kept pressing me on the subject would be slapping him in the face. After all, if the highest-ranking scholar had declared my argument satisfactory, no one could attack my reasoning without challenging the authority of the senior professor. So no one asked any more questions on that subject.

In the first five minutes of an exam that usually takes hours we were done with the only question that threatened my degree. I could not have arranged such a sequence of events. No matter what type of planning and politicking I had attempted, I could not have arranged for that professor at that moment to ask that question that blocked all further challenges. I could not. But God could, and God did. His abilities are beyond our imagining. His ways are beyond our knowing. His solutions are beyond our doing. That is why when the bottom falls out he urges us to seek him first.

The Requirements of Prayer

Daniel teaches us that one of the principles of prayer is to confess our need early. True prayer actually is the simultaneous acknowledgement of our limitations and of our need for God. Daniel urged his companions to pray for God's mercy because he knew they did not have the power to undo the king's decree or avoid its consequences (2:18). Daniel's press for prayer was a confession that the young men required a power greater than their own.

Such petition for God's intervention does not require us to become irresponsible about our duties, actions, and plans. But prayer does acknowledge, "Apart from you, Lord, my plans mean nothing. On my own, Lord, I can't fix this. I can't heal the wound, correct the fault, clean up the mess, or put my life back together without you. God, you must take control if any good is to result. Use me if you will, but you must act—otherwise my power, my brains, and my connections will count for nothing. Only you, Lord, are truly able. I depend on you."

When our hearts are committed to such truths, our actions change. We recognize that before we pick up the telephone, call the meeting, create the priority list, or form a crisis-management team, we must fall on our knees and ask God's help. He is the only true crisis manager.

Prayer is also and inevitably the confession of our weakness. By reaching toward God, we confess our inability to change our world by our own strength or by our own resources. By their very nature our prayers concede that we cannot provide what we most need. But by praying we also affirm our conviction that God can help. With prayer we acknowledge our dependence on God's grace and our trust in his heart of love. We push ourselves out of the way so that God's ways can be revealed.

We may forget how helpless apart from God we truly are. Our society constantly tells us that our efforts make all the difference. In the business world, in our educational experiences, in judicial cases, in our families, and even in the church, our actions are understood as the root cause for success or failure. So when the bottom falls out of our lives, our reflex reactions are focused on self-supplied solutions. We are so accustomed to depending on our own resources that we neglect seeking God's supply when we need it the most. This is even true of "professional" Christians.

Jack Miller, one of the most thoughtful pastors of the last century, once included a simple request in a letter to a friend of mine. Jack wrote, "Please pray for my habitual tendency to trust in myself and what I can do." The request reveals the near-constant struggle we all have to include God in our lives. If such a great man of God can confess his temptation to depend on himself, then we should all recognize how easily we can fall into similar patterns. In our haste to handle everyday problems as well as major crises, we can become so busy, so self-absorbed, so problem-focused, so accustomed to figuring our way out of our difficulties, that we forget God's way out: prayer.

Our prayerlessness can be a poignant reminder (an internal barometer of the soul) of how much we really believe that God can make a difference in our lives. Daniel indicated how important he believed it was to seek God at all times by making prayer the first priority for himself and his friends when the king's command created their crisis (2:17–18). Crises are often the means God uses to get our prayer lives back on track and to remind us that we must seek him always.

Recently, a young man sat in my office. He was broke, out of work, and trying to find some direction for his life. According to society's agenda, he should have been traumatized and troubled, but he was smiling.

"Bryan," he said, "for two months I've been doing everything I can to get back on track. I have tried to get a job using every skill I have. I've searched the classified ads, hit the bricks, called all my contacts, mailed résumés, and driven a million miles to interviews. But nothing was working. I wasn't getting any job interviews. I was running out of ideas of what to do next. And I was getting more desperate and depressed every day. I was so wound up in job hunting that I didn't realize how spiritually dry I had become.

"Then I realized that I had not had a conversation with any Christian friend in weeks. My devotional life was 'zilch.' My church attendance was 'in and out' as fast as I could manage so I didn't waste any job-hunting time. I need God more than ever, but I wasn't giving him any priority in my time and efforts. When I realized how little I was focused on seeking God, it was as though I heard him say to me, 'Stop trying to do this your way. Depend on me, and ask my help.'

"Ever since that moment, I've been praying regularly, and it's hard to fathom the difference it's made. Suddenly God is opening doors I never dreamed would be opened for me. But, even more important, I realize now that God will provide for my needs even if all these doors close. For the first time in my life I know how good it feels to be absolutely confident in God."

We may fear to seek God in time of crisis if we have not sought him regularly before. But we should not let that fear dissuade us from turning to God now. Daniel teaches us that there is never a wrong time to pray. Daniel gathered his friends together for focused prayer after the crisis came. Daniel did not fear to approach God in more fervent prayer when circumstances were more pressing. Crisis can be the very instrument God will use to draw us to greater dependence on him. If the bottom has fallen out and we have not prayed much before, we should pray now. Anytime is the right time to pray. When the bottom fell out for Daniel, he fell to his knees. He didn't let the crisis rob him of his spiritual support, and neither should we. If the bottom has fallen out for us and prayer has not been our first response, we should make it our next response.

The Response of Praise

This second chapter of the young prophet's life also describes a spiritual activity that should accompany prayer during crisis. This activity is as easily stated as prayer, but it may be even more difficult to imitate. Daniel's second response to crisis is recorded in verses 19–23 (NIV):

> During the night the mystery was revealed to Daniel in a vision. Then Daniel praised the God of heaven and said:
>
> "Praise be to the name of God for ever and ever;
>   wisdom and power are his.
> He changes times and seasons;
>   he deposes kings and raises others up.
> He gives wisdom to the wise
>   and knowledge to the discerning.
> He reveals deep and hidden things;
>   he knows what lies in darkness,
>   and light dwells with him.
> I thank and praise you, God of my ancestors:
>   You have given me wisdom and power,
> you have made known to me what we asked of you,
>   you have made known to us the dream of the king."

In the midst of his crisis, Daniel offered personal praise to God. Daniel opposed pressure with praise.

Easy Praise

"Oh, sure!" we may think. "When God tells Daniel what the king's dream is, when the crisis is over, then he praises God. It's easy to praise God when you get the answers." Still, before we dismiss Daniel's experience as irrelevant to our own, we should look more carefully at how the answer God gave the prophet affected his situation. Yes, he received the dream's interpretation. But suddenly Daniel found himself facing a second, equally threatening, crisis *because* he knew what the king's dream meant.

Nebuchadnezzar had dreamed of an enormous, dazzling statue (2:31–33). Its head was made of gold. The chest and arms were of silver, the belly and thighs were bronze, the legs were iron, and the feet were iron and clay. In the dream, a rock cut without human hands struck the statue and pulverized it into dust, which the wind swept away, then grew large (2:34–35). Without hesitation, Daniel related to the king this entire dream. We can imagine the cruel king's response: "Hey, this Daniel is pretty good. He knows my dream even though I did not tell it to him." "Now, Daniel," says the king, "tell me what it means." Daniel will tell the king what the dream means—and there's the rub.

Hard Praise

What does the dream mean? The interpretation Daniel must give to this bloodthirsty king was recorded for us (2:39–45). Nebuchadnezzar's kingdom was to be divided. It was to be replaced by one kingdom after another. Nebuchadnezzar's golden rule in Babylon would be succeeded by the rule of the Medo-Persian empire (a silver era, not quite as lustrous), which would be conquered by Greece (an empire of great strength like bronze that would nevertheless shine less brightly), which would be succeeded by Rome (an empire of iron and clay—strongest of all initially yet eventually made of many different entities that could not hold together). In later chapters of his book, Daniel will be even more specific about the succession of kingdoms (chaps. 7 and 8), but the immediate message for Nebuchadnezzar is embarrassingly clear. Eventually, all this king had possessed and built would be destroyed and scattered like chaff on the wind (2:35, 44).

Now we should put ourselves in Daniel's place to consider how difficult his offer of praise to God must have been. There is a death sentence already on his head. With sword in hand, the commander of the king's guard is at Daniel's side, and the young prophet is supposed to tell ruthless King Nebuchadnezzar that he and all he stands for will soon be as significant as sweat on a flea. Giving this interpretation is neither easy nor safe.

Surely Daniel must have swallowed hard a few times before offering this interpretation to the king. Far from solving all Daniel's problems, God's revelation of the king's dream actually placed the prophet in greater danger than the first crisis when the king had ordered the deaths of all his wise men. In the first crisis, Daniel was one among many wise men in danger. He might have fled the city or slipped into a crowd. But now he stood alone before this powerful king with a message that would seem guaranteed to offend. So it really was not so easy for Daniel to praise God in light of the Lord's revelation of Nebuchadnezzar's dream.

Faithful Praise

Despite the danger involved in interpreting the king's dream, there are three reasons Daniel could still praise God. First, although Daniel does not know how everything will work out in the future, there is already evidence of God's care in the *present*. After all, God had revealed Nebuchadnezzar's dream (2:19). The gods of the pagan wise men had not revealed the king's vision. God displayed his greatness and goodness to Daniel in simply letting his prophet see and understand the dream. What the interpretation of the dream would cause to happen in Daniel's life was still hidden, but God's grace already was evident. Daniel knows that no one else has a clue to the king's dream. There is enough present good to praise God even though the future circumstances remain hidden. Daniel does not ignore the crisis, but neither does he allow it to obscure the good already evident. Daniel praised God for the good he could see, despite the grace not yet fully revealed.

The second reason Daniel could praise God is that the young prophet could remember God's goodness in the *past*. The first chapter of Daniel revealed the faithfulness of God that had preserved Daniel and his friends. God's past faithfulness to this faithful band must have encouraged them to gather together for prayer in this crisis.

God often points his people to past provision to grant reassurance in present difficulties. When Joshua assumed leadership over Israel before the challenges of entering the promised land, he reminded the people of God's faithfulness under Moses (Josh. 1). When Peter addressed his fellow Jews before the challenges of beginning the New Testament church, he reminded them of God's faithfulness to his promises (Acts 2:14–36). And when the church faced persecution, the writer of Hebrews reminded the dispersed people of God's faithfulness amid suffering generations that had preceded them (Heb. 11). The past can provide ample reason for praising God even when the present troubles us. When Daniel offered praise to the "God of my fathers" (2:23), the prophet was calling on God's past faithfulness to strengthen present faith.

But Daniel was not limited to considering God's past and present provision as the basis for his present trust. He knew another dimension of God's care. The third reason for Daniel to praise the Lord stemmed from the prophet's understanding of Nebuchadnezzar's dream: it unveiled a *future* good for which God also deserved praise. The "rock" that endures forever after breaking into pieces the statue whose components represent successive world kingdoms could be none other than our Rock, Jesus Christ. Through Nebuchadnezzar's dream God showed Daniel the ultimate triumph of Christ on earth (2:44).

This "Rock" revelation did not get rid of the present crisis. Daniel and his people were still in slavery. God's temple was still in ruins. God's prophet was still in jeopardy. Still, God displayed his long-range plans to Daniel. Daniel did not know all that would happen in his immediate situation, but God assured him that all things were working toward a grand triumph. So, despite his present danger, there was good in the past, present, and future for which Daniel could praise God.

Likewise, God's goodness displays itself in our past, present, and future. Our lives are filled with reasons to praise God for the good we can see despite the grace not yet fully revealed. One of the most vivid demonstrations of this truth for me occurred when a young man came to me for pastoral advice.

Richard (not his real name) was a young husband, a new father, and a recent convert. He earned a big salary, and he and his wife lived lavishly. They spent every penny they earned, plus more. Their financial excesses became a crisis when Richard's employer got caught in an economic crunch. He chose to eliminate Richard's job.

Richard's house was mortgaged to the hilt. The family car was still being paid off. Without Richard's big paycheck the family would lose everything. There had been other losses recently in their lives as well. Through a series of discourtesies just prior to their conversion, Richard and his wife had alienated their closest relatives. The youth ministry the couple had tried to start in their church had also failed. Though they worked hard at ministering to the young people, the extravagant couple never relationally connected with the high schoolers or their parents.

Every direction Richard looked, he saw failure, rejection, and uncertainty. One day, in a nonstop venting of emotions, Richard unloaded his frustrations in my office. Hurt, anger, and fear poured out of him for forty-five minutes of uninterrupted angst. He ended his anguished monologue by wondering out loud, Why did God "let me down, after I gave my life to him"?

After he finished venting, Richard sank back into his chair, threw frustrated hands into the air, and, speaking of his wife, said, "I just tell Betty that, regardless of what happens, at least we still have each other and kids we love." The despairing words silenced him. They were meant to accuse God. But in the quiet that followed his complaint, Richard's mind began to replay those last words: "At least we have each other and kids we love."

In the silence, Richard remembered the years that he and his wife had longed for children. Once they had even given up on their marriage and separated before the Lord used a Christian friend to draw them back together. The love this couple now shared was so beautiful and real that their past seemed almost like a chapter from other people's lives. Richard remembered the pain, but it was hard now even to recall the thoughts of the man he once was—the man whose self-absorbed selfishness had almost destroyed the family he now cherished.

Richard remembered the shambles of his family in the silence his words now created. That silence made his words echo all the more loudly: "Whatever happens, we still have each other and kids we love." Suddenly, the meaning and magnitude of the words hit him. He bolted upright in his chair and with a sheepish grin said, "I guess God has been pretty good to us after all." When the bottom was falling out of his life, Richard praised God for the good he could see, despite the grace not yet fully revealed.

Having seen God's goodness to him in the past and having praised God for it, Richard experienced something else. The very act of praising God produced in his heart the courage to face the loss of his job. Praise arms God's people to face their foes. Praise so focuses our minds on the greatness of God that our trials are far less intimidating. Trials do not disappear because we praise God, but believers' hearts do not despair when they are praising their God.

Richard was laid off for a time. His family did struggle to maintain their home. They did lose a car. Their financial struggles did force them to restore some relationships with relatives. Most significant, however, Richard and his family learned they could live without some of the possessions they once considered essential. They reevaluated their priorities and recommitted themselves to the Lord's purposes.

Eventually Richard was hired back by the company that had laid him off, but he worked only a few months. He and his wife decided that, if they could do without some "essentials" for a while, God might have a grander purpose for their lives. Richard began studying for the ministry and now has been a pastor for twenty years. There are still trials (finances are not always easy), but this family is not despairing. They have already seen the goodness of God. And they trust him for new graces not yet revealed. They praise God for his past goodness, and the praise grants the assurance of grace for present trials.

Praise is not a cure-all, of course. But if you were to ask Richard what single incident had the greatest impact on his Christian life, he would tell you it was that moment he realized the absence of income and possessions did not mean the absence of grace. The bottom never falls out of God's plan for a believer.

Perhaps the bottom has fallen out of the life of someone reading these words without knowing why or being able to imagine any sensible explanation. It hurts. Maybe the problem is finances, or a family being torn apart, or a loved one suffering an illness—or perhaps something else has gone wrong that hurts so deeply we have trouble even acknowledging it. How do we face such difficulties? We can start by thinking of just one good thing God has put in our lives right now. Then we can praise him for it. Next we can remember something good God has done for us in the past and praise him for that. Finally, we can thank the Lord for the fact that he will yet do good things for us. If we are yet alive, the Lord is not done with us or the witness that we can be to others of his grace.

The truths of Daniel's life assure us that when praise is in our hearts—no matter how deep is the darkness through which we must walk—our hands are in God's hand. He will not let go. He has not departed. We can praise God for the good we can see, knowing there is grace at work that we may not yet grasp—even as he holds on to us.

If there is no good we can identify in our life now (because life can seem so bleak), still we should not give up on the power of praise. The Bible is not asking us to look for a "silver lining"; it allows us to see God. In this account, Daniel praised the Lord for being the "God of my fathers" (2:23). Daniel's wise and powerful God (v. 20) was also a covenant-keeping God who had been faithful to God's people through many generations. That history of faithfulness toward the people of Israel was the basis for Daniel trusting God in the present crisis. But this covenant faithfulness did not just run backward into the past. In the king's dream, Daniel saw that God was using his wisdom and power to bring the reign of our Savior over all the earth (2:44).

What Daniel saw as future is, at least in part, already an element of our past. The rock made without human hands that would crush the powers of this world has been revealed to us as Jesus Christ (Dan. 2:44–45; Luke 20:18). He came and conquered sin and death at Calvary, assuring us that he ultimately rules the greatest powers of this world. More of Christ's rule will cover the earth as the time unfolds, but Christ's kingdom is already here and its progress has already begun.

Despite current hardships and heartaches, the greatest thing possible in all creation has occurred already. Jesus shattered the powers of Satan by taking the penalty for our sins on himself at Calvary. Then our Savior rose in victory over death, showing that he had defeated sin's power. As believers we are forgiven. We need not live under guilt. We are children of the King, and awaiting us is the full flowering of his heavenly kingdom where there shall be no more tears or trials (Rom. 8:18; 2 Cor. 4:17). He holds us in the palm of his hand, and there is nothing that will occur in your life or mine that God will not work for our ultimate good and his glory (Rom. 8:28). This is adequate reason to praise God even when present trials swirl around us. But there is more.

Through Nebuchadnezzar's dream Daniel saw an ultimate and eternal victory of Christ over all the powers and dominions of this world (2:44). Christ's final work will not be complete until his kingdom is established in and over this world. Jesus is coming back to reign. All will be subject to his authority. Our trials will not be forever; his rule shall be. Unfairness, injustice, pain, and difficulty will end. All will be put right. For this future we, too, can praise God, even in present hardship. Our present is bearable because Christ's future glory is guaranteed.

The Response of Proclamation

Glory to God

Because he understands the nature of his Lord, Daniel offered God prayer and praise in a difficult time. Still, Daniel's regard for God had yet to reach its broadest expression. When the bottom seemed to fall out and Daniel's circumstances remained tough, he still proclaimed the greatness of God. Daniel's response to peril was proclamation. He resisted any temptation to take credit for the amazing insight God granted him. When the king asked Daniel if he could reveal the dream, the prophet—who by now knew the dream and its interpretation—made sure the king knew that God alone was to be glorified for the revelation (2:26–28, 45c).

A set of stairs in our first home in St. Louis went straight up between the first and second floors. There was no landing or turn to ease the steepness of the slope or shorten the number of steps down which a person could fall. When our children were small, we sometimes worried about their safety on these stairs. We were particularly concerned for our daughter when she was a toddler and her rambunctious older brothers would race past her on the stairs. Simply because we worried, though, did not mean the steps caused her the slightest concern. In fact, they seemed to act like a magnet for her little body. She always wanted to crawl up.

One day I caught her going up the stairs on her own. Normally she would get scolded for heading up the stairs, but this time she was trying so hard that I did not have the heart to stop her. But I would not let her go alone, either. There was still too much danger. So I quietly stepped behind her and stretched my arms inches below her in case she slipped. She was concentrating so much on grabbing the stair rails to pull herself up that she didn't even notice me. Finally she reached the top of the stairs. You can hardly imagine how proud she looked as she stood at the top of the stairs on her shaky and inexperienced legs. You would need the theme music from a *Rocky* movie to get the proper effect. If she could have talked, she would have crowed. It was as if every bone in her little body was saying, "Look what I did! I got up here all by myself!"

I knew what she was thinking, but I had a rather different perspective. I knew that, even if she believed her grip had gotten her safely up the stairs, the truth was that other hands were also at work. She had no idea how much danger she really was in or how safe she really was. She was safe from the danger not because of the grip of her infant hands but because of the safety provided by my arms beneath her.

The Bible says God is the one who keeps us safe because beneath us are his everlasting arms (Deut. 33:27). We may think that what we have accomplished, or what we are, is a matter of our efforts, arrangements, or abilities—the work of our hands. But the truth is that other arms have been beneath us. Were it not for these arms beneath our lives we would long since have fallen from the heights we thought our abilities had enabled us to climb. Pride and self-acclaim disappear when the true source of human achievement is known. If we are anything, it is only because God climbed the heights with us and kept us from falling.

Daniel knew the truths of God's enabling and keeping. These truths erased all reference to self in his speech. The prophet was so conscious of the work of his God that no explanation of the king's dream excluded proclamation of God as the source of revelation. Even when the young prophet was not yet sure what the cruel Nebuchadnezzar's response would be, God could not be kept from Daniel's lips (2:28). As a result, God could not be kept from Nebuchadnezzar's mind. When Daniel finished interpreting the dream, Nebuchadnezzar not only paid homage to Daniel (because Nebuchadnezzar did not yet understand God), the king also honored Daniel's God. Nebuchadnezzar said, "Truly, your God is God of gods and Lord of kings, and a revealer of mysteries, for you have been able to reveal this mystery" (2:47). Because of Daniel's proclamation, the king knew Daniel's ability was from his God. Nebuchadnezzar's recognition of the power of God was an important product of Daniel's proclamation that would have far-reaching spiritual implications for this despot (see Dan. 4). But there were even more immediate implications of Daniel's proclamation.

Witness to Others: They See God Better

The proclamation accompanying Daniel's revelation made the power and presence of the Lord so real that the king would not touch God's prophet. Daniel's interpretation openly degraded the future of Babylon and its king. Yet instead of ordering Daniel's execution for such an affront, Nebuchadnezzar fell prostrate before the prophet and praised Daniel's God (2:46–47). Nebuchadnezzar was so humbled that the rage Daniel likely expected from the cruel despot never came. Nebuchadnezzar bowed to Daniel. The prophet's proclamation itself became an instrument God used to give perspective to the king and to protect Daniel.

There is an important lesson for us here. So often we neglect the proclamation of God to those around us because we fear the testimony of our convictions will place us at some disadvantage. But Daniel's life makes it clear that God chooses to work most powerfully when his name is most evident. We rob ourselves of God's power when we let circumstances steal his name from our lips. There is never a better time to proclaim God than when the risk seems great because God assumes control of those causes fought in his name. The powers of this world cannot stand when God is clearly, courageously, and solely proclaimed. By our witness others see the Lord better and, as a consequence, our Lord affects their lives. Whether they turn toward him or away from him, they are still being forced to deal with his testimony through our proclamation.

Strength to Us: We See God Better

Even if God's working is not acknowledged by the world, the Lord's proclamation strengthens believers in crisis. We know that Daniel had special insight into the nature and working of God (2:30, 44). Daniel's insights, and the strength he would derive from knowing God's presence and power, always accompanied a passion to make God known. The message for us is this: when we point others' eyes to the Lord, we also see him more clearly.

We can bear almost anything if we only see God at work in our circumstances. Daniel teaches us we may not see God clearly enough to take comfort and strength from our vision until we proclaim him. Proclamation of God clarifies our vision of him. When we learn enough of God to express him before others, we begin to know him well enough to entrust him with our lives. The heart that overflows with knowledge and love of God is never overwhelmed by the circumstances that are already in his hands. Instead, we become increasingly confident of God. That is why Daniel could speak with such certainty about God's work (2:45c). Proclamation to others establishes in us the truths that strengthen our own hearts.

A Shift of Focus

Prayer, praise, and proclamation are all spiritual responses to crisis that shift attention from our abilities to God's. These responses humble us by making us realize we are ultimately dependent on God's influence rather than our initiative. We confess our weakness by prayer, praise, and proclamation so God's strength will meet no barrier of pride in us. For when we acknowledge our need is greater than we are, God's supply is more sufficient than we can imagine.

There is always an element of our being that wants to take charge. When the bottom falls out in our lives, we recognize the futility of that attitude. God is the only one who must be given charge of our lives and our difficulties. Not only is he the only one who can handle our circumstances, he will also work in them to lead us closer to himself. Extreme situations often reflect God's extreme desire for us to know his love more fully. He teaches us to lean on him because when we rest on the One who loves us, we know no greater peace nor can claim any greater contentment. Dependence on God produces a joy so full that crisis cannot exhaust its supply.

Knowing these truths it is sometimes strange to discover how, despite our best intentions, we stop depending on God and resume trusting in ourselves. Shortly after my wife and I left seminary, I became the pastor of a historic church in Illinois. The church was well established. We had a good income, lived in a nice house, and the neighbors—who had a swimming pool—were even members of our church. Kathy and I said to each other, "We have struggled and pinched pennies long enough. Now, we have found the good life."

Because of our newfound security, we decided it was time to get our family started. This decision was not as easy for us as it may be for some because there is some history of birth disorders in my family. As Kathy was expecting our first child, we occasionally winced when friends would say, "What do you want, a boy or a girl? Well, it really doesn't matter as long as the baby is healthy." Inside we thought, "What if our baby is not healthy? We know our child may have some problems. If that happens, are we supposed to feel sorry for ourselves? Will our child not be as precious because he or she is not perfect? Will our baby be worth less because of this prejudice for health?" We resolved that our child would be worth no less to us regardless of what others might think.

As the time approached for our child to be born, we began to prepare ourselves to love and value our child despite others' attitudes. The birth day finally arrived. Everything looked great. All the test results were good. The vital signs of mother and baby were normal. Then, just minutes before delivery, the monitors began to show that the baby was in distress.

When he was born, he was blue—the result of oxygen deprivation. For some reason, in the last stages of delivery the baby did not get the oxygen he needed. The doctor tried to get him to breathe, but he would not breathe. We did not even get a chance to touch him, as the nurses immediately took the baby to special equipment to clear his lungs and air passages. Because this was our first baby, we did not fully understand what was happening. But then I saw one of the nurses look at the clock and begin timing our baby *not* breathing. Suddenly, in a surreal moment of looking from the clock to my wife's fading smile, I realized what was happening. Inside, I cried, "Oh, heavenly Father, I thought I had prepared myself for anything, but I have not prepared for my child to die."

What do you do when your baby starts to die? You suddenly realize how helpless you are. You cannot do anything to control what is dearest to you. You see that all your abilities, your preparations, and your plans really mean nothing. You are not in control. So what do you do? What can you do but pray? I prayed, "God, help him. God, help us. I'm not sure what we will do, or what we will be, if we lose him. God, please, save him."

God did save our child. Praise God!

I can praise God now for his past goodness to our family. There are still the hard times when I am tempted to think that God is not concerned for us, when grace seems far away and not very clear. But in those times I can look at the face of my son—healthy and whole despite some early developmental issues—and I can praise my God. Still, I recognize that the health of my son is not, and cannot be, the only reason I praise God. Life is long, and members of our extended family have faced the loss of children, and we all still have much yet to face. We face what is to come, however, with a greater understanding of our God because of the past circumstances of our first son's birth. But, knowing that not all have been spared the loss of a child, there is more to learn in the provision of another son.

God spared my son, but he did not spare his Son. I only began to sense the pain of the death of a son. God knows the pain. When he was in control and not required to feel pain, my God sacrificed his only Son for a sinner like me—and like you (see John 3:16). May God help us all never to lose sight of that great gift so that when the bottom seems to fall out of our lives we know what to do, whom to trust, and whom to proclaim. When our focus is on the cross rather than on our crisis, our hearts will lead us to the one who purchased our lives with his own and is coming again to take us to his home. We will pray to the God who always loves us. We will praise the God who alone will save us. We will proclaim the God who gave his Son for us. Even when the bottom falls out, prayer, praise, and proclamation will grant us peace for today and confidence for tomorrow.

3

Faith in the Furnace

—— DANIEL 3 ——

Now the spotlight shifts from Daniel, who remains in the royal court, to his friends Shadrach, Meshach, and Abednego. At Daniel's request, they have been sent to an outer province as administrators. So they will have to live their faith without him (2:29). Their actions demonstrate that they are ready.

Despite his recent theology lesson from Daniel, Nebuchadnezzar reverts to idolatry. No longer content to control merely the labor of his Jewish captives, he attempts to control their hearts and minds. The king erects an idol of gold, ninety feet tall. He orders everyone in the province to bow to the idol whenever his musicians play a salute. At least three subjects do not bow. Shadrach, Meshach, and Abednego stand up for their God. Then, despite having administrative rank, the three young men get a blast of the king's wrath. He orders them thrown into a fiery furnace. In their response to these dire circumstances, we learn not only what human faithfulness looks like but also what biblical faith truly is:

King Nebuchadnezzar made an image of gold, whose height was sixty cubits and its breadth six cubits. He set it up on the plain of Dura, in the province of Babylon. Then King Nebuchadnezzar sent to gather the satraps, the prefects, and the governors, the counselors, the treasurers, the justices, the magistrates, and all the officials of the provinces to come to the dedication of the image that King Nebuchadnezzar had set up. Then the satraps, the prefects, and the governors, the counselors, the treasurers, the justices, the magistrates, and all the officials of the provinces gathered for the dedication of the image that King Nebuchadnezzar had set up. And they stood before the image that Nebuchadnezzar had set up. And the herald proclaimed aloud, "You are commanded, O peoples, nations, and languages, that when you hear the sound of the horn, pipe, lyre, trigon, harp, bagpipe, and every kind of music, you are to fall down and worship the golden image that King Nebuchadnezzar has set up. And whoever does not fall down and worship shall immediately be cast into a burning fiery furnace." Therefore, as soon as all the peoples heard the sound of the horn, pipe, lyre, trigon, harp, bagpipe, and every kind of music, all the peoples, nations, and languages fell down and worshiped the golden image that King Nebuchadnezzar had set up.

Therefore at that time certain Chaldeans came forward and maliciously accused the Jews. They declared to King Nebuchadnezzar, "O king, live forever! You, O king, have made a decree, that every man who hears the sound of the horn, pipe, lyre, trigon, harp, bagpipe, and every kind of music, shall fall down and worship the golden image. And whoever does not fall down and worship shall be cast into a burning fiery furnace. There are certain Jews whom you have appointed over the affairs of the province of Babylon: Shadrach, Meshach, and Abednego. These men, O king, pay no attention to you; they do not serve your gods or worship the golden image that you have set up."

Then Nebuchadnezzar in furious rage commanded that Shadrach, Meshach, and Abednego be brought. So they brought these men before the king. Nebuchadnezzar answered and said to them, "Is it true, O Shadrach, Meshach, and Abednego, that you do not serve my gods or worship the golden image that I have set up? Now if you are ready when you hear the sound of the horn, pipe, lyre, trigon, harp, bagpipe, and every kind of music, to fall down and worship the image that I have made, well and good. But if you do not worship, you shall immediately be cast into a burning fiery furnace. And who is the god who will deliver you out of my hands?"

Shadrach, Meshach, and Abednego answered and said to the king, "O Nebuchadnezzar, we have no need to answer you in this matter. If this be so, our God whom we serve is able to deliver us from the burning fiery furnace, and he will deliver us out of your hand, O king. But if not, be it known to you, O king, that we will not serve your gods or worship the golden image that you have set up."

Then Nebuchadnezzar was filled with fury, and the expression of his face was changed against Shadrach, Meshach, and Abednego. He ordered the furnace heated seven times more than it was usually heated. And he ordered some of the mighty men of his army to bind Shadrach, Meshach, and Abednego, and to cast them into the burning fiery furnace. Then these men were bound in their cloaks, their tunics, their hats, and their other garments, and they were thrown into the burning fiery furnace. Because the king's order was urgent and the furnace overheated, the flame of the fire killed those men who took up Shadrach, Meshach, and Abednego. And these three men, Shadrach, Meshach, and Abednego, fell bound into the burning fiery furnace.

Then King Nebuchadnezzar was astonished and rose up in haste. He declared to his counselors, "Did we not cast three men bound into the fire?" They answered and said to the king, "True, O king." He answered and said, "But I see four men unbound, walking in the midst of the fire, and they are not hurt; and the appearance of the fourth is like a son of the gods."

Then Nebuchadnezzar came near to the door of the burning fiery furnace; he declared, "Shadrach, Meshach, and Abednego, servants of the Most High God, come out, and come here!" Then Shadrach, Meshach, and Abednego came out from the fire. And the satraps, the prefects, the governors, and the king's counselors gathered together and saw that the fire had not had any power over the bodies of those men. The hair of their heads was not singed, their cloaks were not harmed, and no smell of fire had come upon them. Nebuchadnezzar answered and said, "Blessed be the God of Shadrach, Meshach, and Abednego, who has sent his angel and delivered his servants, who trusted in him, and set aside the king's command, and yielded up their bodies rather than serve and worship any god except their own God. Therefore I make a decree: Any people, nation, or language that speaks anything against the God of Shadrach, Meshach, and Abednego shall be torn limb from limb, and their houses laid in ruins, for there is no other god who is able to rescue in this way." Then the king promoted Shadrach, Meshach, and Abednego in the province of Babylon. (Dan. 3:1–30)

A New Definition of Faith

How do you win the World Series? Decades ago, when the New York Mets were the underdog darlings of the National League, two young pitchers told the world the secret. Tom Seaver and Tug McGraw borrowed a line from a Walt Disney character and said, "Ya gotta believe." In almost every World Series since, someone takes up the same slogan for the favorite team.

A clever advertising agency also picked up the phrase and has used it to sell peanut butter. The ad says that the way they make their peanut butter is "with a whole lot of peanuts and a little bit of magic" and then one more thing—"Ya gotta believe."

There appears to be a consensus in popular culture that good things will happen if someone just "believes" enough. If you have enough confidence in the outcome, dreams will come true. In order to win a game, make peanut butter, get a job, attract a good-looking boyfriend, or win a ticket to Hollywood on *American Idol*, we really, *really* must believe in the results we want. Unfortunately, the idea that we can make really good things happen by applying a whole lot of faith gets so much play in our culture that people actually begin to believe in such a belief. The idea that adequate faith can trigger God into immediately giving us the best things in life gets transferred to the most serious matters of health, career, family, and faith. Even Bible-believing Christians may begin to assume that they can make good things happen through mustering exceptional faith—and may have been taught this in their churches. Great movements of Christianity across our world have gained steam (only to lose trust later) on the assumption that sufficient faith will result in great success, extraordinary wealth, and excellent health.

I have experienced the consequence of equating exceptional faith with getting exactly what one may want. I had a job working as an assistant to a commercial photographer. For an outdoor project with a local pool manufacturer we needed two days of good weather to take all the photos necessary. My boss, a Christian, encouraged me to pray with him for clear skies. We prayed, and the first day of picture shooting was beautiful.

The next day was wet and ugly. Through the morning we sat in my boss's car, waiting for the rain to pass. But the rain did not pass. And the longer the deluge continued, the more my boss's mood became evident on his face. His countenance transitioned from sadness to dejection and then to anger that spilled into words.

"Yesterday," he snarled, "God gave us a good day because we prayed in faith. Today it's raining even though we need it to be sunny. That means somebody isn't doing his job."

I did not know exactly which "somebody" he had in mind, but there were only two alternatives—us and God. Assuming the reason we had the first good day was because of our exceptional faith, then the reason the second day was rainy was either because our faith was inferior or our God had failed. Either we were not doing our job or God was not doing his.

Assuming that life's difficulties indicate that either our faith is inadequate or our God is inadequate is a sure recipe for despair. If bad things happen because our faith is inadequate, then no one has sufficient faith, because everyone faces problems in this broken world. But if bad things happen because our God is inadequate, then we have no one to turn to in this troubled world. Jesus told us that difficulty invades every life, including that of the faithful (Matt. 6:34; John 16:33; 17:15). We cannot gauge the adequacy of faith by the absence of trials. We need to define faith by standards beyond the popular consensus.

It can seem very spiritual to say, "If you trust God in sufficient quantity or quality, then you will get what you wish." But as inviting as that message may sound, we need to examine whether it is true. Does the Bible teach that if you have adequate faith, you can get exactly what your human heart desires?

At first glance, many of the miracles of the Bible may make us think God's Word teaches that our faith can determine particular outcomes that we desire. We may point to holy men and women of biblical accounts and say, "Why, just look at the wonderful things that happened because of their confidence in what they wanted to occur." But if this kind of special confidence really defined biblical faith, then we would have to skip the third chapter of Daniel.

This chapter of Daniel's history tells us of three faith giants: Shadrach, Meshach, and Abednego. Because of their faith these three young men are unquestionably biblical heroes. Citing such, the writer of Hebrews says, "Through faith . . . [they] quenched the power of fire" (Heb. 11:33–34). With great courage they expressed their faith by refusing to bow to the image of gold. Yet when Shadrach's, Meshach's, and Abednego's obedience put them on the brink of the king's fiery furnace, they did not pretend to know what was going to happen to them. They did not claim to know what their circumstances would hold (v. 17a) or what their God would do (v. 18a). Even though they affirmed that God was able to deliver them, they added, "But if not, be it known to you, O king, that we will not serve your gods" (v. 18).

We may want to correct these heroes of faith by saying, "Oh no, Shadrach, Meshach, and Abednego. Don't say, 'If . . .' No ifs, ands, or buts are allowed for those truly faithful. You should believe without doubting." But Shadrach, Meshach, and Abednego did not operate on the popular notion that faith is exceptional confidence in particular outcomes. By their words and actions Shadrach, Meshach, and Abednego tell us of a more biblical faith.

Biblical faith is *not* confidence in particular outcomes; it is confidence in a sovereign God. We trust that he knows what we cannot discern, plans what we cannot anticipate, and secures our eternity in ways beyond our fathoming. Our trust is not in the quantity or quality of our belief. Our trust in God is not built on insights we possess or wishes we manufacture. The Bible does not teach us to look inward to discern what we should be trusting. Faith is not confidence in our belief but confidence in our God. Any other perspective will ultimately harm our faith.

What Biblical Faith Is Not

One way to get a better picture of biblical faith—the kind of faith that helps rather than harms—is to examine the kind of faith Shadrach, Meshach, and Abednego shared. Their faith will first give us a clear understanding of what biblical faith is *not*.

Faith Is Not Trust in the Quantity of Our Belief

We may be tempted to measure our faith by how much confidence we can pump into our minds (and how much doubt we can bleed from our hearts) so that what we want to happen will occur. We may go through intricate rituals to convince ourselves that we have created enough faith in our brains to eliminate doubt and to bind God to honoring our desires. We may sing a spiritual song, pray long, read Scripture, and scold ourselves for any questioning thoughts in order to fill our minds with as much belief as is necessary to get God to do what we think is best.

In one sense such faith rituals make us like athletes psyching up for the big event (focusing with music playing through their earplugs, imagining the moves ahead, and high-fiving the coach), convincing ourselves that we really, *really* believe. In another sense, we resemble witches, throwing a pinch of song, an ounce of prayer, and a ton of belief into a cauldron of human desires so that God must do what we determine he should do. Our faith is not so much in God as it is in the amount of belief we have conjured up to control him.

I once heard a mother in the depths of puzzled and honest pain express what happens to faith when we trust its amount rather than its object. This young mother was running errands with a tribe of preschoolers in the car. After a couple of stops, she recognized she was running terribly late. She would miss a doctor's appointment if she did not make faster progress. The next stop on the errand list was the neighborhood grocery. She began to calculate what that meant: getting all of the children out of their car seats, into their coats, into the store, into the shopping cart—and the reverse of it all on the way out. This would be a twenty-minute stop for just a couple of items. Then came inspiration, a way to get back on schedule. If there were a parking space right by the front door, then she could leave the kids in the car and watch them through the storefront glass. She could zip in, zip out, never lose sight of the children, and be right back on schedule.

"Lord, please give me a parking space by the door," the young mother prayed. "I know that you can provide a parking space and I believe you will."

Recounting the experience later in our home, she said, "I was praying with all kinds of faith." And she tried to build more faith for herself by saying again and again in her mind, "I believe. I believe. I believe."

She thought that if she just had enough faith, God would do what she wanted him to do. She prayed in earnest for God to honor her faith. Yet when she arrived at the store and turned into the parking lot, she saw immediately there was no parking space near the front door. We may smile at this young mother's naïveté. But when she told my wife and me what had happened, she spoke through tears.

"What's wrong with me?" she asked. "I prayed with all kinds of faith, but God didn't answer. There must be something wrong with my faith."

She had caught herself in the old trap of defining faith as confidence in the quantity of our belief, rather than confidence in God. As a consequence, when something unwanted occurred, she could only assume that her faith was inadequate or that her God was. This Christian mother was too well schooled (and too full of true faith) to believe that God was inadequate, so she assumed her faith was at fault. Simply because what she wanted to happen did not happen, she thought her faith was insufficient or missing. But she had not lost her faith; she had only misplaced it.

What precipitated this spiritual crisis in this young woman's life was the idea that faith resides in creating enough feelings of belief inside of us. But faith is not something we conjure in our brains; it's not a mind game. Faith is not trusting in how much confidence we have about things we would like to happen. Shadrach, Meshach, and Abednego confessed that they didn't know what would happen. They were not sure if they would be thrown into the fiery furnace (v. 17), and, if that was their future, they were not sure if they would live or die (v. 18). Yet they were great men of faith.

These three faithful men understood that faith is not defined by mental gymnastics that strengthen our focus on our desires. Real faith locks onto God. We pray to him for what we think is right but trust him to do what he knows is best. Shadrach, Meshach, and Abednego said that even if God did not deliver them from death, they would serve only him. Their words tell us that faith is not measured by the strength of our expectations but by the substance of our conviction that "whatever my God ordains is right."[1]

Biblical faith calls for each of us to acknowledge God's provision as sufficient, loving, and good even if it falls short of, or contradicts, immediate desires that cannot fully anticipate his plans or fathom his wisdom. Believers whose faith will withstand the trials of this world must be able to affirm, "I may not understand God's provision. I may not expect it or, in this life, know enough even to like it, but I trust my God whatever comes. This does not mean I always know what will come. But my faith trusts that what my God knows is best—not what I think is best."

This insight into faith relieves those who worry that there is something obviously deficient with their faith when what they want to happen does not always occur. We are not lesser Christians because we believe God is wiser than we are. We are not inferior Christians because we trust God's wisdom more than our own.

For too long too many have been victims of the fantasy that adequate faith will relieve Christians of all difficulties. Problems of the faithful supposedly vanish because what they want to happen happens. Sufficient faith allegedly solves problems, removes affliction, and untangles troubles. Sadly, such a presentation of Christianity makes it sinful to weep, hurt, or be disappointed. These emotions automatically imply that things other than what we wanted have happened and, therefore, evidence an inferior faith. As a result, we are inundated with literature and programming that requires hyperenthusiastic

Christianity. This Christianity insists on continuous smiles, perpetually bub-
bling optimism, and never-ending spiritual highs.

Of course there is nothing intrinsically wrong with joyous expressions of our
faith; solemnity is not more holy than enthusiasm. But we should never imply
that anyone not on an emotional high lacks faith. Faith in Jesus Christ is not a
feeling. Feelings change; emotional highs ebb. Faith—biblical faith—does not.

Shadrach, Meshach, and Abednego did not bubble with giddy enthusiasm.
Nowhere in this passage did any of the three say, "Oh boy, here we go into
the fiery furnace. Isn't this great?" They were not happy about going into the
furnace. They were not even filled with confidence about what would happen to them. But they were filled with faith in their God. They believed in his
presence and in his care despite Nebuchadnezzar's intention to burn them
alive. If they lived, they knew their God was near. If they died, they knew
their God was still near.

Shadrach, Meshach, and Abednego trusted their God because time after
time he had delivered their forefathers from enemies despite Israel's sin and
rebellion (2:23). God had been faithful even when his people had not. God
even had promised that he would save his people from their captivity in Babylon (2:44). Although things looked grim in the immediate future, the faith of
Shadrach, Meshach, and Abednego was not shattered because it was rooted
not in present circumstances but in the nature of their God (2:18, 45).

The God whose purposes are loving and eternal can be trusted (3:17).
Shadrach, Meshach, and Abednego were great men of faith not because of
an unusual amount of confidence in easy living and pleasant circumstances.
Their great faith showed in the confidence that God would accomplish his
good purposes through them as they remained faithful during hard times.

This can be our great confidence, too, when we express faith that tragedy
does not mean God has vanished, danger does not indicate that he has failed,
and difficulty does not imply that he is weak. God is in control (2:20–22, 44;
3:17). Because we know his loving nature, we can have faith that there is a plan
and a purpose for whatever we face. Difficulties may still arise, but he enables
us to surmount them. Grief may still come, but he gives strength to bear it.
His hand is never capricious or clumsy. True faith simply acknowledges that
God knows and does what is right. True faith does not pretend to know all
that must be done. Any faith that insists God must do things our way in order
for him to be truly faithful does not fully trust him. Such faith is forced to rest
on limited human insight and ability. Thus, it is a faith that cannot ultimately
evade disappointment and pain.

In a rural community near my home, a family grew dissatisfied with their
church. So they started a church in their home. In this new church, the family

taught that God would bring wealth and health to those with enough faith. The family felt it had proof for such teaching. For several years this farming family had contracted with a large feed company to supply large quantities of grain at a guaranteed price. When other farmers suffered from vacillating farm markets, this family continued to prosper. Any who attended their home church were told the reason for this wealth: great faith.

Some of the family members so believed in the power of sufficient faith to gain earthly desires that they began to promise healing to sick persons in our town. The family members would tell those suffering from illness that they did not have enough faith. Since they believed sufficient faith makes problems vanish, they assumed illness was an automatic sign of insufficient faith.

The family members from the new church meant well, but the consequences of their actions were horrible. People who were terminally ill and desperately in need of the Lord's comfort were told their weak faith was causing God's absence from their lives. The evidence was their illness.

Occasionally I found faithful Christians in our church distraught after they had been visited by members of the family church. Dear saints who were weak and suffering had been terrified by this warped expression of faith. But my concern was not limited to the sick individuals whom the family visited. Eventually the heartache came home to the family themselves.

A child with a birth defect was born to one of the family members. The rest of the family believed that this sadness came because the baby's parents did not have enough faith. They began a process of discipline and shunning the parents for their sin of insufficient faith. Those parents eventually left the family church because their child's suffering caused the constant questioning of their faith. More problems followed.

Our community, along with farming communities all over the country, sank into an economic crisis. Suddenly the big feed company's set price no longer covered the expenses for the grain that the farm family was contracted to produce. The same contract that had provided security for years now became a financial noose around the family's neck. In two years the family went bankrupt, the farm (which had been in the family for generations) was sold, and family members scattered. Today they do not visit hurting families and say, "Look at the health and wealth that will come if only you have enough faith."

We should take no joy or satisfaction from the pain this family experienced. We should grieve for them even as we learn from them. Faith in the quantity of our faith scatters families and shatters lives. We live in a fallen world where illness, difficulty, and tragedy will thrive until Christ returns. Christians are not immune from the consequences of living in this broken world. Teaching that some heroic degree of faith will inoculate us from trial or tragedy destroys the faith that we actually need in the midst of such afflictions. Of course, God can remove disease and difficulty from our lives if he knows that is best, but he may also desire to use our testimonies in the midst of trial and tragedy for purposes more grand and eternal than we can imagine. The choice is his. Our job is to trust him. Real faith is not faith in the quantity of our confidence; it is faith in our God.

Faith Is Not Trust in the Quality of Our Belief

Though we may avoid the misconception that our faith will accomplish what we want if we generate a sufficient quantity of belief, other errors can creep into our expectations. One such error is the idea that God will do as we desire if our desire is righteous enough. We trust that God will fulfill our desires because of the quality of our belief. We expect God to do as we want because we have determined that it is in God's best interests to make this happen. Because the results are "for God's sake," we become convinced that what we would love to happen must occur.

During military training, a member of my family got in a time crunch and was in danger of being AWOL. He needed to get back to his base quickly, but he faced a number of obstacles: he was traveling late at night, on a holiday weekend, in a pickup truck that was almost out of gas. A non-Christian friend was riding with him. When the friend saw the needle on the gas gauge hit empty, he threw up his hands in resignation and said, "We're never going to make it. We are in trouble, for sure."

My family member, concerned not only for getting back to base but also for the spiritual welfare of his buddy, replied, "No, we are going to make it. I have prayed to God in faith. He will get us there."

You can guess what happened. A few miles farther, the engine sputtered, coughed, and died. Now the story seems funny, but at that time the humor was lost on the one from my family. The events of that evening triggered a spiritual crisis in his life.

"Bryan," he said later, "why didn't God answer my prayer? I prayed in faith, believing God. Nothing better could have happened for my friend than for him to see God at work. I wasn't asking for my sake. My friend would have believed in God's power and probably trusted in him for salvation, if only God had answered. Why didn't God act?"

I do not know. But I do know that biblical faith should keep us from being so attached to what we think is right—even if we are convinced that what we want is for God's good—that we think God has failed because he didn't follow our directions. Faith is trust in God and his plan. Faith does not require

God to fulfill wishes as though our desires were his command and our human plans his divine ordinance. God knows what is necessary to bring others to himself, when it is necessary, and how. We do not. Faith does not require God to do what we would love to happen even for the right reasons.

Learning to trust God's wisdom above our own is not an easy lesson. In times of trouble, relying on God's wisdom can try the faith of the most spiritually astute. Christian counselor and author Jim Conway told of his struggle to trust God's wisdom when his daughter, Becki, was stricken with cancer. The doctors said they would need to amputate Becki's leg to save her life. So the family began to pray, asking God to heal Becki. They knew God could heal, so they prayed that he would save the leg as a testimony of his love. Because they desired glory for God, they also prayed that God would heal Becki entirely.

So strongly did the family believe that God would heal Becki that, on the day of the surgery, Jim insisted the doctors test Becki's leg again. The surgeon agreed, and the family went to a waiting room eagerly anticipating the results they were sure would bring great glory to God. Jim later recounted what happened:

> A crowd of friends from the church had come to wait with us. So many came, in fact, that they made us leave the waiting room. When the surgeon came out, I knew (from the look on his face) what he was going to say, and I couldn't face it. I couldn't face all those people. So I ran.
>
> I ran to the hospital basement where no one would find me. And I cried. I yelled. I pounded my fists against the wall. I felt like the God whom I had served had abandoned me at the hour of my deepest need. Was he so busy answering prayers for parking places that he couldn't see Becki?[2]

The experience devastated Jim, but it also drove him back to the Scriptures. There he discovered the problem with a faith that blindly insists on what we would love to have happen—even if what we want would seem to honor God. Such a faith is foreign to the Bible. We must not let an aching desire for something that seems so right make us lose sight of what God's Word plainly teaches. We must never forget the faithful men and women of the Bible who did not have everything go as their desires dictated. If we forget them, then we will define faith in such a way that we and others get hurt.

We should remember, for example, the difficulties of the apostle Paul. No one doubts the faith of Paul. He took the gospel to the gentiles, wrote inspired Scripture, and performed miraculous healings. Yet the Bible records at least four examples of sickness or disaster in his life that God did not prevent. In his second letter to the Corinthians, Paul says that he prayed three times for

God to remove his "thorn in the flesh." We do not know the specific ailment. We do know that God did *not* grant Paul's request but replied, "My grace is sufficient for you, for my power is made perfect in weakness" (2 Cor. 12:9). Perhaps an example of this occurred in Galatia where an illness prevented Paul's travels long enough for his preaching to produce spiritual fruit there (Gal. 4:13–14).

Paul did not respond to his physical afflictions by doubting his faith or his God. The apostle understood that biblical faith does not remove all hardship and suffering from life. He believed that God knew what was best for him and for the ministry of the gospel. Thus, if God's strength was made more evident by Paul's testimony in a weakened condition, Paul readily accepted the "thorn" and even rejoiced in his weakness that made his commitment to Christ more convincing (2 Cor. 12:9b). Paul's attitude reminds us that God knows far better than we what will bring men and women to a saving knowledge of him. The most powerful testimony Christians have at times is not the fact that they live on "easy street" but that their relationship with God sustains them even when their worlds collapse.

If genuine faith were to bring an end to all life's hardships, then Paul's comments in the chapter preceding his reference to "the thorn in the flesh" also make no sense. There Paul recites a litany of his sufferings. He says he has been imprisoned; flogged; stoned; shipwrecked; adrift at sea; endangered by bandits, countrymen, and circumstances of all sorts; sleepless; hungry; thirsty; cold; exposed; and pressured by church concerns (2 Cor. 11:23–28).

How should we respond to such hardships in the life of an apostle? I doubt if anyone would suggest this: "Now, Paul, if you just had a better faith, life wouldn't be so hard." Of course not. We know the apostle's faith carried him through his hard times. He did not expect his efforts to spread the gospel to be without trial or push back. He knew that Satan would oppose spiritual progress, that afflictions often accompany spiritual gains, and that life will not be without pain until we are in heaven. Paul did not expect his faith to erase troubles but to strengthen him for and through them. Good things do not always happen according to our plans, wisdom, or desires—and that does not mean our faith is at fault.

Paul encouraged Timothy to stop drinking only water and use a little wine for the young pastor's stomach ailments (1 Tim. 5:23). Why did the apostle stoop to such "medical" means? Why didn't Paul just miraculously heal Timothy? The miracle would have been a lot more impressive. And a good miracle would have given the young Timothy a lot more credibility in his difficult ministry at Ephesus. Paul had performed healing miracles on other occasions. He had even raised a young man from the dead. Why not heal now? Surely

Timothy would have preferred this solution, and the spiritual benefits of such a miracle seem obvious.

We might think that God's glory and purposes would be better served by Paul's exercise of problem-removing faith. Yet the apostle did not miraculously heal Timothy. Should we assume Paul was lacking in faith at this stage in his life? No. Paul's faith was intact. At the very moment Paul is writing this prescription, he is also writing inspired Scripture. Should we then assume Timothy's faith was to blame? No. Paul commended Timothy in this letter and gave him additional pastoral instruction. If Paul felt Timothy was insufficiently faithful, surely the apostle would have rebuked the young man for his faithlessness and removed him from pastoral office. But there were no such corrections.

Why, then, did Paul not heal Timothy? We do not know. All we do know is that both Timothy and Paul continued to trust God's wisdom and purposes (2 Tim. 1:2, 5). To them, illness was not an automatic sign of weak faith. And they maintained faith in God even when what they would have loved to happen for his sake did not happen.

Paul surely had reason to question divine purposes when he had to leave a helper named Trophimus sick at Miletus (2 Tim. 4:20). Our minds do mental flips when we read these words—particularly if we believe real faith rescues from all ills. "Paul, why did you leave him sick?" we ask. "Why didn't you heal Trophimus?" There are no simple answers to such questions. Neither Paul nor Trophimus are said to have failed the Lord. Elsewhere in the Bible both are identified, without qualification, as faithful followers of Jesus. We are left only with the understanding that at this time, as at other times in Paul's life, illness plagued his ministry (Gal. 4:13, 14). But the difficulties did not damage or impugn his faith. Rather, these afflictions required and produced faith so that God's work might continue despite the trials.

Paul was not the only faithful believer in Scripture who faced trials in the midst of spiritual pursuits. The eleventh chapter of Hebrews is often called the "faith chapter" because it cites believers from many periods of biblical history who are famous for their faith. Added to the list of those well known for faith that resulted in great spiritual victories are descriptions of believers who suffered great hardships. These who have been tortured, flogged, imprisoned, stoned, pierced with swords, sawed in two, made destitute, deprived, and homeless—all are commended for their faith (Heb. 11:35–40). The writer of Hebrews makes it clear that those who are the most spiritual and faithful may not have their earthly desires fulfilled. In fact, the highest spiritual priorities often result in suffering, persecution, and trial. No New Testament writer contends that the presence of difficulty indicates an absence of faith.

Even the greatest of Old Testament saints did not have a faith that removed every human trial. Elisha performed amazing miracles, routed armies, healed the sick, and raised the dead. But unlike his predecessor, Elijah, he was not taken to heaven in a fiery chariot. Instead, without a word of criticism of his faith, the Scriptures simply record that Elisha got sick and died (2 Kings 13:14). So faithful was Elisha to the Lord's work that even after he died his bones had healing powers (2 Kings 13:21). The Bible simply refuses to make illness an automatic sign of faithlessness. Our difficulties do not prove diminished spiritual integrity, and spiritual priorities do not eliminate real trials.

Lest we begin to look for flaws in the faith of Paul, Elisha, or other biblical believers to explain their difficulties, we should remember the example of Jesus himself. He prayed before his crucifixion that God would take "this cup" from him. Still, the trial came. But of course there was no lack of faith on the Savior's part. His faith was in his God's plans, not the absence of pain. He prayed not only that the cup would be taken away but also that "not my will, but yours, be done" (Luke 22:42). Christ wanted the trial to be taken away, but his deepest desire was that God would do his perfect will, even if that meant humiliation and torture.

Some contend that Jesus's prayer was actually a petition for strength to sustain the suffering that would compensate for our sins. If that is the case, then God clearly fulfilled Christ's desires by allowing him to survive until he fulfilled the requirements of the cross. Yet even this explanation makes it plain that faithful prayer and spiritual integrity are not tickets to pain-free lives.

Expressions of biblical faith are not a mental or emotional snapping of our fingers to get God to do what will make our lives easy. Our confidence should be not in what we want God to do but in God. Edith Schaeffer writes, "We need to be willing to let God be God."[3] We cannot presume to direct God's will as if our desires bind his hands. Our wishes are not his commands, and faith should not be so ill-defined as to imply as much. Real faith trusts God's plan and purpose. We do not trust in what we decide is right; we trust that God knows and will do what is right—in his time and according to his wisdom—to accomplish the gracious purposes of eternity.

Faith Is Not Trust in Our Insight

Scripture directs us to do God's will and then to trust him to take care of the outcome. This is precisely what Shadrach, Meshach, and Abednego did. They did not pretend to know what would happen to them. They had no desire to be burned alive and no doubt prayed for deliverance. Still, they recognized their chief duty was obedience, not figuring out what God would do next.

Had they been in charge, the three young men would certainly have had the golden image destroyed, Nebuchadnezzar rescind his edict, the furnace fail to burn, or any number of similar alternatives that would have made life less dangerous. But there were no alternatives. Shadrach, Meshach, and Abednego had to stand on the brink of a blazing, fiery furnace with a readiness to die in order to do God's will. They did not know what would happen, and they certainly did not desire for things to get this desperate. They merely understood that God would use their obedience for his good purpose, and they trusted him for that. Faith results in being faithful despite what comes, not telling God what should come.

Shadrach, Meshach, and Abednego teach us that believers are not more holy because they have a great certainty that something specific will happen or because they have identified correctly what God will do next. Too often Christians try to prove their faith to themselves or others by predicting God's actions. Faith of this sort gets measured by the conviction and precision with which one speaks about how "God will bless."

I once attended a prayer meeting in which a woman praised God because she was sure that he was going to heal her dog. The day the dog got sick she "just happened" to read in the Psalms that God "heals all your diseases." She explained that this apparent coincidence was God's "providential leading," assuring her that he would heal her pet.

This well-meaning but poorly informed woman had tied her faith to her ability to read God's will in the sequence of circumstances. Unfortunately, the circumstances were about to change. At the next prayer meeting, this same woman told the group her husband had just experienced a heart attack. "Obviously," she surmised, "God was not telling me that he would heal my dog; God was telling me in my psalm reading that he would heal my husband." My first impulse, I am ashamed to admit, was to laugh. What if her son got sick the next day? What would God be saying then? What if she read Numbers 14:12 ("I will strike them with the pestilence and disinherit them") next week? Then I remembered how often I had heard similar, if not so naive, expressions of faith from far more mature believers.

Once, when a fierce snowstorm forced me to forego a trip to my home, I stayed overnight at the home of a friend. I stayed up late with this family as they awaited the arrival of a daughter from college. After she was many hours overdue with no word of explanation, the unspoken worry on every mind was that she might have been in an accident. Someone finally spoke our fear, saying, "I hope she's all right." The immediate reply from the mother was, "Of course she's all right. I have faith in God, and I know she'll get here safely." But the daughter never did arrive that night. She did have an accident.

Faith is not made more effective because we predict outcomes in confident words or tones. Well-meaning elders may try to encourage pastors by saying, "Because you are God's messenger for us, and because God wants his message to go out effectively, God will bless your ministry. Our church will grow." But even Jesus did not witness that kind of unqualified success in his lifetime. Zealous, committed pastors may say to their churches, "Because there is the need for an expanded gospel witness in this community, and because God wants the community to hear the gospel, we know God will provide the money we need for this building program [or this broadcasting ministry or this youth outreach, etc.]." But Jeremiah had to preach in the context of Israel's fall, and Isaiah was told that his faithful preaching would not be heard.

Promising the success of human projects based on faith predictions gives divine status to human guesses. This is not faith in God; it is just optimistic wishing. Plans and projects supported with such confidence may succeed, but they may also fail because they are based on human probabilities rather than divine promises. Biblical faith is not confidence in what circumstances tend to indicate or what we hope will happen. These are just human desires parading as trust in God. Such parades may make a lot of noise and receive a lot of cheers, but they always run the risk of trampling the faith of tender hearts when our circumstances turn in unanticipated directions.

Confidence based on assurances that have no scriptural support damage faith more than they accomplish good. People assert such assurances because they believe the mark of strong faith is stating in unequivocal terms what God will do in specific circumstances. Such faith remains strong only as long as the circumstances coincide with our wishes. But human wishes are not the foundation of God's wisdom. God does not intend for us to predict outcomes as much as he intends for us to trust him in all circumstances.

If certainty of outcomes determined the quality of faith, then Shadrach, Meshach, and Abednego had inferior faith. Not one of them claimed to know for certain that they would not be burned alive. They were not concerned to read their circumstances with superhuman insight. They were only concerned to respond to their circumstances in godly ways. Regardless of what the king did to them—and they did not claim to know what that would be—they would obey God.

Shadrach, Meshach, and Abednego define faith for us by their righteous commitment to do God's will rather than by any mystical ability to read God's results. They trusted God in the present rather than trusting their insight into the future. They did not tie their faith to favorable circumstances; they responded to their circumstances with faith in God. The faithful three were more concerned to obey God than to guess his plans. Their faith was marked not by special insight into confusing circumstances but by faithful obedience amid those circumstances.

Shadrach, Meshach, and Abednego demonstrated that God expects us to act in accord with his Word and to trust him to work in accord with his perfect purposes. We do not have faith because all is going well; we do not lose faith because something goes poorly. Our faith is not in what circumstances might indicate but in God's greater purposes.

For more than a century the men and women of the North Africa Mission (now Arab World Ministries) exemplified what it means to trust obediently in God's purposes rather than to be ruled by attempts to read circumstances. This mission agency dedicated itself to reaching Muslims with the gospel of Jesus Christ. In recent years the mission has experienced remarkable success among one of the people groups most resistant to the gospel. The resistance is not new. In 1934, after a generation of work among Muslims, the mission counted more deaths among its missionaries and their children than it could count conversions. What if someone then had equated the quality of their faith with the nature of their circumstances?

Circumstances can never be trusted to indicate with certainty what our actions should be or what God's purposes are. The wisest king who ever lived wrote about the futility of trying to determine God's will on the basis of circumstances. In Ecclesiastes 8:14–9:1, Solomon said,

> There is a vanity that takes place on earth, that there are righteous people to whom it happens according to the deeds of the wicked, and there are wicked people to whom it happens according to the deeds of the righteous. I said that this also is vanity. And I commend joy, for man has nothing better under the sun but to eat and drink and be joyful, for this will go with him in his toil through the days of his life that God has given him under the sun.
>
> When I applied my heart to know wisdom, and to see the business that is done on earth, how neither day nor night do one's eyes see sleep, then I saw all the work of God, that man cannot find out the work that is done under the sun. However much man may toil in seeking, he will not find it out. Even though a wise man claims to know, he cannot find it out.
>
> But all this I laid to heart, examining it all, how the righteous and the wise and their deeds are in the hand of God. Whether it is love or hate, man does not know; both are before him.

If faith were to depend on determining what circumstances mean, then, the Bible makes clear, our faith would be futile.

We do not have to comprehend what will happen or explain why something has happened to have a strong, vibrant faith. We are permitted to be like Shadrach, Meshach, and Abednego and say, "Our God is so great, we trust him even though we don't know what will happen. As long as we do his will, we are in his care. That is sufficient for us." Great faith does not claim to know what only God can know; it claims to know the God who knows. Faith is only as great as its object—and the object of biblical faith is God's eternal care, not humans' earthly expectations.

This can be a message of great comfort to many believers. It means we need not trust in special divinations, revelations, or expressions of sanctified optimism in order to be faithful. We are not lesser Christians because others claim they know more about what circumstances mean than we. We can be content to trust and obey, just like Shadrach, Meshach, and Abednego. If this simple, obedient faith held them in God's care through a fiery furnace, then we can be content with such a faith in our trials. Other Christians may claim confidence in the fulfillment of personal desires, but we are allowed to claim something deeper and beyond: confidence in the infinite wisdom and eternal love of our God. Desire plus optimism does not equal faith. Biblical faith is not the stuff dreams are made of. Real faith is tougher, more resilient, more aware of the complexities of a fallen world, and more trusting of a sovereign God.

By their example, Shadrach, Meshach, and Abednego lay out a simple plan of action to help us faithfully confront the trials we face: (1) we acknowledge our needs without stipulating how God should or will respond; (2) we humbly acknowledge the ability of God either to meet our needs in the way we desire or in a way that he knows is better; and (3) we commit ourselves to uncompromising obedience whatever comes. We simply obey God and trust him to take care of the circumstances. "He rewards those who seek him" (Heb. 11:6). The rewards may not be what we expect, nor come as we anticipate, but faith understands the perfection of God's plan and trusts the love that prepares it so carefully. We need not read the results to rest in him.

Faith Is Trust in God Alone

Faith that honors God above our desires is not simply resignation to our circumstances. We do not shrug our shoulders and say, "What will be, will be." Faith is not fatalism.

We Believe God Is Able

The first reason that we trust God is that we believe he is "able to do far more abundantly than all that we ask or think" (Eph. 3:20). Shadrach, Meshach, and Abednego clearly echo this confidence: "Our God whom we serve is able to deliver us from the burning fiery furnace" (Dan. 3:17). They had good reason for this affirmation. They had testimony of God's supernatural power in the past. They and their forefathers had been preserved by the power of their covenant-keeping God.

In the preceding history of Israel, God had miraculously delivered his people numerous times. The three men knew the rescue stories of the past—God had saved Noah from the flood, Israel from captivity in Egypt, Gideon from the Midianites, David from Goliath, and many more. But they did not need only to rely on history lessons. They had witnessed God's saving hand in the previous chapters of their lives. They had been saved with Daniel when they ate vegetables rather than the king's table fare (Dan. 1). They had prayed with Daniel for the revelation and interpretation of the king's dream (Dan. 2) and knew of God's miraculous provision. Through all of these scriptural accounts we, too, have evidence of the power of our God to do whatever he knows is best. Thus biblical faith affirms that our God is able to rescue—but that is not enough reason to trust him. If he can rescue but is undependable, unkind, or untrustworthy, then faith in him would be worthless.

We Believe God Is Good

To trust God as he desires we must believe that we can entrust ourselves to his care. To do this we need to know that God is worthy of our trust. Biblical faith is not merely the confidence that our God is able; it also requires the confidence that our God is good.

Shadrach, Meshach, and Abednego affirmed God's goodness when they removed all doubt from their assertion of their ultimate rescue from Nebuchadnezzar. They affirm that God is able to deliver them from the fire (v. 17a), but they do not say that he will (v. 18a). Their famous "but if not . . ." is their clear refusal to predict what their circumstances hold or what God will do about those specific circumstances. But there is no doubt about their rescue from Nebuchadnezzar. They declare that "he [God] will deliver us out of your hand, O king" (v. 17).

How can the three young men be so sure of their rescue from the evil king? Is this the kind of certainty about circumstances they have previously avoided? To answer that question we have to consider another question: What are the possible ways that God can deliver Shadrach, Meshach, and Abednego from Nebuchadnezzar's attempts to control their hearts and minds with the worship of an idol? God certainly has the option of rescuing the three from the fiery furnace. But an eternal God can also rescue the three from compulsory idolatry by taking them to himself.

Our human response to such a radical rescue as an immediate heaven is to think, "That doesn't really count as a miracle." But why doesn't heaven count as a miraculous rescue? The realities of heaven are more precious and eternal than anything here on earth—and just as real. The only reason that we do not value the provision of heaven as a glorious and good alternative to suffering on earth is that we do not conceive of it being as great, good, and real as the Bible says. But it is real, great, and good. In heaven all pain and suffering are banished. We are eternally present with loved ones, including our Lord, whose glory offers more beauty and joy than ten thousand years on this earth can provide. By embracing the potential of a heavenly reality as well as an earthly rescue, these three young men are declaring their confidence that God is good regardless of what happens to them. Their faith echoes that of Job, who said of God, "Though he slay me, yet will I trust in him" (Job 13:15 KJV).

Why would Shadrach, Meshach, and Abednego trust that their God is this good when their circumstances were so bad? First, they trusted God in these immediate awful circumstances because God had rescued them before (see Dan. 1). They had experienced the caring hand of their God. By his hand they also knew the threats of a fiery furnace were not their ultimate fate. Through their friend Daniel, God had already revealed that their Messiah would come to establish an eternal kingdom that would displace all earthly kingdoms. Nebuchadnezzar might make their earthly existence difficult, but he did not have the final word over their eternal destiny.

What Shadrach, Meshach, and Abednego learned about God's heart from Daniel's prophecy we also learn from their experience. They were cast into the furnace, but then another appeared with them. Three men were cast in, but Nebuchadnezzar saw four in the fire—and the fourth looked divine (Dan. 3:25).

Nebuchadnezzar did not understand; we do. This fourth person of divine appearance was a biblical demonstration of the Immanuel principle. The angel who announced the coming of Jesus to his earthly family declared, "'They shall call his name Immanuel' (which means, God with us)" (Matt. 1:23). In so doing, the angel picked up a theme from Isaiah, the Old Testament prophet, who declared that God would save his people by coming to be with them (see Isa. 7:14). God consistently demonstrates his good character by his presence. He does not stand far off, but keeps coming closer and closer to sinful, weak, and desperate people until he lives among them, dies for them, and ultimately indwells them through the person and work of Jesus.

Biblical faith remains confident that our God is good not simply because he was present with Shadrach, Meshach, and Abednego in their furnace but also because that was just an echo of the Immanuel principle that was ultimately manifested in Jesus Christ. He came to live among his people on this earth in order to die for their sin, but now he also lives within us by his Spirit to help us conquer sin.

As a consequence of a recent mission trip to Ethiopia, a group of students and I understood more deeply how precious the principle that God comes to be with us in our brokenness is. One day a group of students was asked to minister to a young woman stricken with an incurable cancer. As they visited with her, the woman became too weak to stand and sank to the ground. She was dying. The students wondered how to express the eternal hope of the gospel across the barriers of language, disease, and deprivation. The circumstances were more desperate than words could capture, and the pain more intense than logic could penetrate. How could they express their faith in such awful and inexplicable circumstances?

One student simply chose to lie on the ground, brush the flies from the young woman's face, and hold her hand. This action more than anything we said represented the faith we claim. It is not faith in easy fixes to a fallen world; it is faith in One who chose to enter a fallen world to be with us. Though he could have remained in heaven's remotest realms, he stooped to lie in the dirt of our shame and to hold the hands of those diseased with sin in order to demonstrate his love for us. Because he demonstrated over and over that he was Immanuel, we are confident not only that he is able to do what is right but also that he will do what is best for our eternity because he is so good.

The Immanuel principle appears at some of the most surprising places in Scripture, but the message is always the same: God is with us. The very presence of God was with Shadrach, Meshach, and Abednego in their desperate circumstances. God delivered the three even though there were flames all about them. The same God who delivered these three delivers us. In the person of his Son, God came to be with us, endured the trials of this world, and suffered to deliver us from the flames of hell forever. Now we trust this God, knowing he always has our best interests at heart (Rom. 8:32).

We trust his provision not because our circumstances are always good but because he has demonstrated that he is always good. He entered our lives in the dust of an animal stall. He gave his life on a cross made filthy by the guilt of our sin. Faith now rests in the love his presence has always demonstrated. When our religious optimism has dried up, we can still rest in his love. When we are not certain what the best turn of events might be, we can still rest in his love. When we are unable to predict how he will handle a situation, we can still rest in his love. Because the God who is all-powerful and all-wise has shown how much he cares for us through the cross of Jesus Christ, faith rests in his love even when the mind cannot search out his reasons. We trust him because, through his Son, God has shown how much he loves us. Faith rests in this love.

While I was pastoring a rural church in which farmers and coal miners—people accustomed to hard lives—predominated, I heard a story that taught me much about the nature and foundation of true faith. There was once a miner who, though a stalwart believer, was injured in the mines at a young age. He became an invalid. Over the years he watched through a window beside his bed as life passed him by. He watched men of his own age prosper, raise families, and have grandchildren. He watched, but he did not share the rewards or the joys of others with whom he had once worked. He watched as his body withered, his house crumbled, and his life wasted away.

Then one day when the bedridden miner was quite old, a younger man came to visit him. "I hear that you believe in God and claim that he loves you," said the young man. "How can you believe such things with what has happened to you? Don't you sometimes doubt God's love?"

The old man hesitated and then smiled. He said, "Yes, it is true. Sometimes Satan comes calling on me in this fallen down old house of mine. He sits right there by my bed where you are sitting now. He points out my window to the men I once worked with who are still strong and active, and Satan asks, 'Does Jesus love you?' Then Satan casts a jeering glance around my tattered room as he points to the fine homes of my friends across the street and asks again, 'Does Jesus love you?' And then at last Satan points to the grandchild of a friend of mine—a man who has everything I do not—and Satan waits for the tear in my eye and then he whispers in my ear, 'Does Jesus really love you?'"

"And what do you say when Satan speaks to you that way?" asked the young man.

Said the old miner, "I take Satan by the hand and, in my mind, I lead him to a hill called Calvary. There I point to the thorn-tortured brow, to the nail-pierced hands and feet, and to the spear-wounded side. Then I ask Satan, 'Doesn't Jesus love me?'"

The cross is the warrant for confidence in God, despite a lifelong heartache. Had any of us stood at the foot of the cross and seen the horror, we would have cried out to God to stop the suffering. But God knew better. He did not stop the cruelty until the life of the One who hung there had bled away. The agony did not mean that God failed nor that the faith of the One who died was weak. There was great suffering, but in the suffering was a purpose so loving, so powerful, and so good that our eternity changed as a result—our sins were washed away. When our focus remains on the cross, our faith will not waver though troubles come and human answers fail. Such faith does not depend on emotional intensity, on knowing what should happen, or on a certainty of what God will do. True biblical faith trusts that God knows and is doing what is right, because he gave us Jesus.

4

Me with You

—— DANIEL 4 ——

I magine walking down the street toward a man handing out evangelistic tracts. You reach out to take one of the pamphlets. Then, just as the tract brushes your fingertips, you identify the tract peddler. It is King Nebuchadnezzar of Babylon. You recoil in horror. Not only are you shocked to take anything from a man more than 2,500 years old, you also are amazed that a man like Nebuchadnezzar would have anything good to say about your God. This is the despicably cruel ruler of pagan Babylon. He captured and deported God's chosen people (Dan. 1:1, 2). He enforced his whims by chopping off the heads of his subjects (Dan. 1:10). This capricious king issued death decrees for scores of people simply because they could not interpret dreams he would not describe (Dan. 2:5–12). This idolatrous king created golden statues for worship and ordered the live cremation of all who objected to worshiping them (Dan. 3:11). Surely this is no man to tell others about our Lord.

Still, receiving such a tract from Nebuchadnezzar may not be as unthinkable as his history would suggest. Chapter 4 of Daniel actually is such a tract, bearing Nebuchadnezzar's testimony of our God's work in his life (see vv. 1–2). God did an amazing work in the ancient king's life, and he recorded aspects of it for Daniel. As a result, this poignant account of a man's ruin and restoration dramatically reveals a gospel story of God's mercy toward those who have stood against him. Nebuchadnezzar's "evangelistic tract" is a timeless reminder that God shows his grace to those who stand with him now, even if they have failed to do so in the past.

King Nebuchadnezzar to all peoples, nations, and languages, that dwell in all the earth: Peace be multiplied to you! It has seemed good to me to show the signs and wonders that the Most High God has done for me.

> How great are his signs,
>   how mighty his wonders!
> His kingdom is an everlasting
>   kingdom,
>   and his dominion endures from
>   generation to generation.

I, Nebuchadnezzar, was at ease in my house and prospering in my palace. I saw a dream that made me afraid. As I lay in bed the fancies and the visions of my head alarmed me. So I made a decree that all the wise men of Babylon should be brought before me, that they might make known to me the interpretation of the dream. Then the magicians, the enchanters, the Chaldeans, and the astrologers came in, and I told them the dream, but they could not make known to me its interpretation. At last Daniel came in before me—he who was named Belteshazzar after the name of my god, and in whom is the spirit of the holy gods—and I told him the dream, saying, "O Belteshazzar, chief of the magicians, because I know that the spirit of the holy gods is in you and that no mystery is too difficult for you, tell me the visions of my dream that I saw and their interpretation. The visions of my head as I lay in bed were these: I saw, and behold, a tree in the midst of the earth, and its height was great. The tree grew and became strong, and its top reached to heaven, and it was visible to the end of the whole earth. Its leaves were beautiful and its fruit abundant, and in it was food for all. The beasts of the field found shade under it, and the birds of the heavens lived in its branches, and all flesh was fed from it.

"I saw in the visions of my head as I lay in bed, and behold, a watcher, a holy one, came down from heaven. He proclaimed aloud and said thus: 'Chop down the tree and lop off its branches, strip off its leaves and scatter its fruit. Let the beasts flee from under it and the birds from its branches. But leave the stump of its roots in the earth, bound with a band of iron and bronze, amid the tender grass of the field. Let him be wet with the dew of heaven. Let his portion be with the beasts in the grass of the earth. Let his mind be changed from a man's, and let a beast's mind be given to him; and let seven periods of time pass over him. The sentence is by the decree of the watchers, the decision by the word of the holy ones, to the end that the living may know that the Most High rules the kingdom of men and gives it to whom he will and sets over it the lowliest of men.' This dream I, King Nebuchadnezzar, saw. And you, O Belteshazzar, tell me the interpretation, because all the wise men of my kingdom are not able to make known to me the interpretation, but you are able, for the spirit of the holy gods is in you."

Then Daniel, whose name was Belteshazzar, was dismayed for a while, and his thoughts alarmed him. The king answered and said, "Belteshazzar, let not the dream or the interpretation alarm you." Belteshazzar answered and said, "My lord, may the dream be for those who hate you and its interpretation for your enemies! The tree you saw, which grew and became strong, so that its top reached to heaven, and it was visible to the end of the whole earth, whose leaves were beautiful and its fruit abundant, and in which was food for all, under which beasts of the field found shade, and in whose branches the birds of the heavens lived—it is you, O king, who have grown and become strong. Your greatness has grown and reaches to heaven, and your dominion to the ends of the earth. And because the king saw a watcher, a holy one, coming down from heaven and saying, 'Chop down the tree and destroy it, but leave the stump of its roots in the earth, bound with a band of iron and bronze, in the tender grass of the field, and let him be wet with the dew of heaven, and let his portion be with the beasts of the field, till seven periods of time pass over him,' this is the interpretation, O king: It is a decree of the Most High, which has come upon my lord the king, that you shall be driven from among men, and your dwelling shall be with the beasts of the field. You shall be made to eat grass like an ox, and you shall be wet with the dew of heaven, and seven periods of time shall pass over you, till you know that the Most High rules the kingdom of men and gives it to whom he will. And as it was commanded to leave the stump of the roots of the tree, your kingdom shall be confirmed for you from the time that you know that Heaven rules. Therefore, O king, let my counsel be acceptable to you: break off your sins by practicing righteousness, and your iniquities by showing mercy to the oppressed, that there may perhaps be a lengthening of your prosperity."

All this came upon King Nebuchadnezzar. At the end of twelve months he was walking on the roof of the royal palace of Babylon, and the king answered and said, "Is not this great Babylon, which I have built by my mighty power as a royal residence and for the glory of my majesty?" While the words were still in the king's mouth, there fell a voice from heaven, "O King Nebuchadnezzar, to you it is spoken: The kingdom has departed from you, and you shall be driven from among men, and your dwelling shall be with the beasts of the field. And you shall be made to eat grass like an ox, and seven periods of time shall pass over you, until you know that the Most High rules the kingdom of men and gives it to whom he will." Immediately the word was fulfilled against Nebuchadnezzar. He was driven from among men and ate grass like an ox, and his body was wet with the dew of heaven till his hair grew as long as eagles' feathers, and his nails were like birds' claws.

At the end of the days I, Nebuchadnezzar, lifted my eyes to heaven, and my reason returned to me, and I blessed the Most High, and praised and honored him who lives forever,

> for his dominion is an everlasting dominion,
> and his kingdom endures from generation to generation;
> all the inhabitants of the earth are accounted as nothing,
> and he does according to his will among the host of heaven
> and among the inhabitants of the earth;
> and none can stay his hand
> or say to him, "What have you done?"

At the same time my reason returned to me, and for the glory of my kingdom, my majesty and splendor returned to me. My counselors and my lords sought me, and I was established in my kingdom, and still more greatness was added to me. Now I, Nebuchadnezzar, praise and extol and honor the King of heaven, for all his works are right and his ways are just; and those who walk in pride he is able to humble. (Dan. 4:1–37)

A Shattered Colossus

The poet Percy Bysshe Shelley tells of meeting a traveler from an "antique" land who describes the ruins of a great statue in the desert. The head, half sunk in the sand, lies apart from stone legs still standing on their pedestal. The shattered face yet portrays a sneer of royal arrogance. Words on the pedestal reflect the look on the face:

> My name is Ozymandias, King of Kings;
> Look on my works, ye mighty, and despair!

But beyond these words and relics the poet relates,

> Nothing beside remains. Round the decay
> Of that colossal wreck, boundless and bare
> The lone and level sands stretch far away.[1]

The words of Shelley's fabled Ozymandias echo in Nebuchadnezzar's prideful claims in this fourth chapter of Daniel. Like the king in Shelley's poem, Babylon's king forgot that time and circumstance erode all human accomplishments, making pride absurd. Thirty-two years had passed since Daniel's first interpretation of Nebuchadnezzar's dreams had burst the king's illusions about his greatness (Dan. 2:36–46). Now Nebuchadnezzar needed a reminder about the limits of his greatness and glory. One day he walked atop his palace, surveyed his kingdom, and said, "Is not this great Babylon, which I have built by my mighty power as a royal residence and for the glory of my majesty?" (Dan. 4:30). He was asking for trouble. And what the king asked for, he got.

Months earlier Nebuchadnezzar had dreamed of a majestic tree growing to wondrous heights. In the dream, the tree was cut down and stripped of its branches at the command of a heavenly messenger (Dan. 4:13–14). Only the stump remained, bound with metal bands and drenched with dew. Then, without further explanation, the mysterious messenger said, "Let him be drenched with dew like an animal in the fields, and let him have the mind of an animal for seven years, so that all the living will know only the Most High is truly king" (paraphrase of vv. 16–17).

The dream terrified the king, and he again called for Daniel to interpret the vision. The meaning was as simple as it was scary. Daniel told King Nebuchadnezzar that he was going to have a great fall. He was going to lose his mind, believe himself to be an animal, and live in the fields drenched with dew until he acknowledged that God alone is sovereign. When Nebuchadnezzar ultimately regains his mind and rule, he plainly states what "the peoples, nations, and languages, that dwell in all the earth" (v. 1) are supposed to learn as a result of his demise.

What is in Nebuchadnezzar's evangelism tract for all people—including us? He repeats the answer three times (vv. 17, 25, 32). Verse 17 says it best: this was written "to the end that the living may know that the Most High rules the kingdom of men and gives it to whom he will and sets over it the lowliest of men." Each of the three clauses of this key verse contains an essential truth God intends for us to take from the king's experience.

God Is in Charge—We Are Not

The heavenly messenger first rendered his verdict to the end that "the living may know that the Most High rules the kingdom of men." The Most High God is the only true Ruler of all kingdoms. We use the word "sovereign" to describe this kind of rule, and a number of Bible translations use that word to describe God's rule in this verse. God reminded Nebuchadnezzar that there is only one true sovereign, the King of kings. Though human power and glory may tempt us to believe otherwise, our Lord's dealings with Nebuchadnezzar caution us always to remember what divine sovereignty means: God is in control, and we are not.

Our intellect, abilities, and accomplishments do not ultimately determine our futures or provide our security. This is, of course, a difficult truth for a proud and powerful man like Nebuchadnezzar to accept, but it is not much easier for most of us to accept. In a society where Clint Eastwood, Harrison Ford, and Steve Jobs are heroes, independence and self-reliance become the idols of our pursuits. We want to be self-made men and women. We want self-sufficiency, autonomy, and control. From our youngest years we are taught to take charge of our own lives, to make our own breaks. Study longer, work harder, plan better than the next guy—that is how you get ahead. We all get the message: those who strive for excellence hold their destinies in their own hands.

Of course, there is nothing wrong with striving for excellence. God expects us to make good use of the gifts he gives us. But we should remember that they are gifts. Talent, brains, and opportunity mean nothing apart from God's provision. If we begin to trust only in what we can achieve—to believe that we are the sole cause of our success—then all around us life will begin to whisper the foolishness of our faith in ourselves.

From the time my parents were married until I was married and having children, my father worked for only one company. As a highly skilled farm manager, he turned failing farms into profitable ones or managed farms for absent landowners. He remains one of the smartest, hardest-working, most honest men I know. I do not mind bragging on my father. He climbed the ranks in his company from staff worker to high executive. For thirty years my father excelled. He was tops in his field, secure in his work. Then the company owner retired.

At his retirement, the owner sold his company to a large corporation that had no place for many long-term employees, including my father. After thirty years of service and achievement, my father was without a job. Decisions made entirely apart from him, actions taken over which he had no control, controlled him and stole his security.

Still, my father is an intelligent, resourceful man. He offered to purchase an "unprofitable" region from the corporation so he could manage it his own way. They agreed to the deal, and my father set up his own company. The operation quickly turned a profit. In one year he made more money than he ever made before.

One reason for this near-instant success was my father's ability to get the management contract for a huge farming operation in rural Tennessee. But the area was not going to remain rural very long. Soon after my father acquired the management contract for that large farm, a major automobile company set up a billion-dollar manufacturing plant in that area. Readers can guess which tract of land the automobile company purchased on which to construct the plant. Indeed, they chose the farm that had become the backbone of my father's new business. The owner of the land sold it to the car company, and my father's farm management fees for the property ceased.

For the second time my father had security and success taken from him by forces over which he had no control. He was no less intelligent, able, or hard working than in the thirty years previous, but he was made to realize—as were all in our family—that no one is truly in charge of his own destiny. And we were not the only family to have to face this hard truth. Because of economic realities, the automobile company eventually shut down the manufacturing plant, putting many hundreds more out of work. From line workers to the nation's most respected business leaders, we all learned that there are hidden forces larger and more complex than any person can control. As much as we may want it otherwise, and as often as we may think otherwise, we are not ultimately in charge. Only God is sovereign.

Fragile Power

God uses the experience of Nebuchadnezzar to declare the unreliability of all the human means we may use to assert our sovereignty. The king thought his power, wisdom, and accomplishment were a hedge against the insecurities that face us all. God refuted the sufficiency of each. We can never know enough, do enough, or have enough to have ultimate control over our lives.

Nebuchadnezzar thought his great power made him sovereign (Dan. 4:30). He forgot how fragile all human greatness is. In twelve months this king went from having power over the world's greatest dominion to not having power even over his own faculties. God merely stirred Nebuchadnezzar's thoughts and the life of the king fell apart. A mental disease made him into a wild animal (4:29–33). All his political and military power meant nothing when the true Sovereign of heaven and earth acted. The greatest of human powers is more fragile than we often dare to consider.

Not only do small changes in our minds result in big changes in our lives, but small—even minute—changes in almost any aspect of our lives can have similar results. One of the greatest baseball players ever, Albert Pujols, is honored because of his great batting average. Over the years, he has gotten a hit roughly three out of every ten times he has gone to the plate. Yet the worst player on his team gets a hit slightly more than two out of every ten times he bats. The difference between being a hero and a heel hinges on the slightest differences in human ability. Game-changing plays occur because of flukes and failures. World-changing battles are sometimes determined by weather changes or words misheard. Greatness based on human ability is the most fragile of commodities. Neither the physical power of the greatest athletes nor the political and military power of the greatest kings are reliable ways to control one's destiny.

False Wisdom

Perhaps human strength is not our first resort in difficult situations. We may be able to see the fragility of our power and yet believe that our wisdom will grant security. Words in relief on the Chrysler building in New York City declare, "Wisdom and knowledge are the stability of your time." We can easily be convinced that superior intelligence will rescue us from the insecurities of the world. Nebuchadnezzar surrounded himself with the wise and learned so that he had expert advice for all contingencies (Dan. 4:6). His security, at least partially, rested on human wisdom.

The problem with human wisdom is its limits. Nebuchadnezzar's wise men could not answer all his questions, nor can our wisest answer all of ours. Whether they come in brokers' suits, doctors' scrubs, or with attorneys' fees, the advice of our experts does not insulate us from the world's problems and uncertainties.

Investors who spend millions of dollars yearly getting expert market analyses have certainly discovered the limits of human wisdom. Until recently we thought our home values would always go up. We thought that Lehman Brothers were the smart guys in the brokerage business and that Warren Buffett could not be outsmarted. We thought that "Black Monday" would not come again and that all the regulations were in place to prevent a great recession. Yet, despite all of our timing, subscribing, and consulting, most investors have discovered we are spectators rather than managers in the world of finance. No one can outsmart the market or be certain of its direction.

Those of us who do not play at high-altitude financial pinnacles nevertheless face the same insecurities. I recently visited parts of the country both in the south and in the west where housing starts have gone from thousands per month to zero per month—where onetime owners of multimillion-dollar mansions are shopping at Goodwill. I have been to parts of the world where tsunamis and hurricanes and earthquakes have undone the financial plans of the most savvy investors. I have friends whose house foundations have cracked, whose neighborhood has become a chemical dump, and whose walls have become infested with toxic mold.

Through all these experiences, I have come to the certain conclusion that no one knows for sure what will secure our money or our health or our future. We are all just playing the percentages and hoping that we have been wise enough to guess right. No one can anticipate all the contingencies. We try to do the best we can with what we know, but we know we never can know enough. There is no security in human wisdom. The possibilities are beyond computing.

Vain Accomplishment

When most of us consider the fragility of our abilities and the limitations of our wisdom, our response is to do what we can while we can in order to beat the odds. We resolve to "get while the gettin' is good." Since nothing is secure forever, many of us try to prepare for hard times. We try to amass enough of this world's goods and favors as protection against potential setbacks. We begin to look for security in accumulation. Like Nebuchadnezzar we may begin to survey all we have been able to build to give us assurance of our security (Dan. 4:30). The trouble is, no one can ever amass enough to protect them from all life's vagaries.

Despite earning millions, the great fighters Mike Tyson and Evander Holyfield went broke. But so also have Wall Street executives whose salaries and bonuses made the boxers' winnings look like pocket change. Months before he died, Ben Edwards, the legendary Christian leader of A. G. Edwards investment company, was interviewed by *The St. Louis Business Journal*. He revealed that his investments had been reduced by a factor of ten. "So I don't struggle as much with the temptations of wealth," he said.[2] These men learned what we all know deep down inside: you can never have enough to make you *really* secure.

It seems obvious that our accumulations will not secure us, yet even in the church our actions reveal that we think security comes in collecting what we can. The more we accumulate, the more frantically we try to hold on to our wealth. We heap up accomplishments only to discover we are building mountains with marbles. The more we add, the more we fear that it will all roll away. So as strange as it may seem, the wealthier that Christians become, the less likely they are to give to God's work.[3] A study reported a few years ago by *Christianity Today* similarly indicated that, on average, "Americans who earn less than $10,000 gave 2.3 percent of their income to religious organizations . . . , whereas those who earn $70,000 or more gave only 1.2 percent."[4] In the most affluent nation the world has ever known, "the median annual giving for an American Christian is actually $200, just over half a percent of after-tax income."[5] It seems that the higher we climb on our mountains of accumulation, the more tightly we try to hold on to our marbles. We apparently do not feel more secure because the marbles are piled higher.

My family loves vacationing in Colorado. One of our more unusual activities is touring a stone castle that a man with a peculiar but spectacular sense of purpose is building with his own hands in the Rocky Mountains. The castle has huge stone turrets with winding staircases leading to a breathtaking but precarious mountaintop view. When my sons were little, they would climb the stairs with me, even though there were no banisters. At the lower levels, I often had to remind the boys to hold my hands. But the higher we climbed, the less reminding they needed. By the time we reached the top I felt like my hands were being crushed inside two miniature vises. My children simply realized that greater height meant greater danger. The higher you are, the farther you have to fall. That reality keeps almost all of us acting like my children, clinging to our wealth as they clung to my hand. We strive to heap up things that will make us more secure, only to discover our higher incomes and bank accounts only make us feel greater peril.

A Difficult Confession

We may be more like Nebuchadnezzar than is pleasant to confess. If our abilities or hard work have resulted in success, we may believe our security is due to our efforts. We, like Nebuchadnezzar, may scan what we have built, whether it be in terms of academic, commercial, professional, or church accomplishment, and admire what we have built by our ability and wisdom. "We've done it!" But that is never the whole picture. We must remember how the events behind our successes fell into place. We had to be in the right place at the right time. Someone opened a door or helped us along the way. If we are honest, we can imagine how a different person here or a different circumstance there would have made all the difference.

If we cannot connect the dots in our own lives, then it may help to think about family members, classmates, or peers. Their lives were not the same, though they were just as smart or smarter, just as capable or more so, just as expert or better. We should consider them and then ask ourselves again, did we make all the difference as to why we succeeded and they did not? Or as to why they succeeded and we did not? Although it is difficult to confess that we are not really in charge of our lives, it is a confession that God and honesty require.

God Gives—We Do Not Gain

Nebuchadnezzar's "evangelistic tract" contains a second lesson. Not only does he teach us that God alone is in ultimate control, but he also teaches us that God must grant what we cannot gain. When we begin to see that human power, wisdom, and accomplishment ultimately cannot account for worldly success, a typical response can be to look for something else in us that will justify God's blessing. Pride still wants the cause of success to be something in us.

The particular temptation of Christians is to explain our success by our goodness. To explain our accomplishments, we credit our moral or spiritual superiority. We reason, "If success is not by might nor by power, then it must be by my righteousness." God answers through Nebuchadnezzar to make it plain that our achievements are not by our might nor by our righteousness but by his grace. The seventeenth verse of this chapter of Daniel continues: "the Most High rules the kingdom of men and gives it to whom he will." God not only proclaims himself sovereign, he also declares that he grants kingdoms to whomever he wills. There is no human factor. God provides as he determines best. The Lord uses our obedience to bless us, but he is not obligated by our obedience to grant us earthly success.

An honest assessment of our lives in comparison to those around us should reveal the truth about the significance of human goodness in earthly success. If we have accomplished anything, it requires very little reflection to recall worse people who have done far better—and better people who have done far worse. If we hold up our righteous works before God and say, "For these I am blessed," we speak as fools and against Scripture. The Bible says even our best works are only filthy rags to God (Isa. 64:6). Because of their mixture of human motives and limitations, when we have done all the good works we should do, we are still unworthy servants of God (Luke 17:10).

If we were so foolish as to claim that our accomplishments are because of our moral superiority, then the one who could laugh the loudest at such a claim would be Nebuchadnezzar. He was the richest, most powerful man of his time—king of earth's kings. He was on top of the world. Was it because he was morally good? Hardly. He was a wicked, cruel, vindictive man.

There was no correlation between goodness and success in Nebuchadnezzar's life. Or, if there were any correlation, it was an inverse relationship. His life should make it clear that there is not a cause-and-effect relationship between human goodness and earthly success. For his purposes God blesses as he knows is best. He is committed to taking care of the godly, but—as we have seen earlier in this book—the godly know that this life is not God's only opportunity to bless. The only explanation for earthly success is God's gracious provision. We never gain as much as God gives.

Grace lies behind not only material accomplishments but spiritual attainments as well. God grants Nebuchadnezzar more than an earthly kingdom. By the end of this chapter this king praises, exalts, and glorifies the King of heaven (Dan. 4:37). Nebuchadnezzar speaks as a child of the kingdom of God. A pagan king gets to claim the truths of God's kingdom. Why? Why did God reach down to touch Nebuchadnezzar's heart and turn him toward heaven? Was the king morally better than his subjects? Had he done more good? The answer is no, definitely not. Spiritually, Nebuchadnezzar was a wretched, pagan tyrant. There was nothing in Nebuchadnezzar that made God deal graciously with him.

This truth of God's unmerited mercy to one who possesses no apparent good in himself is gospel gold to mine in the book of Daniel. God makes a pagan king a member of heaven's family by grace alone. The same must be true for us. We become members of God's family simply because of his mercy. Despite our sin and guilt, God loves us. He gives the kingdom to whomever he wills despite our unworthiness. No one is worthy or deserving of the kingdom of an absolutely holy God, yet he claims us. If we have any standing before God, it is because of his grace alone. This may not be a truth we want to hear on our good days—when we are confident of our moral achievements. But it is a truth we desperately long to hear on our bad days—when we are sure of our spiritual failures. When shame dominates more than success, we must not forget that God loves us because of his grace and not because of our goodness. On our bad days our eternal hope and our very lives may depend on whether we remember this grace.

Some time ago a young man who had struggled with life-threatening depression years earlier phoned me, asking to visit. For much of his life this young Christian wrestled with immorality. His struggle was with a particular temptation that can capture lives and twist personalities. Yet by diligently seeking the Lord through biblical counsel, my friend had gained victory over his sinful lifestyle. But he called unexpectedly, asking to see me again, and I could tell from his tone that there was a problem.

He told me the story soon after he arrived. After much career accomplishment, he had experienced some financial and family setbacks. His business began to fail, and with the increased pressure, his family life deteriorated. His world seemed to be collapsing. The pressures became so continuous, so intense, that he felt he had to find some relief. He sought escape in his old lifestyle. He returned to the old perversity. This time the sin seemed even worse because of his abandonment of the Lord's victory.

My friend confessed all this with great grief and many tears, but the despair I anticipated was absent from his voice. This one for whose life I had once wrestled now spoke of his greatest failure without words that made me fear for his safety. The reason was soon evident.

Following the agony of his confession came words filled with wonder. He explained that since his sinful relapse, he had felt the presence of God more closely than ever. He had found the sin so unfulfilling compared to the life the Lord had given him that he knew now it had no more hold on him. He felt free from its grip for the first time in his adult life.

But the wonder was not simply a consequence of feeling more release from the clutches of temptation. Despite his recent relapse, his circumstances were also improving on all fronts. He had a new job. The job led him to a new home away from past temptations. As financial pressures eased, family relationships were healing. He even explained that he was able to see and relate to people at church in a way he previously could not fathom.

My friend's self-image, his business, his family life, even his worship, had all improved from the moment of the worst sin of this young man's life. He was amazed. "Bryan," he said, "it's not supposed to work this way, is it? I betrayed you and all you tried to do for me. I failed God. I turned from his victory in my life. And, now, all he is doing is blessing me, and blessing me, and blessing me. How can this be?"

I had the privilege of telling my friend what we all must learn again and again in our Christian lives: "When the goodness and loving kindness of God our Savior appeared, he saved us, not because of works done by us in righteousness, but according to his own mercy" (Titus 3:4–5). God's love is not conditioned on our goodness. He does not call us his own because we have been better than others. God loves us simply because he loves to do so. This does not mean we should believe we can sin without consequence. It does mean that God will do whatever is necessary to bring those he loves into fellowship with himself. He may use discipline, as he did with prideful Nebuchadnezzar, to turn us from the consequences of sin. Or God may use inexplicable mercy, as he did with my young friend and with the humbled king, to draw us nearer in heaven's embrace (cf. Rom. 2:4). But whether God's means are hard or gentle, his motive is always love. Neither Nebuchadnezzar nor my friend deserved God's grace, so God granted what they could not gain through the means he knew was most appropriate for each heart.

My friend had the great privilege of knowing for certain what it takes so many Christians a lifetime to discover: God loves his children because they are his, not because they are holy. They never could be holy enough to merit his love. When they try to become holy enough for him, tying his love to their goodness, they inevitably become hard and cynical. Like children who believe their parents love them only when they are good, Christians who believe they are loved because of their righteousness grow bitter and resentful.

Persons who believe their heavenly Father's affection is conditional will obey him to earn his blessing, but they do not like him very much. They honor his standards, but their hearts are far from his. Their assurance of God's love rests on the belief that they are morally superior to those around them. As a result, they become judgmental, bigoted, suspicious of others' motives, and the cruelest of gossips. They must always compare themselves to the faults and frailties of others to assure themselves God loves them, and the exercise hardens them in the worst ways. By trying to stand tall on the weaknesses of others, such people sink into pride. By experiencing God's affection despite moral compromise, my friend was spared such pride and came to know the gracious nature of God's love.

I said to my friend, "You never again in your life have to worry if you have become good enough to get, or keep, God's love. Now you know that when you sinned your worst, God blessed you the most. When you were in your deepest, darkest pit of sin, he showed you his love most clearly."

God also showed his love to Nebuchadnezzar when he was at his lowest state. God claimed Nebuchadnezzar not when he was a ruling king but when he was a raging animal. This sequence helps us remember that grace is not applied to those who have earned it. God is not waiting for us to reach him with the latest Tower of Babel. Although pride and guilt both seek to convince us that we must climb to grace, neither speaks truth. When the king stood high, boasting about his accomplishments, he knew nothing of God's salvation (Dan. 4:30). Only when he was so humbled that his eyes could only look up to heaven for help did God make him whole (Dan. 4:34).

We, too, must lift our eyes toward heaven and ask God to save us because we know that we cannot save ourselves by our power, wisdom, or accomplishments. Standing on our righteousness is not helpful either. Although we may fear that God will abandon us because of our sin, we must let God's Word rule over our feelings. We can never do enough to gain God's love. But if we will look up to him—even from a pit of misery that our sin has created—then his grace claims us. We do not have to climb to spiritual heights before God will love us once or love us again. God loves only because he delights to do so.

God has never shared his love on the basis of great potential or holy attainment. God chose Israel as his holy nation not because of its greatness but because it was the most desperate of nations (Deut. 7:6–8). God loved the apostle Paul though he murdered believers (Acts 9:1, 15). God promised David the lineage of Jesus, knowing the young king would sin greatly (2 Sam. 7:11–16). God loved a cruel, pagan king named Nebuchadnezzar when there was no earthly reason to do so. If God so loved these whose lives were so disgraceful, then he can love us, too, though our sin is great. We must not think our sin destroys the love of God, or else, when we need his strength, support, and forgiveness the most, we will suppose him far from us. Our sin is not greater than God's love. We may hold him at arm's distance, but his arms always outreach ours and are always outstretched to receive those who believe.

Of course there are those who believe that, if we will teach that God loves only the "good people," then believers will be spurred on to greater holiness. Nothing could be further from the truth. Obedience provides for the greater experiencing of God's love, but human obedience does not produce more of God's love. Whenever believers seek to earn God's affection, they focus more on their works than on his work. By making good works the warrant for God's love rather than the result of his love, they ultimately diminish the necessity of the cross and the redeeming love of the Savior. By depending on their own holiness they deprive themselves of its one true Source. Holiness and true righteousness spring from hearts fully aware of the mercy of God. The strongest testimonies come from the most grateful people. Those most grateful are ones humbled by the realization that though they could never gain God's favor, he grants it.

Without a Leg to Stand On

So far Nebuchadnezzar's message is as humbling for us as the account is humiliating for him. Through the pagan king's fall we learn that because only God is sovereign and grants his kingdom to whomever he wishes, we cannot stand before him on the basis of our abilities or our goodness. When we have neither of these legs to stand on, we could sink pretty low. But the ancient king has not reached the end of his "evangelistic tract." He knows there is no joy in lowliness—unless we read the remainder of verse 17: "the Most High rules the kingdom of men and gives it to whom he will *and sets over it the lowliest of men*" (emphasis mine).

The lowliest get the kingdom. Here is the encouragement our hearts need. No matter what a lowlife we may think we have become, we are not automatically excluded from God's blessing. If a lowlife like Nebuchadnezzar was granted the kingdom, there is hope for the lowliest of us.

No Matter How Great the Sin

As a pastor, I wrestle as much to convince believers that they can be forgiven as I do to convince unbelievers that they must be forgiven. Some have been helped simply by considering what a spiritual lowlife Nebuchadnezzar was. He was murderous, arrogant, materialistic, idolatrous, and an enemy of God's people. Yet God claimed his heart. Once the king acknowledged his lowliness before God, the Lord restored him (Dan. 4:34). If God reached Nebuchadnezzar, he can reach anyone. Though we may have sinned greatly, we are not likely to have sunk as low in sin as Babylon's king. If God can reach a lowlife like Nebuchadnezzar, there is nothing that can stand between us and God's restoration except a failure to confess our lowliness as this king confessed his.

How deeply the truth of God's love for the "lowly" must penetrate hearts is revealed in the testimony of a young girl from the early years in my ministry. She listened to the gospel as it was presented to her by a college friend. She heard of the sacrifice of Jesus for her sins and, for the first time, faced the seriousness of her condition. Her guilt was overwhelming. Because of past sexual activity, she could not bear to think of approaching God. She said, "God can't love somebody like me. God shouldn't love me." Then the friend said, "It doesn't matter how great the sin, God's love is greater than all our sin." Suddenly the young woman understood what the grace of God really meant. The "lowliest" are loved by God. When we confess that our sin has brought us so low that none but God can restore us, he lifts us up.

No sin is too great for God's love. No truth is more central to our faith. Yet as familiar as these truths are, they seem remote when we sin. In the throes of our shame we wonder if God truly could love us. We may doubt if he should love us. But if we are ever to be truly whole, we must recognize there is no sin we have ever committed, or can commit, that the grace of God cannot cover. The truth of God's matchless forgiveness must overwhelm our hearts, or we shall forever doubt him and fear our futures.

As the leaders of my church gathered together for an annual conference, a familiar song struck me with new poignancy. A thousand voices joined to sing "To God Be the Glory." The second verse of the song is:

> O perfect redemption, the purchase of blood!
> To every believer the promise of God;
> The vilest offender who truly believes,
> That moment from Jesus forgiveness receives.[6]

"There it is," I thought. "There is the truth we must always unite to sing. We must shake the rafters and move the world with this truth: 'The vilest offender who truly believes, that moment from Jesus forgiveness receives.' From that moment of repentance, and for all eternity, God's pardon covers the vilest of sin. We must never stop singing these words. Sin too quickly makes grace a faint echo and forgiveness a distant hope. Our hearts—and the hearts of hurting people all around us—easily despair without claiming this promise of God: there is no sin so great that God cannot pardon it."

No Matter How Hard the Heart

Not only does Nebuchadnezzar indicate that God can forgive no matter how great the sin, he teaches us that God can heal no matter how hard the heart. Nebuchadnezzar was hardened to God's truths. He had heard of Daniel's God for years but rejected the message. Most of us know of such a person who has heard the gospel of Jesus Christ time after time but has never responded in faith. This person is calloused against God's truths. And if we really scratch deeply into our innermost hearts and minds, we must confess that we often believe this person cannot be changed. We believe they never will accept the gospel; they are too hardened. We have given up hope of seeing change. We have stopped praying. Though it is painful to confess, to some extent we have even stopped caring. Whoever it is, we must remember that it does not matter how hard the heart. God can change hard hearts. If he could change Nebuchadnezzar's heart, God can change the hardest heart.

A friend at work told me recently how God had retaught him the power of the gospel to change hearts. My friend's great-aunt died. Though he had not seen her in years, he knew her reputation about matters of faith. A lifetime of selfish and careless living had hardened her to the gospel. For most of her adult life, if someone tried to share the message of salvation with her, she either scoffed or flew into a rage. Her heart seemed untouchable. Neither she nor any of her immediate family accepted any "religion." My friend assumed there was no hope for her.

After the aunt's death, the family gathered at her house one day to divide her personal belongings. In one box on a bookshelf someone discovered some "religious" books. Since my colleague was the only "religious" person present, the family quickly decided this box was part of his share. He took the books home, but they smelled so much of stale tobacco smoke and a stuffy house that he did not even want to touch them. He put the box of books in his attic and forgot about it.

A few months later my friend went into the attic on some now-forgotten errand and stumbled upon the box of books. He took one out and was amazed to discover it was a very fine devotional guide. He took other books from the box. Each was a solid book for Bible study or devotions. While thumbing through a commentary on Ephesians, he came upon a handwritten letter pressed between the pages. The letter was written late in life by the aunt and addressed to God. She wrote the letter as a result of her study of God's Word. In the letter she confessed her sins and claimed Jesus Christ as her Savior. No matter how hard the heart, God can change the heart.

If God can bring Nebuchadnezzar to his knees, God can break the wills and win the hearts of our loved ones. So we must pray for the salvation of those whom God places in our care with the confidence that he is able to break the hardest heart. The battle may be long before it is won. As this chapter begins, it has been thirty-two years since Daniel first began his testimony of God in Nebuchadnezzar's life. Apparently Daniel had developed an affection for the king in the intervening years (Dan. 4:19), but still the ruler had not responded to Daniel's testimony. Another year passed between Daniel's interpretation of this dream and its fulfillment. Seven more years passed before Nebuchadnezzar lifted his eyes to heaven. A total of forty years passed before the king responded to Daniel's witness. But the king finally did respond. The message for us is that we must not cease working and praying for a brother, father, spouse, or friend. Never give up. Never give up. Never give up. It does not matter how hard the heart. God can reach the hardest heart.

Me with You

In private conversation and correspondence a pastor friend of mine tells of why it is so important never to give up believing in the power of God's grace to soften a hard heart. As a young pastor, fresh out of seminary, my friend was asked to visit a dying man in a Washington, DC, hospital. An aggressive bone cancer was eating away the man's life. He was not a Christian.

On the few occasions when the pastor presented the gospel there was no spiritual response, but a friendship formed. Through a number of visits the pastor learned that this dying patient was a remarkable, self-made man. He was raised in Spain by a loving mother who diligently taught her son the truths of faith. He only listened a little. The Franco regime killed his father, and, because Spain's official church supported Franco, the boy spurned Christianity. He fled his country as a young teenager and came to America knowing no English. He worked hard and studied hard. He eventually went to college, to medical school, and then began a highly successful career. Despite his early disadvantages, he became skilled, wealthy, and a respected leader in our nation's most prestigious hospitals. He also became more convinced of his atheism. Then came the cancer.

In just a few months the cancer destroyed the accomplishments of a lifetime. His body, once kept in top shape by miles of daily swimming, was devastated. His skills also began to deteriorate with the advances of the cancer. With his spirit broken and his body wracked with pain, the man ran out of pride and finally tired of his own answers. When the young pastor next visited, the despairing doctor confronted him: "I have treated depression all my life, but I have no answers for what I'm going through. If your God really has some answers, then you must help me with the hell I am going through now. Give me some peace, if you can."

The young pastor could hardly begin to think of what to say. He hesitated, grasped for the right words, and then stumbled forward: "You've gained everything a man could gain in every avenue of life. You have wealth, respect, and achievement. These all may have to be put aside before you gain this last thing you want. In every sphere of life you have succeeded, except the spiritual sphere, and to succeed there you must not follow any of the rules you have used before. You cannot conquer the spiritual world by your efforts. To gain spiritual success you must admit your helplessness and inability. You must confess you have nothing to stand on. To enter God's kingdom and know his peace you must not come as a self-sufficient man but as a helpless child—you must not come as a lion but as a lamb."

Still there was no spiritual response. Little else was said that night. The man talked no more. A few days later the bone cancer progressed to the extent that the man's leg broke spontaneously as he lay in bed. The doctors had to operate to repair the damage despite their patient's weakened condition. On the eve of that operation, unbeknownst to his family, he wrote a note to the young pastor. In a labored scrawl he wrote in Spanish the words that he had memorized years ago at his mother's knee: "I believe in God the Father Almighty, Maker of heaven and earth; and, in Jesus Christ, his only Son, our Lord . . . ," the words of the Apostles' Creed. The note continued in English with these words:

> Jesus, I hate all my sins. I have not served or worshiped you.
> Father, I know the only way to come into your kingdom is by the precious blood of Jesus.
> I know you stand at the door and will answer those who knock.
> I now want to be your lamb.

The man who wrote those words never regained consciousness after his operation. His life was lost, but his soul was won. God can change the hardest hearts and wipe away the darkest sin. He must do it, for we cannot. Our God calls us to put aside all we trust, take pleasure in, or have used to make ourselves worthwhile. He urges us to come to him as a helpless child, and then promises us his kingdom forever. When we call to him, without trying to stand on our accomplishments or goodness, but humbled by his mercy for sinners like us, he responds. His voice is gentle and loving. His words echo our desires. He says, "Forever you are mine. The kingdom of heaven is for humble and lowly such as you."

5

Loving Enough to Warn

— DANIEL 5 —

Chapter 5 of Daniel addresses the question of what would happen if you gave a party and God crashed it.

Nebuchadnezzar was no longer on the throne. A successor named Belshazzar ruled the land. One night Belshazzar hosted a great banquet, and an unexpected and quite unusual guest appeared. The visitor was a disembodied set of fingers. In the sight of all the partyers, the uninvited hand wrote a message on the palace wall. The king was so frightened, the blood drained from his face and his knees knocked. No one could explain the specter or interpret the message. The king's wise men and counselors were called. They were equally baffled. The king grew more worried and pale. Then the queen remembered Daniel.

"O king," she said, "do not be upset. Your predecessor, Nebuchadnezzar, called upon a man named Daniel to interpret dreams and solve riddles. This Daniel still lives in the kingdom. Ask him what the handwriting means" (paraphrase of vv. 10–11).

Belshazzar called Daniel. The prophet interpreted the message, but he did not calm the king. Daniel prophesied judgment.

Chapter 5 of Daniel becomes the flip side of chapter 4. In chapter 4 Daniel used King Nebuchadnezzar's conversion to affirm that the repentant reap the rewards of grace, however bleak their pasts. In this chapter Daniel uses King

Belshazzar's sacrilege to declare that the rebellious reap the consequences of wrath, however secure their present. Two equally evil kings demonstrate two equally vital messages: God's complete pardon for the humble and God's sure judgment for the proud. Here the gospel message that has been developing through the book of Daniel takes an important turn. Previously we have learned that God will remember sinful people (Dan. 1, his grace toward Daniel and his friends), he will rescue an unworthy people (Dan. 2, his ultimate establishment of a messianic kingdom), he remains "right here" with his people (Dan. 3, appearing with Daniel's friends in the fiery furnace), and he can show mercy to the worst of people (Dan. 4, rescuing even Nebuchadnezzar). Now in chapter 5 there is this aspect of grace for us to deal with: God also reveals his judgment on the unrepentant. We must also consider this aspect of the gospel if we are to be faithful to all that Daniel would teach.

King Belshazzar made a great feast for a thousand of his lords and drank wine in front of the thousand.

Belshazzar, when he tasted the wine, commanded that the vessels of gold and of silver that Nebuchadnezzar his father had taken out of the temple in Jerusalem be brought, that the king and his lords, his wives, and his concubines might drink from them. Then they brought in the golden vessels that had been taken out of the temple, the house of God in Jerusalem, and the king and his lords, his wives, and his concubines drank from them. They drank wine and praised the gods of gold and silver, bronze, iron, wood, and stone.

Immediately the fingers of a human hand appeared and wrote on the plaster of the wall of the king's palace, opposite the lampstand. And the king saw the hand as it wrote. Then the king's color changed, and his thoughts alarmed him; his limbs gave way, and his knees knocked together. The king called loudly to bring in the enchanters, the Chaldeans, and the astrologers. The king declared to the wise men of Babylon, "Whoever reads this writing, and shows me its interpretation, shall be clothed with purple and have a chain of gold around his neck and shall be the third ruler in the kingdom." Then all the king's wise men came in, but they could not read the writing or make known to the king the interpretation. Then King Belshazzar was greatly alarmed, and his color changed, and his lords were perplexed.

The queen, because of the words of the king and his lords, came into the banqueting hall, and the queen declared, "O king, live forever! Let not your thoughts alarm you or your color change. There is a man in your kingdom in whom is the spirit of the holy gods. In the days of your father, light and understanding and wisdom like the wisdom of the gods were found in him, and King Nebuchadnezzar, your father—your father the king—made him chief of the magicians, enchanters, Chaldeans, and astrologers, because an excellent spirit, knowledge, and understanding to interpret dreams, explain riddles, and solve problems were found in this Daniel, whom the king named Belteshazzar. Now let Daniel be called, and he will show the interpretation."

Then Daniel was brought in before the king. The king answered and said to Daniel, "You are that Daniel, one of the exiles of Judah, whom the king my father brought from Judah. I have heard of you that the spirit of the gods is in you, and that light and understanding and excellent wisdom are found in you. Now the wise men, the enchanters, have been brought in before me to read this writing and make known to me its interpretation, but they could not show the interpretation of the matter. But I have heard that you can give interpretations and solve problems. Now if you can read the writing and make known to me its interpretation, you shall be clothed with purple and have a chain of gold around your neck and shall be the third ruler in the kingdom."

Then Daniel answered and said before the king, "Let your gifts be for yourself, and give your rewards to another. Nevertheless, I will read the writing to the king and make known to him the interpretation. O king, the Most High God gave Nebuchadnezzar your father kingship and greatness and glory and majesty. And because of the greatness that he gave him, all peoples, nations, and languages trembled and feared before him. Whom he would, he killed, and whom he would, he kept alive; whom he would, he raised up, and whom he would, he humbled. But when his heart was lifted up and his spirit was hardened so that he dealt proudly, he was brought down from his kingly throne, and his glory was taken from him. He was driven from among the children of mankind, and his mind was made like that of a beast, and his dwelling was with the wild donkeys. He was fed grass like an ox, and his body was wet with the dew of heaven, until he knew that the Most High God rules the kingdom of mankind and sets over it whom he will. And you his son, Belshazzar, have not humbled your heart, though you knew all this, but you have lifted up yourself against the Lord of heaven. And the vessels of his house have been brought in before you, and you and your lords, your wives, and your concubines have drunk wine from them. And you have praised the gods of silver and gold, of bronze, iron, wood, and stone, which do not see or hear or know, but the God in whose hand is your breath, and whose are all your ways, you have not honored.

"Then from his presence the hand was sent, and this writing was inscribed. And this is the writing that was inscribed: MENE, MENE, TEKEL, and PARSIN. This is the interpretation of the matter: MENE, God has numbered the days of your kingdom and brought it to an end; TEKEL, you have been weighed in the balances and found wanting; PERES, your kingdom is divided and given to the Medes and Persians."

Then Belshazzar gave the command, and Daniel was clothed with purple, a chain of gold was put around his neck, and a proclamation was made about him, that he should be the third ruler in the kingdom.

That very night Belshazzar the Chaldean king was killed. And Darius the Mede received the kingdom, being about sixty-two years old. (Dan. 5:1–31)

Hard Words

My wife's sister, Karen, is a hospice nurse. In caring for the dying, she has discovered that people face their mortality in many different ways—including turning away from it. She told us of an older woman who refused to talk about the seriousness of her cancer. When doctors or family tried to speak to her about her condition, she would not acknowledge their words or attempt to process the medical reports. Karen, the nurse, was not sure that the woman was capable of hearing what was being said, until one day a friend sent the woman a bouquet of flowers that included snapdragons. When she was a child, Karen and her sisters played with the blossoms of snapdragons. Each blossom is shaped like a set of lips and can be squeezed together to mimic a little puppet speaking. Karen showed the woman how the flower puppets worked and used one to sing her a song: "You are my sunshine, my only sunshine; you make me happy when skies are grey. . . ."

Then the dying woman put a blossom in each hand and produced her own puppet show. One puppet speaking in a rough voice became her doctor saying, "Your blood counts are not good. We can't do anything for you." The other puppet spoke in the voice of a little girl, innocent and carefree: "You don't have to be so mean. I understand." The message that was too hard to hear directly was received when held at a little distance. Those flowers helped the woman move the message to a distance where it could be heard.

This account of King Belshazzar functions similarly. The message is one of judgment. This message follows the truths of the gospel that have unfolded in previous chapters: God's faithful care for his people, his continuing provision for his people, his abiding presence among his people, and his willingness to deal graciously with those who humble themselves and repent. But now this same gracious God must address the consequences of non-repentance. To fail to give such warning would actually endanger the spiritual futures of his people. But how will God make such a message known? That message may be more than a people already suffering in captivity can take. So God moves the message to a caring distance, demonstrating the reality of judgment in the life of a king so proud that he parties with sacred vessels stolen from the temple of God. The message of judgment comes not from the mouths of flowers but in some writing on the wall during the king's party. In this writing is a message that a beloved people must understand so that they will repent of their sin and be saved from its consequences.

It is not an easy message. Who wants to hear about judgment or talk about it? But if sin has no consequence, if evil has no check, if justice never comes, then what good is God and of what benefit is his grace? If grace is amazing, then it must rescue us from something and that something is highlighted in this passage by three words: Mene, Tekel, Peres.

Mene, Tekel, Peres. "Mene" means numbered out; "Tekel" stands for weighed and found wanting; "Peres" warns of being divided and cast down. Though secure in the world, those who are unrepentant before God will ultimately be identified, weighed, and judged.

Belshazzar was a powerful man. He had become the undisputed sovereign of Babylon, the empire that had dominated the ancient world for generations. Outside the walls of his capital a foreign army challenged the king's dominion, but Babylon's ruler was unperturbed. Belshazzar was secure. The Persian invader had been kept at bay outside the city gates for two and a half years. The walls of Babylon were as much as 350 feet high, 87 feet wide, and impregnable to any war machine of that day. The metropolis surrounded by these mammoth walls was itself so spacious that food could be cultivated within the walls. The river Euphrates even flowed through the city, supplying a fresh and ample source of water for people, cattle, and crops. Babylon could not be starved into submission. Belshazzar was secure. So confident was he of his safety that as a slap in the face of his enemy, Belshazzar threw a party. By hosting a feast the king dismissed the enemy as if to say, "You don't worry us a bit. That's because weaklings don't worry us. You call this a siege? Ha! You want to know what I think of your siege? It's not enough to keep me from throwing the biggest bash this kingdom has ever seen. You go ahead and have your little siege. We are going to party."

So arrogant was Belshazzar about his security that he even dismissed God. This king ignored the vivid lessons God taught his predecessor, Nebuchadnezzar. The power of Jehovah of Israel and the sacredness of his temple were disregarded. In a flourish of irreverence, Belshazzar ordered that the holy vessels secured from God's temple during the conquest of Israel be brought as wine cups for Babylon's feast. Belshazzar was secure. So he thought. But his judgment would come that night.

The Persians diverted the course of the river Euphrates and penetrated Babylon's defenses by funneling troops under the city's walls through the drained riverbed. The city was conquered. Belshazzar was killed. The party was over. The prophet's words rang true and echo still: "God is not mocked" (Gal. 6:7); "The wrath of God is revealed from heaven against all ungodliness and unrighteousness" (Rom. 1:18); "God will bring every deed into judgment, with every secret thing, whether good or evil" (Eccles. 12:14).

Beware

God says to every person, "Beware." Beware, because there is no human wall so high, no human fortress so secure, no activity so hidden that it can protect sin from the wrath of God. We must consider this truth not only in the context of this ancient account of an arrogant king but also in terms of our lives today. There are walls we too may try to erect to protect our sin from the wrath of

God. We must see the walls for what they are—foolish defenses that must be abandoned for our own welfare.

Human Security Won't Last

Belshazzar was not the last to believe that his sin was protected by a wall of human achievement. Tiger Woods, Pete Rose; Bernie Madoff, Michael Milkin; Ted Haggard, Jimmy Swaggart. The names change; the message does not. Mene, Tekel, Peres. Mene: numbered out; Tekel: weighed and found wanting; Peres: divided and cast down. Secure in the world, sinful before God, judged. Despite their achievements and apparent invulnerability, those unrepentant before God will ultimately be identified, weighed, and judged. The words still apply even to sports figures, business leaders, and religious leaders. But the words do not accomplish their purpose if we do not think that they have some application to us as well. The cautionary tales of these public figures are only items of titillating gossip if we do not hear the echoes of Mene, Tekel, Peres for our own lives.

Daniel's message should be moved to focal distance for us so that we can read the writing on the wall of real life: power, position, prestige, peer approval, wealth, wisdom, wonderful potential, amazing accomplishments, even esteem in the church will not shield us from an all-powerful, all-knowing, holy God who brings every dark thing to light and judges sin. The names change, the situations vary, but the consequences do not. The judgment of God is sure. God's Word still whispers, "Mene, Tekel, Peres."

Of course, a disadvantage of taking our cues from headline-making figures is that their fame, power, and wealth may make them and their stories seem unreal and inapplicable. Until we see the reality of God's judgment in lives that seem "real," we may be interested or impressed by God's actions but unchanged in our own lives. So consider the account of another man, a man more like us—a man whose life demonstrates the reality of a living God.

He was an incredibly able businessman. Beginning as a driver for a road construction company, he saved every spare penny he earned. Before he was twenty-five he had saved enough to buy his own dump truck and become his own boss. He kept on saving. He bought another dump truck and then another. By the time he was thirty he owned a truck line. His business went so well that eventually he bought the road construction company that first had hired him as a driver. With a virtual monopoly on road construction contracting and trucking services in his rural Tennessee community, the man became wealthy beyond his dreams.

He was a Christian man. As his business prospered, the local church leaders recognized the advantages of his involvement. They asked him to become an officer in the church. They asked repeatedly. He always turned them down. He was busy about other things. These other things more and more began to dominate his life.

He was a man under pressure. Rumors began to circulate in town about shady business deals and contracts improperly handled. His personality became more intense. His anger boiled more quickly. He began to drink more. The tension between the man and his wife became common gossip. The oldest daughter fled the pressures inside the family and too soon married into an ill-considered relationship. Two sons, following the worst of their father's instincts, turned wild, turned to drugs, and tuned out responsibility.

The business still occupied the father. But there were new pressures there, too. The rapid expansion of the construction company caused cash flow problems. Banks, listening to more rumors about mismanagement and misappropriation, became reticent to loan money. So the man finally turned to the church, but it was not spiritual help that he wanted. He asked old friends in the church to trust him and invest in his business because it was "totally secure." Many believed him, and some invested their life's savings in the firm.

Then he became a man in ruin. For reasons that are still not clear, the younger son one day "borrowed" a company car. Joyriding down a rain-slickened country road he crossed the center line and plowed head-on into oncoming traffic. He lay in intensive care for nine months. The hospital costs were astronomical and continued to mount because the son's spinal cord was severed in the accident and his paralysis required round-the-clock care.

The court battles between insurance companies, the hospital, and others injured in the accident continued for years. But while the litigation awaited settlement, no one paid anything, except the family. In the first year after the accident, the family was charged $750,000 in medical bills. The man lost his struggling road construction business and the investments of his church friends. In the second year he lost his truck line. In the third year he filed for bankruptcy. Today the once-wealthy businessman pumps gas at a service station in his hometown under the scorn of former investors and the ridicule of former friends.

The trek from truck driver to millionaire took about forty years. The plunge from community leader to service station attendant took about four years. The accident that caused the empire to fall took about three seconds: Mene, Tekel, Peres.

There is no human wall so high, no human accomplishment so great, that it is secure against the judgment of God. God will bring every deed into judgment. No matter how great the man, how hidden the means, or how long the practice has continued, God ultimately will prevail. His Word is true, and his justice is sure. In the Bible, in the newspaper, in the lives of the people we know, God warns us to beware his holy judgment.

Spiritual Insulation Won't Work

Since God speaks so plainly to warn us of the consequences of sin, why, then, do so many continue to ignore him? One reason, of course, is that many do not believe in a living, just God. But there must be other reasons. Daniel tells King Belshazzar that through his predecessor, Nebuchadnezzar, the new king "knew all" about God's judgment, and still "you . . . have not humbled your heart" (Dan. 5:22). The clear message is that simple knowledge of God does not insulate us from the consequences of an unrepentant life.

Even those who think of themselves as Christian need to remember that simple knowledge of God does not insulate them from the consequences of sin. To turn us from the greater dangers of a sinful path, God may well allow us to experience the consequences of sin. Always the intention of such discipline is to save his children from greater harm. Still, we must also face the reality of what a continuing lack of repentance may mean. Even as we acknowledge that those who are truly the Lord's are eternally secure in him despite their sin, we have to remember to whom these promises apply. God promises his abiding care to those who love him, and those who presume on his grace do not demonstrate love for him. We have no certainty of a lasting relationship with the Lord if we persist in unrepentant actions or attitudes.

Some may say that this text has no application to us because it only addresses God's rage against an enemy of his people. But though the text is written about Belshazzar, it is for God's people. The Babylonians and the Persians were not going to read the book of Daniel. The book was written to be read by God's people. They are yet being disciplined in captivity for their previous idolatry. While the people of Israel may rejoice that their enemy gets his just deserts, they cannot avoid the plain evidence that their sin has also resulted in much pain. There is no Scripture that says God's children will never face earthly consequences despite rebellion against him. There is no Scripture that says those in personal, unrelenting rebellion need not worry because they have the complete assurance of God's abiding love. No claims could be further from the truth of Scripture or of greater offense to God than pretending that sin doesn't really matter to him.

Belshazzar praised the gods of silver, gold, bronze, iron, and wood—the gods of his own making (Dan. 5:23). He continued in sin because he trusted the gods he made to protect him. Sometimes contemporary people continue in sin because of a god they invent to protect them. They believe that because they say that Jesus died for their sins and God forgives whatever they confess, they can do as they please. Such people reason, "God doesn't want us to be 'real bad,' but the ordinary business lies, the ungodly entertainments, the academic compromises, the residual anger toward a brother, the neglect of church obligations—these things don't really count. After all, God knows we're just human." Such "believers" smear the truth about Christ's blood on their sin, believing this will insulate them from its consequences. They only fool themselves. The god that they imagine will protect them is not the God of Daniel.

Notice at what moment in this account of Belshazzar's feast God inscribed his judgment. The writing appeared when the king used the vessels from the temple to drink his wine and praise his gods. God revealed his wrath at precisely the moment when what was intended to be kept holy was used for sin. We who are Christians are called God's vessels (see 2 Cor. 4:7). God intends for our lives and testimonies to be holy. If we begin filling with sin the vessels God has made sacred with the blood of his own Son and using them for unholy purposes, we should not imagine that we have any security against his disciplining wrath.

No Scripture says that because we are believers, God will never allow consequences for unrepented sin. The Bible says that to whom much is given, much is required (Luke 12:48). Israel was given the promise of the covenant, but for its sins it languished in this Babylonian captivity.

To us has been given the fulfillment of covenant promises in the provision of God's own Son who died for our sins. Surely it is foolish to think that we could now take the shed blood of Jesus and smear it over continuing greed, lust, and anger with impunity? Surely we cannot sensibly imagine we could dip our hands in his blood to use it for personal advantage, evil excuse, and deliberate sin without expecting the righteous anger of the Holy Father who provided the sacrifice of his Son. If we really knew the God of Daniel, we would not abuse his Son this way. Yet how often do we, with the cross before our eyes, dip our hands into Christ's wounds to gather his blood to spread as insulation over our lives when we wish to continue in sin? And when we do so, do we not look to God and say, "This makes it OK, right? You don't really mind, do you, Father?" If we see what we are really doing and saying to the Father who sacrificed his Son to provide that blood, we should not doubt his righteous wrath.

The knowledge of spiritual truths is no insulation against the wrath of God. Only months ago one of our denomination's most able church planters acknowledged years of homosexual activity—he, his church, and family now face so much hurt. Spiritual activity did not insulate a Christian leader from the consequences of sin: Mene, Tekel, Peres.

The stories of the immorality of former National Association of Evangelicals leader Ted Haggard were as instructive as they were salacious. Tales of power, payoffs, and adultery are more sad than spicy. Somewhere in their vast material and ministerial successes, good people lost their way. I felt that more keenly and sympathetically when one of my own best friends in ministry was discovered with an addiction that wound him into an awful web of deceit, theft, and family pretense. In the ruin of reputations and ministries that follows the scandals, the Word of God still speaks without confusion: Mene, Tekel, Peres.

But these news accounts are again of persons whose extravagancies and extraordinary ministries may make God's message seem remote. It may be painful to bring the truth closer to home, but Daniel's warning must not go unheeded. Only weeks before I began writing this chapter, two young friends acknowledged extramarital affairs and are out of the ministry. Pornography has claimed at least a half dozen more. Alcohol addiction has led to the fall of three more. Loss of integrity driven by greed or ambition has two more out of ministry. I weep for them. I weep with them. God weeps, too, and says, "Mene, Tekel, Peres." And we all must listen, including me.

The fact that these are my friends is itself all the more devastating, for I realize these men are close to me because they are men like me. I am not different; I am not better; I cannot pretend their error is due to some flaw in them that I do not share. If I do not see the consequences, I will not avoid the sin with appropriate horror. I am scared by their failures. I should be. But my greater fear is that we may no longer even be horrified. The prevalence of sin in our increasingly secular culture may make us calloused to its evil. So God says with unmistakable force and clarity, "Be sure your sin will find you out" (Num. 32:23); "God will bring every deed into judgment, with every secret thing, whether good or evil" (Eccles. 12:14). Mene, Tekel, Peres.

Even though Belshazzar did not know the meaning of these words, his knees knocked and his face turned pale when they appeared. How much more should a holy fear of sin seize us who know what the words meant for him and mean for us?

Grieve

Daniel's message includes more than a warning of sin's consequences. With the warning is weeping. It may be difficult to perceive his grief until one remembers the narratives that precede this passage and the language that permeates it. Four times in chapter 5 the biblical writer reminds us that Nebuchadnezzar was the "father" of Belshazzar's rule. While the term signifies "predecessor" more than actual father, its repeated reference implies something even more profound. For more than forty years Daniel nurtured, loved, and ultimately became God's instrument for changing the heart of Babylon's mightiest king. But a generation later the impact of so great a change seemed lost. The successor, Belshazzar, was as corrupt as his "father" ever was. The change was changed back. How Daniel's heart must have grieved, as repeatedly he directs our attention to the spiritual victory in Nebuchadnezzar's life in contrast to Belshazzar's subsequent surrender to wickedness.

The grief the prophet must have felt over another's sin is even more evident when the purpose of this book is considered. Daniel wrote as God's spokesman to instruct God's people in all times. God is reminding us that sin can reinfect a people, because so often this happens. Israel was purified time after time, only to sink again into contamination. Israel was in bondage throughout Daniel's lifetime because of repeated idolatry. God pointedly warned Israel again, with the object lesson of Belshazzar, that sin results in judgment. This was evidence of his desire that Israel not be harmed by continuing in evil. By indicating this great concern for his people, God discloses how much grief he himself experiences when people sin. Our awareness of his grief for our sin and its consequences should increase our love for him and strengthen our resistance to sin (Eph. 4:30). Perhaps it is in part because we do not often share this sense of grief over others' sin and consequent hurt that the church seems so powerless against evil today.

Daniel grieved over the judgment that surely would follow Nebuchadnezzar's sin (Dan. 4:19) and lamented the decline of Babylon's commitment (Dan. 5:22). Daniel's grief—which reflected God's grief—was recorded to turn God's people from sin. Is it possible that today's church has lost the power to turn God's people from sin precisely because we do not sincerely grieve for the effects of sin in their lives? Are our friends and family members wandering away because they know no one will really grieve if they are lost or damaged by their wayward choices? We are quick to point out evil, quick to judge, glad we are not caught in such sin—but are we grieving for those whom sin has led astray? Have we so concerned ourselves with our own blessings that we have lost the capacity to weep for those who have wandered? There is much for which to grieve. And until we again see clearly and feel deeply the reasons to weep, we will have little influence with those who need our message of God's care. When we do not grieve for the sinner, we have little power over the sin.

The consequences of our inability or refusal to grieve over the effects of sin may be most evident in the church's handling of its own young people. We wonder why our teens do not listen when the church says "tsk, tsk" to promiscuity. We wonder why telling them that premarital intercourse is wrong and dangerous does not curb their sexual activity. Seventy-two percent of young men and seventy percent of young women in this country are sexually active before marriage.[1] Christian youth leaders like Josh McDowell say the figures are not significantly different for young people in evangelical churches than for the surrounding unbelieving culture. Why has the church lost power over sin amid its most precious members, its children? We can blame many causes. The church can blame parents for not monitoring their children's entertainments. Parents can blame the church for not providing better youth programs. Parents and church can blame a culture that inundates the young with sexualized entertainments, secular values, and selfish priorities. We have been blaming a long time, though. It does not seem to have done much good. Blaming is easier than grieving, but not more powerful.

Until the church learns to express grief as eloquently as it vents rage, we shall have little power over sin. We must grieve for children having children, for children having abortions, for children so desperate for affection that they do not even know when they are being used.

Our children leaving the church, bingeing on alcohol, controlling their emotions by cutting their flesh, or vomiting their calories—the list of youthful struggles and sins could go on and on. But are we more concerned for our shrinking churches or for the pain of those leaving? Are we more anxious about our failures or the emptiness our children feel that makes them try anything to try to feel something—anything?

When Jesus looked over the people of Jerusalem, so immersed in sin and so hardened to his message that they soon would murder him, he wept. Jesus knew how to express rage and umbrage, but his first response to the devastation of sin was grief: "O Jerusalem, Jerusalem. . . . How often would I have gathered your children together as a hen gathers her brood under her wings, and you would not!" (Matt. 23:37). Grief for sin drove Jesus to the cross, where sin was overpowered. If we are to have power over sin today, grief must at least drive us to our knees. It is not difficult to be angry with sin. It is easy to blame. Grieving for sin is hard work, calling for the deepest searching of our own hearts and motives. Still, we must seek this rending of our hearts as though it were a rare, life-giving potion that alone could save a dying child. For without grief over others' pain we are powerless in combating the sin that threatens God's children.

As a pastor, I saw a young girl in our congregation grow in the Lord over a period of years. I will call her Debbie (not her real name). A young teen, she came to us soon after her abusive and alcoholic father had abandoned her family. She had almost no Christian background, but through Sunday school and church-camp experiences Debbie eventually committed her life to the Lord and blossomed in him. She became a leader in our youth group and a wonderful testimony to other young people. She often took special care to befriend young people who had troubled family backgrounds like hers. Debbie shared her own life and the Lord's love.

When she graduated from high school, however, Debbie confronted the harsh realities facing many young women in poor small towns. Without the means or desire for college, and without good job opportunities, she decided to get married. Sadly, her choice reflected the only family relationships she had known. The young man to whom she became engaged already had an alcohol problem, had bounced from one dead-end job to another, was currently unemployed, and, worst, was not a Christian. When I heard that a wedding was likely, I went to Debbie and expressed concern. She acknowledged that her "friend" was not a believer, said she remembered the Bible's instructions that believers should marry "only in the Lord," and promised to obey God's Word in her choice of whom she would marry. Three months later she came asking me to marry her to the very same young man.

Debbie assured me that her fiancé had become a Christian, and we set a time to talk about his faith and their plans. In the meantime, the two already had begun living together. Further, the conversation at our meeting made it very evident the young man did not have the slightest idea of what a Christian was and was not the least interested. Debbie later indicated she had decided to coach the young man on what to say to trick me into marrying them. Debbie was defying the Scriptures openly, had broken her word to me, and was now actively trying to deceive me.

The whole situation made me furious. After another frustrating meeting, I said that I could not in good conscience marry the two unless both agreed genuinely to commit themselves to the Lord. Their response was to be married in a church down the street where the pastor did not know them and did not ask questions. Debbie's explanation of the turn of events to friends and family, of course, was not quite the same as mine. My name was mud. And hearing of her slander, I got angrier.

It was not until months later that I saw my sin. My decision was biblical; the Scriptures clearly forbid the wedding of believers and unbelievers (Matt. 19:5; 1 Cor. 7:39; 2 Cor. 6:14–7:2). But I am convinced now that my attitude was wrong and therefore made me increasingly helpless in dealing with Debbie. I became angry, but I did not grieve. Here was a young woman who had known alcoholism and abuse all her life. She knew no other family world. Now, when she had the opportunity to make a new family world, she chose to marry back into her nightmare. She did not even have the perspective to know she was in a nightmare. It was all she knew. And yet I did not grieve.

I was so blinded by rage and vain concern for my own reputation that I lost sight of Debbie's pain. Is the reason she did not listen—could not listen—that she saw that I did not care enough about her to grieve? I will never know for sure in this life. But I now recognize that anger is no substitute for tears. Without weeping, the walls of sin are impenetrable, however righteous our indignation may be.

Among the saddest words of Scripture are those echoed three times in the first chapter of Romans: "God gave them up . . ." (Rom. 1:24, 26, 28). The words remind us that sin is so awful that its worst punishment can simply be to let it run its course. God simply may let people have their way when they persist in sin. I have pastored long enough to know just what this means. I have seen the troubled marriages that inevitably result when believers marry unbelievers. I have seen the scars on children's children. I have tried to comfort believing wives when tears of pain stream down their faces over children who are following the paths of unbelieving husbands. I have watched in helplessness as shallow faith becomes a sham of faith when a believer marries a non-Christian.

When God's people disobeyed, the Old Testament prophet Ezekiel saw the Lord's glory leave the temple. When God's people disobey him, the experience of his blessing still departs their lives. Until we see the tragedy of sin as clearly as Ezekiel, we will not pray, work, and love as we should, for we will not have grieved as we ought. It is not enough that our knees quake in fear of sin's consequences. If our knees do not give way in grief over the tragedy of sin, we are powerless to confront it or correct it.

Repent

Where is the grace in all of this? Are warnings to fear and grieve all Daniel can offer from God in this chapter? No. The mercy of the previous chapters has not vanished. God's warnings are proof of God's love. If he did not care, he would not warn. Remember, even though this account is written about a pagan king, Daniel writes for the children of God. The Babylonians and Persians were not the intended readers. God inspired these words for us to read. We are to read the warning as an expression of God's care for us.

When growing up, I loved the evenings that the children in our family would sit by my father's chair while he read stories to us. One of our favorites was the poem "The Highwayman."[2] The poem tells of an adventurer who robs the coaches of English aristocrats. The daring highwayman is in love with an innkeeper's daughter, and, by night when the coast is clear, he courts her. The authorities learn of the romance, and one twilight before the highwayman arrives, British soldiers invade the inn. They tie the innkeeper's daughter at the window so the highwayman will see her and believe the way is safe. Then, lest she try to warn her lover in any way, the soldiers gag the maiden and tie a musket at her heart that will fire at the slightest movement. Then the highwayman comes riding.

Unaware of the muskets that wait to cut him down, the highwayman gallops ever closer to his destruction. He sees his love at the window. She hears his horse's hoofs on the lane. The soldiers cock their muskets. Nearer to the arms he loves, nearer to his destruction, the highwayman comes riding. Then, just as he is about to enter musket range, a premature shot rings out warning him to turn back. The highwayman reins and turns as the frustrated soldiers shoot a futile volley. All the muskets fire, but only one found its mark. The one true shot was from the musket that fired the warning, the musket aimed at the heart of the innkeeper's daughter. At the expense of her life, she expressed her love in giving that warning.

Daniel's warnings also express such love because they are the early strains of a clarion call echoing through history and culminating at Calvary. There at the cross, our Lord demonstrated how great his love is when he sacrificed his life to warn us of the destruction that awaits us if we do not turn from sin. His was not the first warning, only the most poignant. Through Daniel's accounts of Nebuchadnezzar and Belshazzar, God has previously warned that repentance leads to blessing and rebellion to destruction. God warned in the writing on the wall that we all live in a just universe where sin will be punished. The message of the cross completes that warning. The hymnist Thomas Kelly points to the cross on which the Son of God died and writes,

> You who think of sin but lightly
> Nor suppose the evil great
> Here may view its nature rightly,
> Here its guilt may estimate.[3]

The cross stands both as God's ultimate warning of the consequences of sin and as the greatest expression of his love for sinners. If God did not love, he would not so graciously warn. The cross is the fatal cry of a Savior to those he loves to turn from what will do them great harm.

Mene, Tekel, Peres is not ultimately the handwriting against Belshazzar; it is the handwriting of God for us. By his hand God warns us of our sin. On the cross of Jesus we see that handwriting in its boldest and brightest strokes, for there the script is written in the blood of God's own Son. But the glory of that blood is that it does more than warn. In his letter to the Colossians the apostle Paul tells us it is the same blood that blots out the handwriting that was against us (Col. 2:14). God warns us of his judgment so that we will seek the Son who already has assumed it. The blood of Jesus beacons and beckons. It beacons a warning to all who will look, testifying that God judges sin. "Turn back," the blood warns, "turn back from the sin that leads to your hurt and this destruction." At the same time the blood beckons. It beckons sinners to be covered and cleansed by the crimson flow that God lovingly provides for all who truly repent. "Come," cries the blood, "come away from your guilt and enter the forgiving, comforting, strengthening presence of the Savior."

Grow in Grace

Sin is pleasant only for a season (Heb. 11:26); it has a limited appeal. God knows this better than any of us, and so he warns us as clearly as possible about sin—its consequences and his judgment. The warnings may seem harsh, but their intent is clear. God only wants us to turn from the sin that will hurt us and to return to the arms that will hold us in safety. As a father lovingly reserves his sternest warnings for the greatest dangers his child will face, our heavenly Father carefully measures his terms to warn us of dangers to our growth in grace.

The message of God's judgment is never pleasant; still, we must listen. However dark or hidden away our sin, however secure we think we are in it, we must listen. God says, "Your sin will surely find you out, for I bring every deed into judgment including every hidden thing. You must turn from it, my child. Go back, go back from the sin that will destroy what is most precious to you and to me. I judge sin. I desire to show mercy. I love you. I gave my Son for you. Come to the arms that will embrace you with love and life. Come, my child. Come to me."

When Lieutenant Colonel Brian Birdwell spoke at our city's prayer breakfast, he recounted his harrowing experience of being in the section of the Pentagon that was struck by the 9/11 attackers. The hallway in which he was walking was immediately enveloped in flame as an 80-ton aircraft traveling at 520 miles per hour struck the building. The force of the impact knocked him from his feet, and he temporarily lost consciousness. He awoke surrounded by fire, on fire, and without orientation. He said that he knew he was facing a ghastly death and wanted to flee but did not know which direction to run. The wrong choice would send him deeper into the flames, but he had to make a choice. So he ducked his head and ran, screaming, "Jesus, I am coming to see you." Then, whether he headed toward life or death, he still knew he was heading the right direction. It turned out to be the right direction for more life here.

We do not have to wonder what direction to run. In his mercy the Lord has shown us the consequences of sin and the mercy of his Son, so that we will run toward him. I write here as clearly as I know how about the reality of the judgment of God, but I want to make clear the reason. God shows consequences so that we will not experience them. Judgment need not be our destiny. Whatever our lies, whatever the evil we have allowed or are being consumed by, there is a direction to run. We must run to our Savior. When we do, he will receive us and hold us and help us. He loves us enough to point to the consequences of sin and say, "Mene, Tekel, Peres." And he does so to express with all the love in his heart, "Not that way. Come to me. If I love you enough to warn you, then you know that I love you enough to receive you. Come to me." Turn from the sin and run to him.

6

The Song of a Broom

— DANIEL 6 —

Sunday school pictures of a ruddy-faced lad in a lions' den bear scant resemblance to the actual situation described in this chapter of Daniel's life. Daniel was more than ninety years old when these events unfolded. You might think that he had earned a little rest and relaxation for those "retirement" years, but God still was using the faithful prophet. Age apparently is no barrier to spiritual usefulness. In Daniel's case, glorious gospel truths that have been building through the chapters describing his life in Babylon reach a climax here.

As we come to the end of act one in the book of Daniel (chaps. 1–6 describing Daniel's life), it is helpful to review the scenes that prepare us for act two (chaps. 7–12 describing Daniel's prophecies). Each previous chapter had a key image or event that plays a pivotal role in piecing together the gospel message of Daniel:

In chapter 1, Daniel and his friends were kept healthy on a politically dangerous diet of vegetable soup, as God communicated to his people, "I remember you."

In chapter 2, Nebuchadnezzar's multilayered statue was displaced by a heavenly rock, as God assures his people, "I will rescue you."

In chapter 3, one "like a son of the gods" appears with Daniel's friends in a fiery furnace to demonstrate the God's Immanuel principle: "I am right here with you."

In chapter 4, Nebuchadnezzar's restoration from animal-like insanity communicates God's vital message to his own idolatrous people: "I restore the humble."

In an important but gracious contrast, chapter 5 reveals the writing on the wall that humbles an arrogant King Belshazzar and discloses God's loving warning of judgment to all people in all times: "I judge the proud."

Now as we come to this concluding chapter of the biographical portions of the book of Daniel, the final brick in the foundation of Daniel's gospel message gets laid, preparing us for the glorious prophecies of God's future work in the chapters that remain. What is the final gospel truth that a loving God will unveil in this chapter? It's not complicated. The Lord allows the aged Daniel to face his greatest challenge in a lion's den to say to his people then and to us now: "Trust me."

Here is how that message unfolds: A new king reigned over Babylon. Darius the Mede was the conquering ruler who, like the Babylonian kings before him, recognized the wisdom of Daniel. Darius selected the aging prophet for his cabinet. Daniel became one of only three administrators who governed Babylon. But Daniel's new rise to power was still incomplete. Daniel so excelled at his cabinet post that the king decided to put him solely in charge of the whole Babylonian government.

Other cabinet members and lesser officials were not pleased. They tried to dig up some dirt to ruin Daniel. But he was too honest. No trumped-up charge would stick. Then the growing jealousy of the evil officials mutated into a warped ingenuity.

"Let's use Daniel's religious convictions to trap him," they plotted.

The officials appealed to the pagan king's pride.

"O king," they said, "you are so great no one should pray to anyone but you. It is actually an insult for anyone to recognize any being greater than your magnificence. Why not issue a royal decree proclaiming punishment for anyone who would insult your greatness by praying to anyone but you?"

The king's pride trapped him. He ordered the lions' den for those who would pray to any god but him. Little did the king anticipate the fate his pride had determined for his friend Daniel.

The decree was issued. The lions' appetite was whetted. And Daniel faced his greatest trial yet:

It pleased Darius to set over the kingdom 120 satraps, to be throughout the whole kingdom; and over them three high officials, of whom Daniel was one, to whom these satraps should give account, so that the king might suffer no loss. Then this Daniel became distinguished above all the other high officials and satraps, because an excellent spirit was in him. And the king planned to set him over the whole kingdom. Then the high officials and the satraps sought to find a ground for complaint against Daniel with regard to the kingdom, but they could find no ground for complaint or any fault, because he was faithful, and no error or fault was found in him. Then these men said, "We shall not find any ground for complaint against this Daniel unless we find it in connection with the law of his God."

Then these high officials and satraps came by agreement to the king and said to him, "O King Darius, live forever! All the high officials of the kingdom, the prefects and the satraps, the counselors, and the governors are agreed that the king should establish an ordinance and enforce an injunction, that whoever makes petition to any god or man for thirty days, except to you, O king, shall be cast into the den of lions. Now, O king, establish the injunction and sign the document, so that it cannot be changed, according to the law of the Medes and the Persians, which cannot be revoked." Therefore King Darius signed the document and injunction.

When Daniel knew that the document had been signed, he went to his house where he had windows in his upper chamber open toward Jerusalem. He got down on his knees three times a day and prayed and gave thanks before his God, as he had done previously. Then these men came by agreement and found Daniel making petition and plea before his God. Then they came near and said before the king, concerning the injunction, "O king! Did you not sign an injunction, that anyone who makes petition to any god or man within thirty days except to you, O king, shall be cast into the den of lions?" The king answered and said, "The thing stands fast, according to the law of the Medes and Persians, which cannot be revoked." Then they answered and said before the king, "Daniel, who is one of the exiles from Judah, pays no attention to you, O king, or the injunction you have signed, but makes his petition three times a day."

Then the king, when he heard these words, was much distressed and set his mind to deliver Daniel. And he labored till the sun went down to rescue him. Then these men came by agreement to the king and said to the king, "Know, O king, that it is a law of the Medes and Persians that no injunction or ordinance that the king establishes can be changed."

Then the king commanded, and Daniel was brought and cast into the den of lions. The king declared to Daniel, "May your God, whom you serve continually, deliver you!" And a stone was brought and laid on the mouth of the den, and the king sealed it with his own signet and with the signet of his lords, that nothing might be changed concerning Daniel. Then the king went to his palace and spent the night fasting; no diversions were brought to him, and sleep fled from him.

Then, at break of day, the king arose and went in haste to the den of lions. As he came near to the den where Daniel was, he cried out in a tone of anguish. The king declared to Daniel, "O Daniel, servant of the living God, has your God, whom you serve continually, been able to deliver you from the lions?" Then Daniel said to the king, "O king, live forever! My God sent his angel and shut the lions' mouths, and they have not harmed me, because I was found blameless before him; and also before you, O king, I have done no harm." Then the king was exceedingly glad, and commanded that Daniel be taken up out of the den. So Daniel was taken up out of the den, and no kind of harm was found on him, because he had trusted in his God. And the king commanded, and those men who had maliciously accused Daniel were brought and cast into the den of lions—they, their children, and their wives. And before they reached the bottom of the den, the lions overpowered them and broke all their bones in pieces.

Then King Darius wrote to all the peoples, nations, and languages that dwell in all the earth: "Peace be multiplied to you. I make a decree, that in all my royal dominion people are to tremble and fear before the God of Daniel,

for he is the living God,
   enduring forever;
his kingdom shall never be
   destroyed,
   and his dominion shall be to the
   end.
He delivers and rescues;
   he works signs and wonders
   in heaven and on earth,
he who has saved Daniel
   from the power of the lions."

So this Daniel prospered during the reign of Darius and the reign of Cyrus the Persian. (Dan. 6:1–28)

The Song of a Broom

Four more days and she would be seventeen. It would be her father's birthday, too, but this year there would be no party. America was mired in the Great Depression, and her father was dying. Instead of gathering presents, the family (a mother and seven children) gathered around a rickety bed and prayed over the sound of his labored breathing.

On the day of the funeral, the girl's mother with her seven children trudged through the mud to a simple grave. A small crowd of women friends also came; the men could not or would not afford the time off work. The teenage girl, who could only find work as a maid, had to borrow a dress for the occasion. When the family went home, she carefully folded it smooth and lay next to it on her bed.

A sense of desolation seemed to crush her. It was over—not just the funeral. Everything was over. Seven children, no real income, the house so heavily mortgaged it would not be theirs for long. She was old enough to know these things, and to despair because of them. Even the silence of the room seemed to weigh on her and choke hope out of her.

And then she heard it. Breaking the oppressive silence came the tentative *whisk-whisk* of a broom on the kitchen floor. Then the sound came again, more determined this time: *whisk-whisk*. Her mother who had not spoken for three days was reassuming her household duties. The broom went *whisk-whisk*, and the sound said more than her mother could voice: "Life goes on. All is not lost. We have trusted the Lord and still we will. We will press on and live again." Later, the girl would write in her diary of how powerful the gentle sound of her mother taking up that simple household task was in kindling new hope and faith in the child's heart.

"The world is not entirely fallen in, all is not lost, there is hope, life will go on." All of this was said in the sound of a broom that indicated there were still things worth doing. Her mother was pressing on. The assumption of the duties of everyday life was itself an expression of a faith that there was a future. In the gentle rhythm of the broom came a song of hope and triumph over trial. *Whisk-whisk* went the broom and in the repeat of each stroke and counter-sweep it whispered to a wounded heart, "Trust and live, trust and live."

It was enough. The girl rose from the bed ready to take up her own tasks and resume her life with new courage and hope. More difficulties lay ahead, of course. The reverberations of tragedy were not over. She would face more tragedy later in life—as would the writer who tells this story. For far away from this Depression-era account, a primitive people in South America would kill the missionary husband of Elisabeth Elliot, leaving her in a situation even more desperate than the teenage girl whose story she tells. But for neither woman—the deprived widow or the despairing teen—would life remain empty, hopeless, or purposeless. All the "what-shall-we-do" and "what-comes-next" questions were being answered in the faith song of a trusting mother's broom: "Trust and live, trust and live." Many times later in life each woman would recall that song and would sing it in her heart to reclaim the hope and courage needed for the challenges of a new day.[1]

This young woman's story, as it is recounted by Elisabeth Elliot, seems to capture many of the truths of this final chapter of Daniel's biography. The attitudes and actions that lead the prophet from trial to triumph echo in the broom's song. These same truths are meant to lead us from difficulty to victory in our lives. We cry out in our anguish, "O God, tell me what to do. What do you expect of me?" Against such adversity that threatens to crush faith and life from us the Bible provides the calming echo of a prophet's broom. He sweeps away the confusion of our circumstances and the complexity of our questions with this gentle reminder: "Trust and live."

Trust

The Signs of Trust

PRAYER

The most evident sign of Daniel's trust is his faithful prayer. When the decree comes forbidding prayer upon pain of horrible death, Daniel does as he has always done. "He got down on his knees three times a day and prayed and gave thanks before his God, as he had done previously" (v. 10). When devotion seemed only to promote disaster, Daniel remained faithful. His prayer was public, as a testimony to others of his faith. His prayer was also persistent. We should remember Daniel encouraged similar prayer at an earlier phase of his life in the face of Nebuchadnezzar's threats (2:18).

From his youth to old age, in crises and out of crises, Daniel prayed for God's help. In addition, the Bible says Daniel "gave thanks." So much does he trust his God that Daniel gives thanks for the grace surrounding him despite the crisis that now envelops him. It is almost as though the aging prophet has already read the words the apostle Paul will write in a future century: "In everything by prayer and supplication with thanksgiving let your requests be made known to God" (Phil. 4:6). Daniel did not question whether praying was the wisest course of action or whether the probable consequences outweighed God's requirements. He simply turned to God in trust as he always had.

DEDICATION

Daniel's prayer in the face of threat is so obvious a sign of trust that we may miss another sign that also is evident. We should remember why Daniel is being set up by his detractors. He has lived with integrity and applied his gifts of insight and management with excellence for the sake of the land his people inhabit (v. 3). Knowingly or unknowingly he has honored the previous instruction of the prophet Jeremiah. At the beginning of Israel's captivity, Jeremiah urged the captives to seek the welfare of the city of their captors (Jer. 29:7).

Jeremiah's instruction and Daniel's example have embroiled God's people in ethical discussions ever since. How can God ask us to work for the good of those who stand in opposition to him, and what are the limits of such work? The answers can be complex but the principle is not. We are to bring the righteousness, grace, and rule of our God to all dimensions of our lives. Paul writes, "So, whether you eat or drink, or whatever you do, do all to the glory of God" (1 Cor. 10:31). The world—even the enemies of our God (which we once were)—must know his nature and his heart by our reflection of his wisdom and character in all places: where we live, where we work, and even where we struggle.

We live to reflect our God and to reclaim the world that he is redeeming for his own glory. Daniel showed his dedication to his God by doing his very best to exemplify God's standards in his occupation and in his religious duties. He trusted God enough to serve him in secular endeavors as well as religious ones. He refused to recognize walls that would separate secular from sacred obligations, demonstrating that he would trust God enough to serve him in every context of life.

The sign of Daniel's trust was not merely a valiant stand in a crisis (v. 23) but a life of dedication exhibited across decades, before a succession of empires, and without the support of his own people. His was the kind of life one author has described as "a long obedience in the same direction."[2] His trust was evident in a path of godly service that extended in every context over a lifetime. Perhaps such prayer and dedication on the part of Daniel strikes us as neither significant nor relevant to ordinary Christians like us. After all, Daniel was a prophet, a supersaint. He was supposed to be incredibly committed. But stereotyping this man's trust with such a "superspiritual" label actually ruins his testimony. By making Daniel's trust unrealistic, we rob ourselves of the help we need when reality makes such trust seem impossible.

The Tests of Trust

Bible teachers often refer to Daniel as one of the great "success" stories of the Scriptures. Such a perspective results from a very selective gathering of facts from the prophet's life. A more honest weighing of all the facts will cause us to speak less of "Daniel the Great" and more of "Daniel the Tested." No victory lasts. No triumph makes more than the most fleeting of spiritual impressions on Daniel's history, culture, or circumstances. As far as he knew, his life had been spent in fruitlessness.

UNCHANGED PAGANS

Daniel ministered in this pagan land for most of a century, and what did he have to show for it? Almost nothing. The account says that "all" the officials of the king turned against Daniel, and King Darius also was willing to endorse their idolatry of himself (v. 7). The people of this land were no more believers in Daniel's God than when the prophet entered the land as a young man. No spiritual awakening was recorded to have swept the land during his long life. Babylon was unchanged. Though some kings listened to him, their successors did not. Kings and kingdoms had come and gone, but still the rulers were idolatrous, wicked, and cruel.

Daniel's positions and influence seemed to come and go with purposeless frequency. Yes, he had offered a lifetime of honest administration and godly counsel in government service, but what was his reward? For all his wisdom, integrity, and faithfulness, Daniel is an old man facing the jealousy of peers, the idolatrous arrogance of a king, and a death sentence in a lions' den.

UNCHANGED PEOPLE

Still, all the trials might be considered worth the suffering and disappointment if there were some evidence of the fruit of his ministry among Daniel's own people. But there was no fruit. Not only was Babylon unchanged, Israel seemed unchanged. There is no uprising to rescue him, and no crowd petitions the king to save their prophet. Daniel is the only one mentioned who still prays to his God in the face of the king's edict (v. 13).

Daniel's life seems to have had little effect on the spiritual progress of his own people. No revival was recorded among them. No repentance sweeps through them. The chosen nation remained in captivity despite Daniel's political power, and the Israelites' hearts seem similarly bound despite his prophetic ministry. When these "chosen people" returned to Israel after Daniel's death, their spiritual understanding had so eroded that they could not even remember the language in which God's law was written, much less the standards and traditions it described.

Daniel trusted the Lord and served long, hard, and faithfully. But the only fruit of his faith is jealousy, accusation, and advancing years that make him too old ever to go back to his homeland. His circumstance could well justify his asking the question Leonardo da Vinci asked on his deathbed: "Did I do anything?" For despite the intelligence and designs of the Renaissance man, very little actually resulted from his efforts within his lifetime. And despite all Daniel's trials and failures, God called on the aged prophet to face yet another threat to his life and faith.

The full story of Daniel's life does not seem to inspire much trust. This is certainly not the "blessed" life that prosperity preachers promise to crowds of people longing for easier lives and instant success. Yet in Daniel's life we discover the contexts of reality that make trust in our God both difficult and precious.

UNEXPLAINED CIRCUMSTANCES

In a church I pastored, there was an older man named Earl. He was one of those special men that pastors come to identify as foundation stones of the churches they serve. Pastors come and go. The church goes through triumphs and tragedies, disputes and wrangles, but the foundation stones stand firm, and the church stands because of them. Earl was a foundation stone of foundation stones. He was simply there week in and week out, year after year, for more than three-quarters of a century. When pastors erred (as a result of staying too long or coming too young), when sheep wandered, when wolves crept in and scattered the flock or attacked him personally, Earl remained faithful to his God. Wherever his gifts were needed—whether for higher office or lower—he served gladly and without complaint. When others who were less mature or jealous for the respect given him slandered his name, Earl responded with silence and compassion. He simply and faithfully did his duty out of love for God.

Yet despite his great contributions to the life of the church, I recognized with sadness that Earl's own life contained much personal tragedy. He married late in life—not because he was not attractive or intelligent or able. Earl had more than his share of these qualities. He would have been considered "quite a catch" in his younger days. But Earl put aside his own interests and career as a young man to take care of the family farm for his ailing parents. He spent his early years taking care of their waning years. Eventually, after his parents died of prolonged illnesses, Earl married and raised his family in a modest lifestyle provided by the small farm that had consumed his early career opportunities and adult life.

In his later years, however, it seemed as though Earl's sacrifices might finally pay off. The local coal industry was booming and his farm lay right over a huge vein of coal. A mining company began to work the vein on an adjacent property and the value of Earl's land skyrocketed. The coal company offered Earl a premium price for his entire farm. Earl sold his land. For the first time in his life he knew financial security and success. But it was the nature of this man to sacrifice for others, so again he sacrificed.

He purchased homes for the children he loved. There was still money left over, and, wanting to protect his future, Earl wisely invested in building homes for the community, which was expanding with new mining opportunities. He built quality homes—homes characteristic of the man.

But no one knew that the mining boom was about to go bust. The most prudent community investments would soon look very foolish. Changing federal pollution standards would soon make the soft, high-sulfur coal of the region extremely difficult to market. The marketing difficulties put many miners out of work. Instead of needing new homes to house the anticipated influx of new mining families, the housing market was flooded with the older homes of families departing the region. Besides the mining decline, the rural economy experienced the double hit of a national farm crisis. Family after family went bankrupt and moved away. Earl's quality homes did not have a chance of selling.

He went broke. Earl not only lost the money invested in the new homes, he also lost his own home and his children's homes. No one ever would know fully how painful all of this personal tragedy was for Earl. He never said, and he never complained. But Sunday after Sunday I watched Earl as any pastor watches a man whom he loves and respects go through suffering. I learned to read what was behind the firm handshake and jovial greeting. Somewhere deep in those eyes, always full of compassion for others, were hints of frustration and pain. Those eyes confessed, "All I have done has been undone. I have lost the family farm, the money from it, my home, my children's security. All I have done all my life is fail and fail and fail."

What did Earl do in the face of this great personal tragedy? He did just as he had done before. He remained a foundation stone. When the unscrupulous offered him quick ways out of his financial difficulties, he maintained his integrity. When the church was being racked by the tensions and transitions created by the devastation of the local economy, Earl was steady and faithful in his support of the Lord's work. The temptations came to give in to bitterness, fear, and pessimism, but Earl never wavered from godliness. In those difficult years I believe we remained a church more because of Earl's commitment to duty than because of any pastoral effort or financial plan or building program. He remained solid, and, as a result, we kept standing.

Perhaps to some, Earl's duty seems foolish and fruitless, especially in the light of his own personal difficulties. But I know better. Because of his faithfulness during his losses, our church survived. Earl became more than a foundation stone; he became a beacon of hope and Christian maturity for younger men in our congregation who also were losing jobs and homes. They lost a great deal, but with Earl's example and encouragement, they did not lose faith. From that church eight young people have now gone to seminary to train for ministry. And Earl's once-young pastor (who goes by the name of Bryan Chapell) now teaches at that seminary, in part because of supposed successes he experienced in that church (though this pastor/professor knows who truly provided the stability to make the successes possible). The lives of all these young men in ministry will literally touch hundreds, perhaps thousands, and many will come to know Jesus as a result. Earl would have gladly given up all he lost—and more—if only one person would commit his life to Jesus Christ as a result. Instead, thousands have lived for Christ as a result of Earl's faithfulness.

Earl never saw the spiritual fruit of his labors; he died still trusting that his God would bring the spiritual fruit of his faithfulness when the time was right. Such trust in the face of events that test our faith has always been the driving force behind the greatest of spiritual movements. That is why Martin Luther wrote in his hymn "A Mighty Fortress":

> Though this world, with devils filled
> should threaten to undo us,
> We will not fear for God has willed
> His truth to triumph through us.[3]

Through the faithfulness of his people, God determines to overcome the dark forces of this world. Our trust does not eradicate all present trials. But when we believe the tears of today will be dried by the triumphs of tomorrow, we will find the strength to live for our God. Frustration and tragedy still may come, but they cannot overwhelm the purposes of our God or the usefulness of our lives when we continue in the duties he sets before us. For these reasons, the account of Daniel in the lions' den encourages us not only to trust in God but also to live for him.

Live

Because he trusted in his Lord, Daniel was able to live for God in a great variety of circumstances. The circumstances that climax his life and most capture our hearts are those that require great courage. We should recognize that these accounts are recorded precisely for this purpose. Through Daniel's example, the Bible inspires us to live with courage when circumstances and threats tempt us to compromise. Theological sensitivity should keep us from praising Daniel's courage apart from the God who granted it, but the scruples that keep us from aspiring to Daniel's heroism are mistaken. Our trust in God should fill us with the courage to live for him.

Live with Courage

When It Will Cost Everything

Daniel knew the consequences of his prayers (v. 10). The prophet knew that his commitment to his God would cost him everything: his respect, his position, his life (v. 7). Still he continued his spiritual disciplines. Devotion to God trumped personal safety. In contexts where the greatest consequence of spiritual devotion is the ridicule of family or friends, we may forget the costs that others have paid for their faith or that may be required of us if Christ is really about more than the promotion of our personal gain.

As I have had opportunities to meet with global leaders of Christ's church through the Lausanne Movement, I have been humbled and inspired by how many have been threatened, persecuted, and imprisoned for their faith. What would it mean for North Americans now to join the ranks of those nineteenth-century missionaries who packed their belongings in coffins before sailing to Africa because they expected to give their lives for God? What would it mean for us to lose all respect in the eyes of peers because we gave our careers for the lives of those abandoned to shame like Amy Carmichael—who fought for the lives of children forced into temple prostitution in India during the Victorian era when her mission was scandalous to mention in churches? In an era where the sex trade and sexual slavery is the greatest in world history, the question is worth asking of today's Christian leaders.

Those of us who are called to preach should not forget that we may also be called to risk everything. Nations near ours have made the biblical discussion of homosexuality outlawed hate speech. As the United States polarizes over politics, expectations of what preachers should or should not say in the pulpit also increasingly raise emotions and cost careers. And as our culture pluralizes, calls for tolerance make preaching the uniqueness of salvation in Jesus Christ the one thing increasingly not tolerated. Archbishop Henry Orombi of Uganda once warned that one of the most dangerous things to the American church is that we have ceased to believe in evil—and therefore have become blind to its real threats.[4]

We who know grace may have to preach in a dangerous time. Great preaching has always seen its greatest effects in such times. We may forget that John Wesley's preaching was against church as well as political establishment, and against impious living as well as for a new piety. As a consequence, his preaching was responsible for fifty riots in his lifetime. Once when a riot broke out, a man rose to strike him. But just as that man rose, another threw a stone at Wesley. The stone struck the man who was about to strike Wesley. And the great Methodist preacher called out in great Reformed theology, "Isn't the providence of God wonderful?!"[5] Yes, the providence of God is wonderful, but that does not mean that the stones will never strike us. They struck Paul, Stephen, and thousands of others who faithfully lived with courage when it cost them everything.

We may want to give our lives for Christ's work, and we may resolve to make a difference. And we may really mean it. But we are not really ready to live with courage if our only resolution is to live for the Lord even if it costs us everything. Daniel is teaching us something even harder. We are being called to live for the Lord not only when it costs us everything but also when it changes nothing.

When It Will Change Nothing

Daniel's faithfulness to duty was challenged by more than personal tragedy. Not everyone can identify with the internal struggles that must have confronted Daniel, but we can all identify with him in his struggle against external forces of evil. Daniel did his duty in the face of great institutional sin. Consider how imposing the forces aligned against him were. He was alone in his stand of faith against all the other advisers of the king (v. 7). The law—the unchangeable decree of the Medes and Persians—opposed Daniel (v. 8). Even the king had no power to alter this law (v. 15). Injustice ruled. Idolatry dominated. Israel remained in powerless captivity. And there is no record of any of his countrymen rising to give him support. What could one man do against such overwhelming, institutional, and national evil? What would it matter for one person to take a stand against an entire nation, culture, and tradition of godlessness? Who would even care if Daniel did his personal duty to God? So if duty made no difference, why do it?

Daniel faced the temptation that argues, "Because it will make no difference what I do, it does not matter what I do." It is the game children play with their parents (and adults play with God) when we want to get away with what we know is wrong. A young teenager asks his parents about going to see a movie with questionable content. His mother replies, "No, John, you know we don't support that kind of entertainment." What is John's likely reply? "Aw, c'mon, Mom. They're not going to close down the theater just because we don't go." What is the implicit argument? Because it will make no difference, it does not matter.

Adults use the same argument. We say to ourselves, "Because this product or practice or stand for integrity and justice will make no difference, it does not matter. Since what I do will affect nothing, there is no duty required." Such reasoning leads countless people in lockstep into desperation.

What do each of the following organizations or people have in common? Enron, AIG, Freddie Mac, Goldman-Sachs, Martha Stewart Inc., the Securities and Exchange Commission, the Pittsburgh Steelers, the Atlanta Falcons, Lehman Brothers, Toyota, the Republican Party, the Democratic Party, the National Baptist Church, the Roman Catholic Church, the Presbyterian Church in America, Illinois governors, Richard Nixon, Bill Clinton, David Letterman, Newt Gingrich, John Edwards, Arthur Anderson, Abu Ghraib Prison, Pat Tillman. If you tire of reading this list, recognize it could be much longer. As diverse as the individuals or organizations in the list may seem, they actually share something in common. Each person or institution cited gained notoriety in the national news as either a party to, or a victim of, scandal. People determined to allow or do what they knew was wrong because they believed such wrongdoing was common and their objection would make no difference.

Daniel teaches us that duty remains even when sin seems unaffected by it. Even when the sin is so large that our efforts to oppose it seem meaningless, God requires our faithfulness. The sin may be so large and powerful that to oppose it places us in positions of ridicule and personal jeopardy. Still, God says to stand our ground and live for him.

The book of Daniel is as much about courage in the face of overwhelming odds as it is about divine rescue. In fact, it is about the importance and worth of courage *because of* divine rescue. If all I were to tell you would be that a grace message will be warmly received, causing your church and your reputation to flourish, I would betray you. Christians sometimes serve in hard places where the church will not thrive, where the community will oppose, where our families will question, where we will feel alone, and where we will wonder if there is any obligation because our lives seem to make no difference. For such times and places, Daniel is a great grace. He is God's provision of hope—the message that individual lives can make a difference in difficult places.

We who may face life in difficult places and who wonder if the evil is too great ever to turn back should remember that Daniel was not the last of a faithful clan who gave themselves to God's purposes when it seemed no purpose would be served. When it seemed as though a culture could never be retrieved, the Lord called a man named Timothy Dwight to Yale College in 1795. The awakenings experienced under his grandfather, Jonathan Edwards, were long forgotten. Yale had come under the influence of the French Enlightenment, and the students' heroes were not Peter and Paul but Voltaire and Rousseau. The school founded to be a Christian institution was known not only for drunkenness and infidelity but also for its vehement opposition to all things related to Christ. Lyman Beecher reported that Christian students identified themselves to one another with secret notes because it was dangerous to be known as a believer. Into this hotbed of French philosophy and Christian antipathy, Timothy Dwight began to preach and teach on the trustworthiness of Scripture. He stayed on this same subject for six months. The result was first ridicule, then rage, and then revival. When he courageously put position and prestige on the line, even when it seemed that the stand would cost him everything and change nothing, the Lord changed everything.

Live in Hope

Believing that the Lord can change everything through us, beyond us, or after us is what should keep us living courageously because we are living in hope—the confidence that our God will fulfill purposes through us if we will stand for him.

For one family vacation, we visited the Great Sand Dunes National Park in Colorado. The dunes in this park are not mere sandpiles. These shifting mountains climb as high as nine hundred feet and run for miles as a result of wind-driven sand funneled through a great mountain pass. Through the dunes runs a river—a tributary of the Rio Grande. The water of the river is dispersed by the quantity of sand into so many rivulets that the entire river broadens and shallows out to wading depth. Even our children could walk across this river. They loved the giant, fast-flowing wading pool. When our Jordan was only three or four years old, he particularly enjoyed standing firm in one of the rivulets against the current that threatened to bowl him over. It was laughable to watch—a child trying to hold back a river. Yet a minor miracle occurred whenever our son stood his ground. When Jordan would stand firm, the sand in the current would begin to pile up against him. The sand would gather at his feet and then heap up around his knees, and eventually the river would go around him. When the child stood his ground, the river was turned away.

Our society's sin can seem like a river that threatens to overwhelm God's children. The river that threatens may be a crisis of integrity, the pressures of immorality, or some other institutional sin. It may be a seemingly overwhelming problem on the job. The world says, "Give in. The stand you take will make no difference. Why get yourself in trouble? Why sacrifice for nothing?" God says, "Dig in. Plant your feet firmly on my Word and let me triumph through you."

The trials may be at school, at work, or in the family, where others are pressuring us to abandon a personal stand for the Lord. The value or results from such a stand may be hard to see. Still, we must stand! We carve a piece of the kingdom of God out of this world whenever we claim any corner of it for him. God can use us to build his kingdom if we stand our ground because we are never alone in our stand for him.

Notice how the Scriptures record the direction Daniel prayed during his daily devotions. Daniel prayed "where he had windows in his upper chamber open toward Jerusalem" (v. 10). Why did Daniel direct his prayer to the holy city of Israel? Did God dwell only in Jerusalem? No, of course Daniel did not believe that God, who had miraculously saved him time after time in Babylon, resided only in Jerusalem. Why, then, did Daniel focus on Jerusalem?

Remember, Daniel is a prophet. Following this final chapter of the prophet's life history are Daniel's amazing prophesies of the victories to come in Jerusalem. The captives from Israel will return to the holy city. Jerusalem will be restored, and from the former ruins will rise the Savior. This Savior will defeat forever the enemy who prowls the earth "like a roaring lion, seeking someone to devour" (1 Pet. 5:8). As Daniel did his duty, his physical eyes could see only ruin, despair, and danger. But through the eyes of faith, Daniel saw much more. By focusing on Jerusalem he saw sure victory, future triumph, and certain hope. Through the eyes of hope, ruined Jerusalem shone yet as the great symbol of God's abiding faithfulness to those he would defend. Daniel was faithful in the face of the threat of roaring lions because he trusted in the One who shuts the mouth of the great lion called Satan.

The sign of God's faithfulness that we all remember is Daniel's rescue from the lions. But the greater sign that proves the value of Daniel's hope for his nation and for us is almost hidden in the last words of this chapter. The chapter ends with these words, "So this Daniel prospered during the reign of Darius and during the reign of Cyrus the Persian" (v. 28). The name of the final ruler is most important because under this ruler the people of Israel began to return to their homeland. And because they returned to Israel, ultimately a Child would be born in the city of David who would be Christ, our Lord. Daniel's influence and God's promise finally were fulfilled according to the hope Daniel maintained into his old age.

The message to Daniel's people and to us is that our hope in God is not misplaced. Though we may have to wait to see the results of our faithfulness—and may never see them until we are with him—our God will accomplish his purposes. So we trust him and live for him. Because we know that God shut the mouths of lions for Daniel, and subsequently shut the mouth of the raging lion who seeks to devour us (1 Pet. 5:8), we trust our Savior and live for him. We always live in the hope of the ultimate and eternal victory he will provide for us.

Like a steel locomotive hurtling through history, the gospel progresses on the timeline God has designed to rescue his people. Institutions may fail to reflect him, empires may conspire to oppose him, and his own people may reject him, but the gospel prevails as God has designed. Pastor Wyatt George of Carbondale, Illinois, tells of an amazing Christmas card he received from retired missionary friends Vincent and Margaret Crossett. In the 1940s the Crossetts were missionaries in mainland China. They struggled against poverty and paganism in a remote village to tell others about Jesus. The work was slow and painstaking. Yet after much sacrifice, a small church (we might call it a simple Bible study) seemed almost established. But right on the threshold of this small triumph for the kingdom of God, Satan began his prowl. The communist Chinese took over mainland China in 1949. All foreign missionaries were forced to leave the country.

The Crossetts hated to leave. Their fledgling flock of believers hardly seemed ready to stand the coming onslaught. An atheistic, dictatorial government dedicated to wiping out all Christian influence began its rule with ruthless power. How could the little church survive? The situation seemed impossible. What could the Crossetts do? From a worldly perspective there was nothing to do. The church appeared destined for extinction. But the Crossetts did not see as the world sees. They saw no reason to despair because, through eyes of faith, they saw a God who is faithful to those who honor him.

The Crossetts continued to do their duty. Yes, the walls of China went up and the missionaries were closed out—but not their prayers. For nearly forty years the Crossetts daily kept their spiritual prayer windows opened toward China. They did their duty in the faith that God could triumph even though an institution of sin had swept the land like a mighty river. The Crossetts heard nothing from and knew nothing of their friends for four decades, but still they dutifully prayed for God to be victorious in the church they had left behind.

Finally, the walls of China came down. As the political winds changed, this ancient Eastern land again opened to the West. The Crossetts returned. They hastened to the village where they had left the tiny, struggling group of believers. There was no small church in the village anymore. Instead, from that Bible study had grown a church of four thousand people. This church had spawned other churches. In the surrounding region nearly a dozen churches had sprung up, each with a membership of no less than a thousand people. All the Crossetts did was pray—it was all they could do. But with their faith and duty God triumphed. He turned back the flood of evil. He shut the lions' mouths. The God of Daniel is alive and well. The victories of God are as near as faith and duty.

What, as Christians, are we facing today? It may be sin around us, or in us, that is so great that we cannot see the sense of fighting it. But we must fight. We must stand our ground. We must do what is right and let God take care of the rest. He can. He will, because in his time and for his glory, God shuts lions' mouths. There may be so much wrong—so much upheaval and confusion—that we wonder what to do. And even if we know what to do, we may wonder what the use is. We may think that nothing could change our boss, or our marriage, or our circumstances. Things can appear to be such a mess that there seems to be no chance of ever straightening them out. But, however confusing the circumstances are, however obscure solutions may seem in the dirt and clutter of our situations, God still explains clearly what he expects.

We cry out in anguish, "What do you want from me, God? Surely you have some new answers for this mess. Tell me what you want me to do."

God answers. He is speaking now, softly and gently. Listen: "*Whisk-whisk.*"

No matter what the trial, God asks us to listen to the sound of a broom, a broom described by Daniel. That broom is sweeping away all the clutter of our situations and the confusion of our questions. Will we listen? The broom whispers, "*Whisk-whisk.*" It calls, "trust and live." We must trust the Lord and live for him. He does not ask us to solve the problem. He simply sweeps clean the path to his purpose. His broom sings, "*Whisk-whisk.*" His Word echoes, "Trust and live." His promise rings, "Mercy and victory." These promises are ours forever. So trust and live.

7

The Big Picture

— DANIEL 7 —

The seventh chapter of Daniel begins the dangerous part of his book. Daniel has just come out of the lions' den. That was dangerous for him, of course. But what's dangerous for preachers and commentators is moving out of the biographical portions of Daniel and into the prophetic portions. So far we have been reading the adventures of Daniel and his friends Shadrach, Meshach, and Abednego. But now it's time to enter the world of Daniel's visions and dreams, a world that has puzzled and humbled commentators and preachers for generations.

We should enter the visionary world of Daniel 7 with the recollection that it is a reflection of an earlier chapter in the book. In Daniel 2, King Nebuchadnezzar dreams of a great statue with a head of gold, shoulders of silver, belly of bronze, and legs of iron. Then a rock—cut without human hands—comes and strikes the statue's feet of iron and clay, causing the entire statue to fall over and shatter into pieces that were blown away like chaff in the wind. The dream awakens and troubles the king, who ultimately learns from Daniel that the statue represents successive world empires, including Nebuchadnezzar's Babylonian empire. These empires will rise and fall until all are vanquished by "the Rock" that has no human origin.

Now it's Daniel's turn to dream. In this parallel dream, the aged prophet sees four beasts rise out of a churning sea: a lion with wings, representing Babylon (an image still prevalent in modern Iraq); a bear, representing Persia, which would defeat Nebuchadnezzar's son in Daniel's lifetime and allow the Israelites to return to Zion; a leopard, representing Greece, which would conquer the civilized world with amazing speed under Alexander the Great, who would die at age thirty-three; and a final beast, not identified except to say that it has five times the normal number of horns of an animal of power—a beast with ten horns and teeth of iron, representing Roman alliances that would include the most vicious of the ancient rulers over Israel. Daniel predicts these events and their implications in this account:

In the first year of Belshazzar king of Babylon, Daniel saw a dream and visions of his head as he lay in his bed. Then he wrote down the dream and told the sum of the matter. Daniel declared, "I saw in my vision by night, and behold, the four winds of heaven were stirring up the great sea. And four great beasts came up out of the sea, different from one another. The first was like a lion and had eagles' wings. Then as I looked its wings were plucked off, and it was lifted up from the ground and made to stand on two feet like a man, and the mind of a man was given to it. And behold, another beast, a second one, like a bear. It was raised up on one side. It had three ribs in its mouth between its teeth; and it was told, 'Arise, devour much flesh.' After this I looked, and behold, another, like a leopard, with four wings of a bird on its back. And the beast had four heads, and dominion was given to it. After this I saw in the night visions, and behold, a fourth beast, terrifying and dreadful and exceedingly strong. It had great iron teeth; it devoured and broke in pieces and stamped what was left with its feet. It was different from all the beasts that were before it, and it had ten horns. I considered the horns, and behold, there came up among them another horn, a little one, before which three of the first horns were plucked up by the roots. And behold, in this horn were eyes like the eyes of a man, and a mouth speaking great things.

"As I looked,

> thrones were placed,
> and the Ancient of Days took his
>   seat;
> his clothing was white as snow,
>   and the hair of his head like pure
>   wool;
> his throne was fiery flames;
>   its wheels were burning fire.
> A stream of fire issued
>   and came out from before him;
> a thousand thousands served him,
>   and ten thousand times ten thou-
>   sand stood before him;
> the court sat in judgment,
>   and the books were opened.

"I looked then because of the sound of the great words that the horn was speaking. And as I looked, the beast was killed, and its body destroyed and given over to be burned with fire. As for the rest of the beasts, their dominion was taken away, but their lives were prolonged for a season and a time.

"I saw in the night visions,

> and behold, with the clouds of heaven
>   there came one like a son of man,
> and he came to the Ancient of Days
>   and was presented before him.
> And to him was given dominion
>   and glory and a kingdom,

that all peoples, nations, and
languages
should serve him;
his dominion is an everlasting
dominion,
which shall not pass away,
and his kingdom one
that shall not be destroyed.

"As for me, Daniel, my spirit within me was anxious, and the visions of my head alarmed me. I approached one of those who stood there and asked him the truth concerning all this. So he told me and made known to me the interpretation of the things. 'These four great beasts are four kings who shall arise out of the earth. But the saints of the Most High shall receive the kingdom and possess the king-dom forever, forever and ever.'

"Then I desired to know the truth about the fourth beast, which was different from all the rest, exceedingly terrifying, with its teeth of iron and claws of bronze, and which devoured and broke in pieces and stamped what was left with its feet, and about the ten horns that were on its head, and the other horn that came up and before which three of them fell, the horn that had eyes and a mouth that spoke great things, and that seemed greater than its companions. As I looked, this horn made war with the saints and prevailed over them, until the Ancient of Days came, and judgment was given for the saints of the Most High, and the time came when the saints possessed the kingdom.

"Thus he said: 'As for the fourth beast,

there shall be a fourth kingdom on earth,
which shall be different from all
the kingdoms,

and it shall devour the whole earth,
and trample it down, and break it
to pieces.
As for the ten horns,
out of this kingdom ten kings shall
arise,
and another shall arise after
them;
he shall be different from the former
ones,
and shall put down three kings.
He shall speak words against the
Most High,
and shall wear out the saints of
the Most High,
and shall think to change the
times and the law;
and they shall be given into his hand
for a time, times, and half a time.
But the court shall sit in judgment,
and his dominion shall be taken
away,
to be consumed and destroyed to
the end.
And the kingdom and the dominion
and the greatness of the kingdoms under the whole heaven
shall be given to the people of the
saints of the Most High;
his kingdom shall be an everlasting
kingdom,
and all dominions shall serve and
obey him.'

"Here is the end of the matter. As for me, Daniel, my thoughts greatly alarmed me, and my color changed, but I kept the mat-ter in my heart." (Dan. 7:1–28)

In 1601 Michelangelo Caravaggio painted *The Supper at Emmaus*. The scene depicted is of the event that follows Luke's account of the risen Jesus walking with some disciples along the road to Emmaus. On that walk the Lord has revealed to the disciples the big picture of the Bible, explaining that all the Law and the Prophets have led to him. But though the Scriptures reveal him, these disciples do not recognize him. They do not understand that it is Jesus who is with them until that moment at supper when Jesus breaks bread before them.

In witnessing the performance of that most Christlike of ministries, the scales fall from the disciples' eyes and they see with understanding that the risen Lord is communing with them. But Caravaggio breaks the conventions of his time to depict that moment. Jesus has neither beard nor halo. He looks like one of us. And the disciples do not sit back in glassy-eyed wonder. Instead, they are painted rising from their seats, energized, muscles taut, with faces intent and resolute. They realize not only that the river of all history has flowed to this point but also that they are now a part of the flow; it envelops them, inspires them, and compels them to be a part of the story by telling the world Christ's story. They who had lost hope now have purpose. They who had been discouraged now take courage. They who had been preoccupied with sad and fearful events in their immediate context suddenly see the big picture: these immediate circumstances are not the end, God is fulfilling his purposes, our Savior lives, he will be the victor, and we are in his plan.

The painting is a reminder of how important it is to keep sight of the big picture. We can too easily focus on our immediate circumstances—an election, an economic downturn, a career disappointment, a family dispute—and in the face of our immediate concerns, remove ourselves from the great purposes of God that he promises to further with our own lives.

Daniel is painting a similar big picture so that the Israelites in exile under an evil ruler will not lose hope but, seeing God's certain victory, will rededicate themselves to his great purposes. The text is complicated, but the message is simple: despite present difficulties, we are part of God's big picture—so we must not lose hope but instead rededicate ourselves to his purposes.

How can we believe that we are a part of the big picture when we are struggling with the significance of the immediate? Think of what was immediate to God's people in Daniel's era: they are in captivity in a foreign nation due to their own sin. They have lost their land, their families are decimated, and they have forgotten both the language and laws of their faith. How will Daniel reach them or teach them in the face of such significant losses? He will do it by reminding them that, though their pain and failures are difficult, their God is great and can still accomplish his purposes through his people.

Our God Is Great!

The Scene

To make God's greatness plain, Daniel describes a courtroom scene that God has revealed to him. It is an unusual court because the seats of the judges that are put in place are described as "thrones" (v. 9). Yet the passage makes it clear this is a courtroom. The end of verse 10 tells us, "the court sat in judgment, and the books were opened." Daniel next begins to describe those who have roles in this great judgment scene.

The Judge

Then the chief judge appears, and Daniel's description reveals this judge's true greatness.

HE HAS GREAT WISDOM

He is described as the "Ancient of Days" (v. 9a). He has seen it all before. Nothing surprises him. His days are beyond our accounting. His time precedes ours. His experience is vast. Empires have come and gone, rulers have risen and fallen, economies have prospered and faltered, but he endures beyond and above it all. He ordained our days before any one of them came to be (Ps. 139). He knows because he always has been. His white hair (v. 9b) signifies the wisdom of years, and he is wise enough to judge all because he is the Ancient of Days.

HE HAS GREAT RIGHTEOUSNESS

The white hair signifies not only great age but great purity. His robes are white, too (v. 9). He is without stain or tarnish. Nothing impure or evil touches or smudges him. But even these images do not fully capture the degree of purity the prophet wants to convey. The picture of righteousness is not complete until we understand that the purity of the Ancient of Days is so radiant that it bursts into fire (v. 9c).

Similar images occur when Isaiah describes his vision of heaven where the six-winged seraphs fly around the throne of heaven—with two wings they fly, with two they cover their eyes, and with two they cover themselves, as even the angels cannot bear to look upon or be exposed by the radiance of the holiness of God. But instead, even the seraphim, whose name means "burning ones," fly around the pure radiance of the throne of God singing, "Holy, holy, holy is the LORD of hosts; the whole earth is full of his glory!" (Isa. 6:3). The God of Daniel and Isaiah has great righteousness in addition to great wisdom, and both of these attributes are expressed with great power.

He Has Great Power

The throne blazes but is not consumed, reminding us of the burning bush by which God showed Moses his supernatural power (Exod. 2). Additionally, the throne has flaming wheels (v. 9d), displaying that the Ancient of Days can take his wisdom and righteousness anywhere. This pervasive power of judgment is emphasized by the river of fire that flows from the throne (v. 10a), showing that his judgment and power are not limited but envelop the whole world before the throne. Further evidence of power is shown in the multitudes that attend him—thousands upon thousands (v. 10b), and the greater multitudes that honor him—ten thousand times ten thousand stood before him (v. 10c). Finally, his power is made evident because the court reports to him: the record books of judgment are opened before the Ancient of Days. His is the power to judge, and the accused are brought before him.

The Accused

Though the accused have great power, they are brought before the Ancient of Days and cannot escape his judgment. The culminating power of evil is represented by "the horn" that speaks boastfully before the Ancient of Days (v. 11a). This horn has been previously described in verse 8. He is so powerful that he displaces three other horns of the great beast and boasts of his power (cf. v. 8). Commentators debate whom this greatest of the successive horns represents. Is he the antichrist of the end-time or is he Antiochus Epiphanes, an ancient Roman-allied ruler of Syria who tried to annihilate the religion of the Jews by having them worship Zeus?

Whatever the identity of this boastful horn, there is no question of his destiny—he is executed and his body thrown into blazing fire (v. 11b). In addition, the other beasts are stripped of their authority (v. 12). The overall picture is simply that whatever opposes the Ancient of Days is ultimately destroyed. Kings and kingdoms may rise and fall, but our God remains on his throne and rules over all with wisdom, righteousness, and power.

The clear message we are to take from these descriptions is that we cannot allow the circumstances of the moment to eclipse our understanding of the eternal stage upon which God is fulfilling his purpose. The unchanging nature of the Ancient of Days should give us perspective on both current events and our personal lives. Election results, economic earthquakes, stock market trends, family circumstances, medical reports, personal trials—these will all change, but our God does not change. Though the earth gives way and the mountains are cast into the sea, our God reigns and he does not change (Ps. 46:1–2).

The significance of the truth of God's unchanging character was voiced in our church at a recent Thanksgiving service. In our church, we celebrate Thanksgiving by giving everyone an opportunity to give a word of thanks about something God has done in the past year. A mother in the faith rose and talked about the medications that were not working against her breast cancer. She admitted the discouragement she felt when she saw the list of changed medications, signaling not only past failure but future misery. Then she said she understood that the list of changed medications was an instrument of Satan to cause her despair. So what she did (and if you knew her, you would know she was describing exactly what she did) was to hold the list of new medications above her head and to scream at Satan, "But my God does not change!" The big picture of the eternal nature of a God who is great in wisdom, righteousness, and power was the perspective she needed and claimed to face her immediate personal trial.

But why should we believe this big picture of Daniel? The answer is before us. The biographical descriptions of what God has done in the life of Daniel and his friends are what give credence to the vision of what will happen in the future. The last narrative we have in the life of Daniel is his rescue from the lion's den. In response to Daniel's deliverance, the pagan King Darius says, "People are to tremble and fear before the God of Daniel. . . . He delivers and rescues; . . . he who has saved Daniel from the power of the lions" (6:26–27). God's personal salvation of Daniel gives credence to what Daniel says about the big picture, and what we know about the big picture is what gives us power and resolve for the trials that we personally face. This is the accordion nature of divine promise (large and small provisions successively making the music of God's great providence). Personal salvation confirms the larger divine plan and the divine plan equips us for our personal challenges. We must not forget these varying ways that God communicates his power to us. Awareness of both our personal rescue and God's eternal purposes are necessary to maintain daily faithfulness. To neglect either is to negate the power that God provides for us to fulfill his purposes in our lives.

But perhaps what will make us hesitant to see ourselves in the big picture is our struggle not just with the significance of immediate events but with personal sin. How can God use us if we are not as pure as he or we desire? The answer lies in remembering that our God is not only great but also good.

Our God Is Good!

In verse 13 another person enters the courtroom. Who is he? Daniel describes him as one who is "like a son of man" (v. 13a). The description "son of man" simply means that he is human. In C. S. Lewis's *The Lion, the Witch and the Wardrobe*, boys are described as "sons of Adam" and girls as "daughters of Eve." The designations simply mean that they are human. This one, too, is a son of man. He is like us.

The "son of man" terminology is made more special when we remember that this is also the designation that Jesus would use most often for himself. Eighty-one times in the Gospels (forty-one times in Matthew alone), Jesus refers to himself as the Son of Man. For example, he said, "Foxes have holes, and birds of the air have nests, but the Son of Man has nowhere to lay his head" (Matt. 8:20). Jesus came as one of us to experience the world we know. He came as a Son of Man.

But the One who enters the courtroom is not fully described by his human origins; he is "*like* a son of man," but he appears before Daniel "coming with the clouds of heaven" (v. 13b). He is like us, but he is also like God. God appeared to the people of Israel in the clouds that covered Mount Sinai. He led the people of God from that mountain with fire at night *and* with a pillar of cloud by day. And when Christ ascended to heaven in a cloud, the angels said to those who watched, "This Jesus . . . will come in the same way as you saw him go into heaven" (Acts 1:11). Jesus said the same in previous testimony before his accusers: "Then will appear in heaven the sign of the Son of Man, and then all the tribes of the earth will mourn, and they will see the Son of Man coming on the clouds of heaven with power and great glory" (Matt. 24:30). The clouds tell us that although the Son of Man has human likeness, he also has heavenly origins. He is like us, and he is like God.

What is his job—this God-man?

He is to have a universal dominion.

To explain the purpose of this manlike God, Daniel writes, "And to him was given dominion and glory and a kingdom, that all peoples, nations, and languages should serve him" (v. 14a). He rules over all, and all honor him.

He is to have an eternal dominion.

Daniel also says, "His dominion is an everlasting dominion, which shall not pass away, and his kingdom one that shall not be destroyed" (v. 14b). To whom did God promise an eternal kingdom prior to this passage in Daniel? God made this promise to King David. David was promised a kingdom that would outlast the rising and falling of all others and that would be victorious over all. The Lord said to David, "Your house and your kingdom will endure forever before me; your throne will be established forever" (cf. 2 Sam. 7:12–16).

The Son of Man who comes on the clouds is the fulfillment of the Davidic promise that God made to the people of Israel. Why is that so important? Because they have sinned, turned from him, failed to keep his commands, and been led into captivity. But though they have failed and been faithless, God remains faithful. His people have sinned against him, but he is good to them. He is the Rock that does not change but comes to crush and topple the evil that threatens his people, even when the evil is from them.

The Rock with Two Sides

This Rock that crushes the kingdoms in Nebuchanezzar's dream, and that comes on the clouds in Daniel's vision, has two sides. He is very great and he is very good. Both sides of the Rock are on display in Daniel's vision, and we need both sides. Steve Corbet, a college professor of my children, explains from his own life experience.

Some years ago Steve received from God a daughter with Goldenhar syndrome, a malady that causes some children to be born without facial bones. For the Corbets that meant they had a daughter with no facial bones on the left side and no left eye.

In the early years of loving and raising their precious child, Steve said that he and his wife needed a rock to cling to. The rock they reached for was Christ, but Steve said that only made sense when they embraced both sides of the rock—the side that was very great and the side that was very good. They had to cling to the greatness of God to have strength for tomorrow, and they had to cling to the goodness of God to trust him with today.

Always the same challenge lies before us. When our trials and disappointments are great—when our challenges threaten to overwhelm—we must remember that we cling to a Rock that is very great and very good. He has shown us in his coming as the Son of Man that he is both good enough to care for us—to sympathize with all that we experience—and that he is great enough to fulfill the promises of God despite our failures and challenges of the moment. He came to be with us, and he comes again for us. We are not alone, and the story is not done. For these reasons we can take hope, step forward, and stand for him.

The Mystery and Message of the Thrones

Our job is not done, but the victory is already won. The certainty of our purpose and the victory of our great and good God are evident in the mystery of the thrones. We are told at the beginning of Daniel's vision that "thrones" (plural) are placed in the courtroom (v. 9). The Ancient of Days sits on one, but that does not explain the presence of other thrones. Surely one throne is also prepared for the Son of Man, for Jesus says in his trial before the Sanhedrin, as he prepares to offer himself for us, "I tell you, from now on you will see the Son of Man seated at the right hand of Power and coming on the clouds of heaven" (Matt. 26:64). But still we have not identified all the occupants of the thrones of this heavenly judgment hall.

The apostle Paul tells us who will also sit on thrones with the Ancient of Days. Paul says, "Do you not know that the saints will judge the world? . . . Do you not know that we are to judge the angels?" (1 Cor. 6:2–3). Our Savior sits on his throne with the Ancient of Days to judge heaven and earth, and we will sit enthroned with him. The message is that we shall have ultimate victory over the evil of this world. The victory does not come immediately, and its certainty may not always be apparent. We may not be ahead in every inning, but the Bible assures us that we are on the winning team because we are the people of the One whose dominion is universal and eternal. This knowledge and assurance are for our inspiration and resolution and mission. We know that we are part of God's eternal plan and purpose, and because he will prevail, we know that our lives have purpose regardless of the challenges we now face. Our great and good God is accomplishing his purposes through his people so that when he judges all that oppose him, we shall be colaborers with him in his final judgment because we have been colaborers with him in his unfolding victory.

More than seven decades ago, two sailors began meeting with a lumberyard worker for Bible study in the garage of a Texaco service station in Lomita, California. In a few weeks, those two were joined by two other sailors who were new believers. With these four, the lumberyard worker, named Dawson Trotman, began to share a vision for how they could be part of God's plan to reach the world with the gospel of Jesus Christ.

It was really a silly dream: reaching the world for Christ with four sailors, two of whom were new believers and all of whom were coming for the baked-bean dinner as much as for the Bible study. But by year's end those four asked the lumberyard worker to quit his job. They said, "We will split our salaries to support you if you will become a missionary to the fleet."

He did quit and ministered to those four and their friends for a brief time before they were deployed to Pearl Harbor. In the December 7, 1941, Japanese attack, their ship was destroyed, but the four survived—so that they and their friends were dispersed across the Pacific fleet with the message of the gospel. When they returned to the United States after the war and entered college under the GI Bill, the gospel was dispersed again. And so began the ministry of the Navigators, which has spread the gospel across the world through the witness of college students and those in military service.

How did such amazing things happen? In a famous speech given years later, Dawson Trotman explained: "The need of the hour, as far as I'm concerned, is to believe that God is God and that He is a lot more interested in getting this job done than you and I are. Therefore, if He is more interested in getting the job done, has all power to do it, and has commissioned us to do it, our business is to obey Him—reaching the world for Him and trusting Him to help us do it."[1]

Why trust him? Because he is very great and he is very good; he came to save and he comes to judge. In addition, we have the privilege of participating in his plan of vanquishing all that opposes his will. The need of this hour and every hour is to believe that God is God, that he is faithful to his purposes through those obedient to his will, and to believe—beyond our immediate circumstances and personal sin—that he will use us, if we will but trust him. He is that great, and he is that good.

8

When the Big Rocks Fall

— DANIEL 8 —

A line that has stuck in my brain from a novel that is now lost to my memory declared, "At the moment of decision, most of the decisions have already been made." It is a simple reminder that we are prepared for great challenges by how we have met the ones that have come before. The eighth chapter of Daniel is functioning as one of those pre-challenges. There is a not a lot of drama in this chapter—no encounters with lions or fiery furnaces or enticing details about the end of the world. And for that reason Daniel 8 does not get a lot of attention. In fact, some sermon collections on Daniel skip this chapter entirely. But this is actually a watershed chapter, because what you believe about Daniel 8 will largely determine what you believe about the rest of Scripture and what God actually promises about the rest of your life.

What you believe about Daniel 8 will answer two key questions that are decisive for all the faith decisions ahead of you. First, can God speak supernaturally in his Word?—a question related to how you will handle scriptural truth. And second, can God work supernaturally in your life?—a question related to how you will handle personal pain.

The truth question relates to the precision of Daniel's vision. In the first verse, he says that he is writing in the third year of King Belshazzar's reign.

This means that the Jews are still captive to the Babylonians and the conquering Persians have not yet come. But what does Daniel see in his vision?

He sees a battle between a ram and a goat. The ram has two horns, one short and one long—the long one grows later than the short one. The ram runs west, north, and south, and no one can stop him until a goat comes from the west with one large horn. The goat attacks the ram and shatters both of its horns. But at the height of the goat's power, its one horn is broken off and becomes four horns—and out of one of the four comes another horn. It starts small but becomes so great that its power reaches the "glorious land" (Dan. 8:9) where it throws the starry hosts to earth, challenges the Prince of the hosts, defiles the temple, throws truth to the ground, stops the sacrifices, and substitutes an abomination until 2,300 days pass and the temple is reconsecrated.

What does all that mean? The angel Gabriel comes to answer that question, as Daniel explains:

In the third year of the reign of King Belshazzar a vision appeared to me, Daniel, after that which appeared to me at the first. And I saw in the vision; and when I saw, I was in Susa the citadel, which is in the province of Elam. And I saw in the vision, and I was at the Ulai canal. I raised my eyes and saw, and behold, a ram standing on the bank of the canal. It had two horns, and both horns were high, but one was higher than the other, and the higher one came up last. I saw the ram charging westward and northward and southward. No beast could stand before him, and there was no one who could rescue from his power. He did as he pleased and became great.

As I was considering, behold, a male goat came from the west across the face of the whole earth, without touching the ground. And the goat had a conspicuous horn between his eyes. He came to the ram with the two horns, which I had seen standing on the bank of the canal, and he ran at him in his powerful wrath. I saw him come close to the ram, and he was enraged against him and struck the ram and broke his two horns. And the ram had no power to stand before him, but he cast him down to the ground and trampled on him. And there was no one who could rescue the ram from his power. Then the goat became exceedingly great, but when he was strong, the great horn was broken, and instead of it there came up four conspicuous horns toward the four winds of heaven.

Out of one of them came a little horn, which grew exceedingly great toward the south, toward the east, and toward the glorious land. It grew great, even to the host of heaven. And some of the host and some of the stars it threw down to the ground and trampled on them. It became great, even as great as the Prince of the host. And the regular burnt offering was taken away from him, and the place of his sanctuary was overthrown. And a host will be given over to it together with the regular burnt offering because of transgression, and it will throw truth to the ground, and it will act and prosper. Then I heard a holy one speaking, and another holy one said to the one who spoke, "For how long is the vision concerning the regular burnt offering, the transgression that makes desolate, and the giving over of the sanctuary and host to be trampled underfoot?" And he said to me, "For 2,300 evenings and mornings. Then the sanctuary shall be restored to its rightful state."

When I, Daniel, had seen the vision, I sought to understand it. And behold, there stood before me one having the appearance of a man. And I heard a man's voice between the banks of the Ulai, and it called, "Gabriel, make this man understand the vision." So he came near where I stood.

And when he came, I was frightened and fell on my face. But he said to me, "Understand, O son of man, that the vision is for the time of the end." And when he had spoken to me, I fell into a deep sleep with my face to the ground. But he touched me and made me stand up. He said, "Behold, I will make known to you what shall be at the latter end of the indignation, for it refers to the appointed time of the end. As for the ram that you saw with the two horns, these are the kings of Media and Persia. And the goat is the king of Greece. And the great horn between his eyes is the first king. As for the horn that was broken, in place of which four others arose, four kingdoms shall arise from his nation, but not with his power. And at the latter end of their kingdom, when the transgressors have reached their limit, a king of bold face, one who understands riddles, shall arise. His power shall be great—but not by his own power; and he shall cause fearful destruction and shall succeed in what he does, and destroy mighty men and the people who are the saints. By his cunning he shall make deceit prosper under his hand, and in his own mind he shall become great. Without warning he shall destroy many. And he shall even rise up against the Prince of princes, and he shall be broken—but by no human hand. The vision of the evenings and the mornings that has been told is true, but seal up the vision, for it refers to many days from now."

And I, Daniel, was overcome and lay sick for some days. Then I rose and went about the king's business, but I was appalled by the vision and did not understand it. (Dan. 8:1–27)

He had already killed four people when he broke into her house. In March 2005, Brian Nichols broke into the house of Ashley Smith, a widow and young mother who was struggling with her crystal meth addiction by reading the Bible and Rick Warren's *Purpose Driven Life*.[1] While holding her hostage, Nichols gave her a chance to read, and she read to him the first paragraph of a chapter on the purpose of our gifts and talents. "Read it again," he said. She did. Then she asked Nichols what he thought was the purpose of his gifts. He said, "I think it's to talk to people and tell them about [God]."[2]

That's not bad theology for a four-time murderer and hostage taker. He believed that despite his great sin and even against his intention, he still had a part in God's plan. In this chapter of the Bible, the prophet Daniel is intent on saying much the same to God's people, including us. There is a great story of redemption unfolding across time and history, and those who are both enemies and advocates of God are swept up into its telling. Each one has a part, even if he or she does not intend it, because God is bringing the story to the conclusion that he intends. The part of the story that Daniel tells is not without challenge. It was troubling to him, and it is troubling to us, because the plot is not without a few twists. But because we know the conclusion, we are able to live the story and love it, even when the twists involve us.

What is the first twist that involves Daniel and his people?

Evil May Have Its Day

Even in God's great story, there are times when his enemies hold sway, and usually it is because the people of God have given way to evil. Daniel is himself a character in the larger story of Israel in a time that the nation is being disciplined for turning from God. For seventy years they live in this captivity.

Babylon (the lion with wings in Dan. 7) has its day. Then, through the evil of King Belshazzar, the hope of reform that once glimmered in his predecessor, Nebuchadnezzar, will fade.

Then Media-Persia (the ram with two horns in this chapter) will have its day. The remnant of Israel will return to the land of promise. The Persian empire will continue in its evil until Greece rises to power.

Then Greece (the goat with one prominent horn that ranges so far) will have its day through Alexander the Great and his successors—the four horns—until their Roman enemies and allies reign.

Rome will have its day until God fulfills his promise in the time of Caesar Augustus, when all the world will be taxed and Joseph will register for the taxation with his wife, Mary, in Bethlehem—and there a Child in a manger will come to be the King of all kings.

The plot twists as evil rises again and again to resist God's rule, but the story moves irresistibly forward to the conclusion God intends.

In microcosm, that is what happened in the little apartment where Brian Nichols confronted Ashley Smith. His intention was only to have a few hours of relaxation before confronting the authorities and killing as many as he could before they killed him. Brian told Ashley that he needed to relax, and so, to delay and appease him, she said, "I have some drugs." It did slow him down and give them time to talk. Later she said that she didn't know why, but that the words had *just come out of her mouth*.

She said she didn't know why the words came. He told her he didn't know why he had chosen her apartment. "It was just random," he said. But as the two considered the words about God's purposes in the book they were reading, each concluded there was something more than randomness at work.

Ashley had been on crystal meth for years. Her husband died of its usage. Her sin and desperation were clear. She wrote later, "The crystal meth was actually an idol that I had been worshiping for two years. It had rotted my teeth, thinned out my hair, and made me give [away] custody of the child that I loved most. I lost so much. I lost my family—I lost myself, really."

But God had not lost sight of her, even though she said, "For a long time I thought God doesn't want to have anything to do with drug addiction and he's just not big enough to handle this."

Instead of doing drugs with Brian Nichols, Ashley believed what she had read, believed there was a purpose for her life, and began to think that Brian was there to assure her that God was giving her another chance to live and that she needed to stop doing drugs.

When she talked to Brian about why he specifically chose to go to her apartment building and to hold her hostage, he had no explanation other than, "Maybe you're my angel sent from God." In his sin, he thought that she was God's angel to help him. At the same time, she thought he was God's means to help her overcome her sin. Both were in terrible circumstances, and both had turned from God, but God was using each to fulfill his purposes for both. Both the murderer and the addict were still in God's plan. The final chapter of their story had not been written; both yet had a role in taking it to its conclusion.

Ashley said, "I believe that it was God's purpose for me to help Brian turn himself in and I also believe that God had a purpose for him coming into my life—and changing my life, too. I don't know that if Brian Nichols would have not come to my house that night and had a gun and me be faced with the decision of whether to do the drugs or not, that I would have stopped. I don't know that my life wouldn't be changed right now. I believe that not only did God save me from Brian Nichols, and save him from hurting other people, but he saved me from a drug addiction."

And the results do not end there. The plan is bigger than those two and what happened in that apartment. Ashley said later, "I've had a lot of people come up to me and say, even if they don't have an addiction to drugs or something like that, 'You really helped me realize that even with all this little . . . junk in my life, God wants it [my life] too and I need to let him guide my life.'"

This is God's message to us, too. We all have junk in our lives. We may believe that because of it God has no interest in us and that the problem is beyond him. It is not. There is hope. There is love. There is a story yet to be written for our lives and for eternity.

What God is saying through Daniel is that what happened in that apartment and in individual hearts is happening on a global scale through history and for eternity. That's what Daniel is seeing. Like Ashley, Israel represents a believing people who have sinned and turned from God. Brian Nichols is like the murderous nations abusing them. It was all wretched, but it was not beyond God's purpose of redemption. Each had a role in the greater story being told. But why should we believe the greater story? Because not only does evil have its day, but God also will have his say.

God Will Have His Say

Daniel's vision seems to twist in wild gyrations without control. The enemies of God have their day, the honor of God goes away, the people of God suffer, and all of it seemingly without purpose. How do we make sense of it all? We begin by recognizing that none of it surprises God. Evil may have its day, but God will have his say about the evil. And what God says is that he knows the measure of evil and he knows how and when to end it.

God Knows Evil's Measure

The precision of Daniel's predictions about the temporary triumphs of evil across the world is the hard aspect of this prophecy. Interpreting the vision is not hard. All that hard work is done by the angel, Gabriel. He tells us that the ram with the two horns is the Median and Persian empire. He tells us that the goat is Greece. The trouble is not understanding the vision; the trouble is accepting it.

Through the centuries, critics of the Bible reject this prophecy because it is too good, too accurate. The level of specificity refutes the idea that these predictions could be the product of human speculation. To believe Daniel is writing prophecy, as he claims, and not history, as the level of detail would seem to suggest, would require belief that what is written was supernaturally inspired. And if God has thus spoken, then his Word has far more authority over our lives than we may wish, and his far-reaching knowledge is far more real than we may want on the days that we want to go our own way.

What is the measure of evil that God knows? Remember, this is in the third year of Belshazzar's reign, before the writing on the wall that declared he had been weighed and found wanting for his desecration of the utensils of the temple.

Daniel sees seven things:

- A ram with two horns (one longer than the other) that will carry destruction west, north, and south (vv. 3–4), just as the Medo-Persian empire did.

- A goat with one horn that comes from the west with great speed to destroy the Medes and the Persians (vv. 5–7), just as the Greek Alexander the Great did.

- The goat's one horn is broken off at the height of his power (v. 8), just as happened to Alexander the Great, who had conquered the known world by age thirty-two before dying at age thirty-three.

- The one horn of the goat is replaced by four horns (v. 8), just as Alexander's Greek empire was divided and ruled by the four Greek generals that followed him.

- From one of the four horns comes one small horn that grows in power and moves south and east and toward the glorious land, Israel (v. 9), just as Antiochus Epiphanes, a Seleucid ruler from Greek and Median descent, who ultimately bowed to Roman power, did.

- This one horn of power commits various abominations: throwing some of the starry hosts to the ground and trampling them (alluding to the fact that Abraham's descendants, who were to be as numerous as the stars, were vanquished—v. 10), and setting itself up against the Prince of the hosts, stopping the daily sacrifice, defiling the sanctuary, and throwing truth to the ground (vv. 11–12). All of this Antiochus Epiphanes did as he invaded Israel, slaughtered thousands, murdered any circumcised infant, sacrificed a pig on the altar of the Lord, put a statue of Zeus in the sanctuary, and cut up and threw down the holy scrolls of the law of truth.

- And this desecration of the temple lasted just over six years—or, to be precise, 2,300 days, just as verse 14 says. (Note: the temple was reconsecrated on December 25, which is why the Feast of Dedication [which we know as Hanukah] is celebrated at Christmastime. [Jesus also celebrated the Feast of Dedication in John 10:22–23.])

It is not speculation that this is what these symbols stand for. Gabriel clearly says that the two-horned ram is Media-Persia (v. 20), and that the goat is Greece (v. 21). He even says that the final horn that stands against the Prince of princes will be destroyed but not by human power (v. 25), as happened to Antiochus Epiphanes when he died of bowel disease so odious that it also drove him mad.

The precision of the prophecies that were given hundreds of years before actual events occur is truly amazing. We are left having to conclude either that the Bible lies when it says these words are prophecy rather than history or that the Bible is truly supernatural and that God has communicated his Word to us in ways that give it profound authority in our lives.

God Knows Evil's End

The reason we want God to have authority is that his Word says he not only knows the measure of evil, he also knows its end—and will bring it. God can raise up and destroy without human power, and he does.

- Babylon the great falls.
- Alexander the Great dies young.
- Antiochus Epiphanes (whose name means "Illustrious One," or more precisely, "God Manifest") gets more than he ever wants of God's manifest presence in the form of a terminal disease beyond the power of his armies to stop.

None is greater than God. God is not bound by the knowledge or power of humans. What we cannot stop, he can. Evil does not have the final word. Restoration is not impossible. Renewal is the future.

God not only knows the measure of evil; he also knows its end and can bring it about when his purpose determines that it is right to do so. The confidence we gain by understanding that God knows the measure and end of evil enables us to endure and trust him through it.

To the lessons we learn from Daniel's predictions of evil's end, I need to add a few comments relating to Antiochus Epiphanes. Many thoughtful commentators have understood these words from Daniel also to have some kind of reference to the antichrist of the end of the ages. Does the angel's statement in verse 26 that this prophecy applies "to many days from now" [i.e. "the distant future" (NIV)] mean that these words do not apply to Antiochus Epiphanes? No, clearly not; the details are too specific to him.

So is this a "double prophecy" of something near and far? We must be careful here, because if we begin to interpret single texts with double fulfillments, then we can end up trying to make the level of detail we know about the nearer prophecy also apply to the end-time where we do not have the same level of detail. The result is the intrigue with and abuse of prophecy that we have witnessed to a great degree in the often-fanciful marketing of end-time revelations whose full meaning God has not yet made known. Daniel's ability to predict events many days "distant" is still impressive even if those days constitute the hundreds of years until Antiochus Epiphanes rather than the thousands of years until the climax of mortal history.

But so much about Antiochus Epiphanes does remind us of what we know about the nature of the antichrist. Just as much of the Old Testament reveals God's gracious character in order for us to recognize Christ's character and mission in the New Testament, so also this Old Testament prophecy tells much about the nature of evil—its arrogance, its cruelty, its need to defile, its need to set up worship contrary to God—so that when the antichrist comes we may recognize his nature and intentions also (see further discussion of these matters in chapters 11 and 12 of this book).

My reason for addressing these end-time issues with respect, but not delving into detailed debate, is to focus on the gospel principles that should be evident to all: God not only knows the measure of evil, he also knows its end—and will bring it to pass. Though evil may have its day, it will not triumph. God will have the final say. Our knowledge of these uncontroversial truths enables us to continue to live faithfully within the larger story of the gospel whether we are in the day of evil or can see how we are part of God's triumph. What we can know with certainty is that there is a great plan and that we have a part in that great plan.

How should this ultimate good news affect us? Though it may surprise us, it knocked Daniel for a loop. We learn in verse 27 that the vision made him exhausted and ill, and that he was appalled by it (the word "appalled" can also be translated "devastated" or "horrified"). Why? Because the vision meant that the people of Israel would not have immediate relief, that they would not have their final victory until the succession of empires, and that the Messiah's ultimate victory was far in the future.

Even a prophet would want an end to sin and suffering in his own day. We should not blame him for that. But even though he wanted a far more immediate end to Israel's difficulties, he did not want a different God. That is important. In his humanity, Daniel blanches at the suffering of a broken world and sinful people, but, with his understanding of his God's ultimate triumph, Daniel deals with the day of evil without losing his faith. In fact, knowledge of the evil on earth that must be faced makes Daniel even more intent on understanding the God of eternity and also explains the prophet's coming visions.

Daniel's response to short-term disappointment is as instructive to us as his long-term revelation. What he reveals for us is two mistaken notions.

MISTAKE 1: FAITH RESULTS IN EARTHLY BLESSING

This first mistake is the idea that the presence of great faith will necessarily result in earthly blessing. Daniel does not see an end to his people's suffering in his lifetime, nor for generations to come. His world is fallen, his nation is being disciplined, and his enemies will continue to prosper. Though he may live to see the beginning of the unfolding of God's plan as a remnant returns to Israel under Cyrus, Daniel's vision convinces him that his people have generations of suffering ahead of them.

I recently heard a prosperity preacher say that we will always reap the blessings of the seed of suffering sown by our predecessors. My response to his words was to wonder why they didn't get the blessing of the seed of suffering sown by their predecessors and how I would know that I am a blessing-reaper rather than a suffering-sower. His claims made no sense logically or biblically.

The Bible never promises that we will have an easy life because we have great faith. Daniel had great faith but foresaw the suffering of God's people and the triumph of God's enemies for many generations to come. I am often befuddled at how prosperity preachers that promise earthly blessings can read Hebrews 11:37–38, which says of faithful people, "They were stoned, they were sawn in two, they were killed with the sword. They went about in skins of sheep and goats, destitute, afflicted, mistreated—of whom the world was not worthy—wandering about in deserts and mountains, and in dens and caves of the earth." Such preachers of affluence and ease do not seem to realize how they disrespect the sacrifice of Christian martyrs, who still in our time are being persecuted and slain for their faithfulness in many nations.

Christians should be faithful not because of the promise of an easy life now but because Daniel 8 (which speaks of earthly suffering) comes in the context of Daniel 7 (which speaks of an eternal kingdom). In Daniel 7, God revealed the big picture: the seed of David has been promised; his is a universal and an eternal dominion; his kingdom will come; and we will rule with him. But until that time we live by a "raw faith," a faith not necessarily cushioned with a problem-free life, but a life of purpose in a larger plan that most assuredly will unfold as God intends for the glory of his name and the salvation of many.

The former presidential press secretary Tony Snow died of cancer at age fifty-three, leaving three children. While dying he wrote,

> We want lives of simple, predictable ease, smooth, even trails as far as the eye can see, but God likes to go off-road. He provokes us with twists and turns. He places us in predicaments that seem to defy our endurance; and comprehension—and yet don't. . . .
>
> Picture yourself in a hospital bed. The fog of anesthesia has begun to wear away. A doctor stands at your feet; a loved one holds your hand at the side. "It's cancer," the healer announces. The natural reaction is to turn to God and ask him to serve as a cosmic Santa. "Dear God, make it all go away. Make everything simpler." But another voice whispers: "You have been called." Your quandary has drawn you closer to God, closer to those you love, closer to the issues that matter, and has dragged into insignificance the banal concerns that occupy our "normal time."
>
> . . . The moment you enter the Valley of the Shadow of Death, things change. You discover that Christianity is not something doughy, passive, pious, and

soft. . . . The life of belief teems with thrills, boldness, danger, shocks, reversals, triumphs, and epiphanies. . . .

We get repeated chances to learn that life is not about us, that we acquire purpose and satisfaction by sharing in God's love for others. . . .

. . . God doesn't promise us tomorrow, he does promise us eternity, filled with life and love we cannot comprehend, and that one can, in the throes of sickness, point the rest of us toward timeless truths that will help us weather future storms. Through such trials, God bids us to choose: Do we believe, or do we not? . . . We don't know much, but we know this: No matter where we are, no matter what we do, no matter how bleak or frightening our prospects, each and every one of us who believe, each and every day, lives in the same safe and impregnable place, in the hollow of God's hand.[3]

At any time we may face the loss of loved ones, the stress of finances, the uncertainty of career futures, and various kinds of health crises. We do not need someone to tell us that real faith always results in good times. We need raw faith in a good God who is still God in the hard times because they are part of his big plan to turn hearts from striving and clinging to the hopes of this world so that they will have the hope and promises of the next. This raw faith is the true faith of Daniel and the one that he shares with us, even as he weeps for his people.

But the weeping does not destroy his faith. Sickened by his own vision, Daniel nonetheless focuses on God, and in future chapters will see his truths even more clearly. Read again that seeming paradox reflected in what Tony Snow wrote: "Your quandary has drawn you closer to God, closer to those you love, closer to the issues that matter, and has dragged into insignificance the banal concerns that occupy our 'normal time.'"

Isn't it odd that the trials and suffering do not turn us *from* God but *to* him? The trials refine for us what is real and true and most important. We need to know that this is the case or we will presume that people in trials are always ready to turn from God rather than to him. While it is certainly true that suffering can cause any of us to doubt God and rage at him, it is also true that a hurting child wants nothing more than the comfort of a parent. A pastor friend of mine said there is one common denominator of every adult conversion he has ever known. He said, "Everyone who has come to faith in Christ as an adult says, 'My life was going along fine and then this big rock came and fell on me.'" People who are made desperate by the trials of this life become desperate for something greater than their own resources; and only at this point do many begin their search for God. This reality leads us to consider the second mistaken notion that Daniel's response to earthly disappointment reveals.

MISTAKE 2: FAITH DISAPPEARS WITHOUT EARTHLY BLESSING

Just as we should not presume that the presence of faith will lead to the absence of earthly trial, we also should not assume that the absence of earthly blessings will destroy faith.

While serving as a hardened news anchor for the Fox News Network, Brit Hume experienced something that broke through his hardness to God: the suicide of his son, Sandy. We might presume that his response would be anger at God and the questioning of all religious truth. These were certainly possible, and certainly are the responses of many people to such tragedy. But this is what Brit Hume said in an interview with Brian Lamb on C-SPAN:

> I grew up in Washington. I went to St. Albans School nine years. Church school. Baptized and confirmed in the Episcopal church. I was a kind of nominal Christian all those years.
>
> Suddenly this unspeakable tragedy hits. And at a moment like that you find out what you really believe. And the one thing I recognized almost instantly was that I believed in God and I believed that God would come to my rescue.
>
> And I remember I said to people and it was kind of a half in jest, but it—there was truth to it, that I kept expecting in the days after what happened to Sandy that the phone would ring. And I'd pick up the phone and the voice on the other [end] would say, this is God. This is what this was about, because it seemed so inexplicable.
>
> And it seemed so undeserved for him, for me and for everyone else in the family. Well, obviously, nothing like that [phone explanation from God] occurred, but something did occur.
>
> Somewhere in the middle of that, I felt closer to God and to Christ than I had ever felt in my life, which is in a sense paradoxical. But there it was. And it was unmistakable. . . .
>
> [What I got rather than a phone call was] 973 letters, prayer cards, expressions by mail to me of sympathy, support and so on. . . .
>
> So, somehow, this event touched these people and somehow they found in them to respond. I consider it to be sent a miracle. And it was—and I, I mean, I just felt so buoyed by it. So supported. So loved. And I thought, thank you, God.[4]

Maybe we haven't received 973 letters from God, but we have received 66—in a Bible that we must decide is either supernaturally given or not. One of the letters is from Daniel, who does not shrink from telling us that in the big plan there is trial and tragedy before we finally arrive at heaven and eternity. Evil may have its day, but God will have the final say. We may want something easier, safer, cleaner—but deep down we know that if there were no evidences of the fall, no consequences of sin, no tragedies in this world, then some would see no reason to turn to God—and all of us would have less motivation to rest in his eternal love. In the midst of all these tragedies and trials we must also decide if pain denies him or if it is the reason that we (and others) must trust him.

For when the tragedies come—as they will—we can question and weep and rage, but inevitably for those in whom the Spirit dwells, all of that clears our heads about what is really dear and important and eternal. Maybe the reason that such mysterious things of God come so clearly to Daniel in the next chapters is the stark nature of this one that clears away all illusions about the hopes of this world. The trials Daniel now knows his people will face in earthly time make his focus more intent on the matters of heaven and eternity. That's the way real life works: trials will break some and enrage some, but for others the difficulties will focus hearts on the goodness and grace of the kingdom that is not of this world.

We must not let people's tragedies keep us from sharing with them the eternal comforts of the gospel. In the furnace of suffering, the eternal refreshment of the gospel may be most evident and powerful. Brit Hume confirmed this when he announced his retirement from Fox News. He said, "I feel like I was really kind of saved when my son died—by faith and by the grace of God, and that's very much on my consciousness." He knew people would wonder why he would leave such prestige and money. He simply said, "Christ is a big piece of it," and said that his plan was now to help others know the God of the Bible. Daniel tells us about that God, too, so that his ultimate triumph over all things evil becomes our basis for hope and strength in the immediate trials we will inevitably face.

9

Entering Their Pain

— DANIEL 9 —

We learn a lot about how to use Scripture by observing how those in Scripture use the Word that was available to them. This is an important aspect of the Reformation principle that "Scripture interprets Scripture." We learn something of that principle by observing how the prophet Daniel reads the prophets who have preceded him.

Daniel is reading Jeremiah and learns that the captivity he is experiencing is supposed to last seventy years. He suddenly realizes that the seventy years are nearly completed and that he and his people had better get ready. Getting ready is about more than packing bags; it involves preparing hearts. For this reason Daniel begins to pray, and his prayer results not only in an amazing vision of what will come but also in remarkable insights into how the people of God, then and now, should live. This is what Daniel says:

In the first year of Darius the son of Ahasuerus, by descent a Mede, who was made king over the realm of the Chaldeans—in the first year of his reign, I, Daniel, perceived in the books the number of years that, according to the word of the LORD to Jeremiah the prophet, must pass before the end of the desolations of Jerusalem, namely, seventy years.

Then I turned my face to the Lord God, seeking him by prayer and pleas for mercy with fasting and sackcloth and ashes. I prayed to the LORD my God and made confession, saying, "O Lord, the great and awesome God, who keeps covenant and steadfast love with those who love him and keep his commandments, we have sinned and done wrong and acted wickedly and rebelled, turning aside from your commandments and rules. We have not listened to your servants the prophets, who spoke in your name to our kings, our princes, and our fathers, and to all the people of the land. To you, O Lord, belongs righteousness, but to us open shame, as at this day, to the men of Judah, to the inhabitants of Jerusalem, and to all Israel, those who are near and those who are far away, in all the lands to which you have driven them, because of the treachery that they have committed against you. To us, O LORD, belongs open shame, to our kings, to our princes, and to our fathers, because we have sinned against you. To the Lord our God belong mercy and forgiveness, for we have rebelled against him and have not obeyed the voice of the LORD our God by walking in his laws, which he set before us by his servants the prophets. All Israel has transgressed your law and turned aside, refusing to obey your voice. And the curse and oath that are written in the Law of Moses the servant of God have been poured out upon us, because we have sinned against him. He has confirmed his words, which he spoke against us and against our rulers who ruled us, by bringing upon us a great calamity. For under the whole heaven there has not been done anything like what has been done against Jerusalem. As it is written in the Law of Moses, all this calamity has come upon us; yet we have not entreated the favor of the LORD our God, turning from our iniquities and gaining insight by your truth. Therefore the LORD has kept ready the calamity and has brought it upon us, for the LORD our God is righteous in all the works that he has done, and we have not obeyed his voice. And now, O Lord our God, who brought your people out of the land of Egypt with a mighty hand, and have made a name for yourself, as at this day, we have sinned, we have done wickedly.

"O Lord, according to all your righteous acts, let your anger and your wrath turn away from your city Jerusalem, your holy hill, because for our sins, and for the iniquities of our fathers, Jerusalem and your people have become a byword among all who are around us. Now therefore, O our God, listen to the prayer of your servant and to his pleas for mercy, and for your own sake, O Lord, make your face to shine upon your sanctuary, which is desolate. O my God, incline your ear and hear. Open your eyes and see our desolations, and the city that is called by your name. For we do not present our pleas before you because of our righteousness, but because of your great mercy. O Lord, hear; O Lord, forgive. O Lord, pay attention and act. Delay not, for your own sake, O my God, because your city and your people are called by your name."

While I was speaking and praying, confessing my sin and the sin of my people Israel, and presenting my plea before the LORD my God for the holy hill of my God, while I was speaking in prayer, the man Gabriel, whom I had seen in the vision at the first, came to me in swift flight at the time of the evening sacrifice. He made me understand, speaking with me and saying, "O Daniel, I have now come out to give you insight and understanding. At the beginning of your pleas for mercy a word went out, and I have come to tell it to you, for you are greatly loved. Therefore consider the word and understand the vision.

"Seventy weeks are decreed about your people and your holy city, to finish the transgression, to put an end to sin, and to atone for iniquity, to bring in everlasting righteousness, to seal both vision and prophet, and to anoint a most holy place. Know therefore and understand that from the going out of the word to restore and build Jerusalem to the coming of an anointed one, a prince, there shall be seven weeks. Then for sixty-two weeks it shall be built again with squares and moat, but in a troubled time. And after the sixty-two weeks, an anointed one shall be cut off and shall have nothing. And the people of the prince who is to come shall destroy the city and the sanctuary. Its end shall come with a flood, and to the end there shall be war. Desolations are decreed. And he shall make a strong covenant with many for one week, and for half of the week he shall put an end to sacrifice and offering. And on the wing of abominations shall come one who makes desolate, until the decreed end is poured out on the desolator." (Dan. 9:1–27)

Some years ago, I taught preaching to pastors in Senegal, West Africa. Senegal is primarily a French-speaking, Muslim nation with a mix of animistic tribal religions. As a result, Christianity there struggles to break free of a performance-for-acceptance perspective. God is easily perceived either as waiting to love us until we have done enough to appease him or doing what we want him to do after we have done enough to manipulate him. So as I was teaching about the imperatives of Scripture always being based on the indicatives of unconditional grace, I was getting a lot of resistance. I left one morning session feeling like a failure and wondering if I was making any difference to these pastors.

Through the afternoon my host took me to lunch and then sightseeing. As we returned to his home for dinner, we passed the meeting place where I had been teaching in the morning. It was still filled with pastors! I asked my host why they were still there. He said, "Many of the men struggled to understand what you were saying today, and the men who do understand are explaining it to the others. No one will leave until everyone understands."

I was supposed to be the one teaching, but I learned a lot about the nature of the Christian life that day. I learned that sharing life in mutual covenant with God involves more than just saying that we are in the same family. Those in a family are integrally bound together. One does not prosper if the others do not. These believers seemed to understand better than I that personal growth and community understanding are necessarily interwoven in a family of faith. God binds us together in his covenant of grace so that our corporate relationships are helping to shape and mature our individual faith.

Living the implications of this covenant-union that embraces all of us believers in Christ is both beautiful and challenging. If we really are united to Christ and to each other by a work of the Spirit, then that means we are not able to be as mature as we should be if our fellow believers also are not as mature as they should be. Capturing the essence of our spiritual union is the African saying, "I am because we are." This is a key reason we are compelled to live for one another. But how far should we go with this living for one another?

Should we rejoice with those who rejoice? Yes. Weep with those who weep? Yes. Should we sacrifice for one another? That is harder, but we know the answer is yes. What about this: Should we confess one another's sin? Should we in some way share the load of mutual failings in corporate repentance? Is it possible that we have not repented as we should unless we have repented corporately? If that is true, then not only do we need to repent for each other's sake, we also begin to echo quite remarkable things about the covenant community that are clearly reflected in the prayers, petitions, and vision of the prophet in Daniel 9. The first of these beautiful and challenging truths of our covenant-union is that confession is not just about the individual.

Confession Is Not Just about Me

In the preceding vision (Dan. 8), Daniel learns that the nation of Israel will go through generations of suffering. Perhaps the normal human reaction is to say, "But, Lord, I didn't do anything wrong. Please excuse me from this discipline. It's not my fault. This is not about me." We presume that we are not responsible for sin that we did not commit. But Daniel makes no such presumption. Instead, as a spiritual leader, Daniel assumes responsibility for sin that he did not commit. We need to be very clear about what has happened and what Daniel now does in light of the facts of this chapter (Dan. 9).

Everyone Is Involved

Who has sinned? Apparently a lot of people have sinned: those from the south and the north ("Judah" and "Israel," v. 7); those both near and far (v. 7); those both small and great ("us" and "our kings," v. 8); both authorities and families ("princes" and "our fathers," v. 8); both those present and those past ("we" and "our fathers," v. 16); and all (v. 11—foreshadowing Rom. 3:23, "All have sinned and fall short of the glory of God," and Rom. 3:10, "None is righteous, no, not one").

Everyone Has Rebelled

What have "all" these people done? Daniel says these people have rebelled and acted wickedly (vv. 5, 9, 11, 15). He also says they have not listened to the prophets God sent to correct them (vv. 6, 10).

Leaders Confess

Who confesses? Daniel repeatedly says "we" or "us" (see the repeated "we" of vv. 5–15). But why does Daniel confess? He may have some problems in his life, but it seems unlikely that this brave spokesman for God needs to confess serious sin. God repeatedly and miraculously rescues Daniel and grants him heavenly visions. Surely this Daniel is not guilty like everyone else who "acted wickedly and rebelled" (v. 5) or have "not listened to . . . the prophets" (v. 6). After all, the reason he is praying is that he has been reading Jeremiah.

We have to make a choice. What is the reason that Daniel uses the phrase "we" when he confesses? His word choice is either rhetorical, representative, or real.

If we assume that his word choice of "we" is rhetorical, then we simply say that this is the way preachers and prophets talk. They say the word "God" with deep-toned reverence and frequently use the "royal we," referring to themselves in the plural, as in the question, "Did you appreciate the sermon that we preached last week?" Polite people don't ask, but they think, "What do you mean, 'we'? Do you have a mouse in your pocket?" However, it is clear that Daniel is not referring to himself alone when he says "we," because he includes other people in the confession: kings, fathers, families, and so on.

So we may conclude that Daniel's use of "we" is representative. In this case, we assume that he has not personally sinned but that he speaks on behalf of the people who have and thus says, "We have sinned and have done these wicked things." We cannot automatically exclude this possibility because Daniel is obviously referring collectively to a body of people (rulers, citizens, fathers, and families) who have sinned as citizens of the nation of Israel. Since he is a part of that nation, Daniel may simply be using "we" to refer to all who share that citizenship, even though he is not personally guilty, similar to the way sports fans say, "We won the World Series last year," even though most people who say that did not actually play on the team.

The final possibility is that Daniel's confession is real. This alternative does not exclude the idea that his words are representative, but it also means that he really thinks that he personally has something to confess along with the corporate sins of his people.

Which of these is the right answer? Perhaps all of them. Prophets do say "we" rhetorically and representatively to confess the sin of those to whom they minister. Isaiah says, "All we like sheep have gone astray; we have turned—every one—to his own way; and the LORD has laid on him the iniquity of us all" (Isa. 53:6). Surely there is both rhetorical and representative intent there. But Isaiah's words include personal confession, and the same is true of Daniel. This is unmistakable in verse 20, where Daniel says that a messenger of God appeared to him "while I was speaking and praying, confessing *my sin* and the sin of *my people*" (emphasis mine).

Why does Daniel confess personal sin as well as the sin of those to whom he is ministering? There are at least two reasons. The first relates to the holiness of God. When Daniel confesses the sinfulness of his people, he simultaneously declares the opposite nature of God (cf. vv. 4, 9, and especially 7: "To you, O Lord, belongs righteousness, but to us open shame"). Apprehension of the true holiness of God always results in the acknowledgment of our unholiness.

These words of Daniel echo Isaiah, whose heavenly vision allowed the earlier prophet to see God on his throne while the seraphim circled and sang, "Holy, holy, holy is the LORD of hosts; the whole earth is full of his glory!" In response, Isaiah said, "Woe is me! For I am lost; for I am a man of unclean lips, and I dwell in the midst of a people of unclean lips; for my eyes have seen the King, the LORD of hosts!" (Isa. 6:3–5). God's holiness produces confession of both personal and corporate sin. In the light of God's radiant purity, Isaiah perceived his own desperate condition as well as the unworthiness of his people. In a similar way, having professed the righteousness of God, Daniel perceives the reality of his own sin as well as his people's sin.

The second reason Daniel joins in the confession of those to whom he is ministering is the calling of God. Daniel confesses the reality of his sin and the people's sin because he has been called to carry their burden as his own even though he did not cause the burden. He feels responsible for the people under his care. This is evident in a change of terms in back-to-back verses of his prayer. First, Daniel, speaking to God, refers to the people of Israel as "your city and your people [who] are called by your name" (v. 19 NIV). One might conclude that Daniel is simply separating the people from himself by giving God the responsibility for them. But then the prophet says in the next verse that he is confessing the sin of "my people" (v. 20). Daniel retains possession of these people for the sake of their spiritual welfare. In doing so, he takes responsibility for them.

Daniel pre-echoes the words of Paul to the Corinthians, when the apostle says to those obstreperous people, "You yourselves are our letter" (2 Cor. 3:2). Paul recognized that his own ministry—for good or for ill—was etched in the lives of the people to whom he ministered. They were his responsibility, and thus he carried responsibility for their sin as well as their triumphs. This is Luther's theology of the cross, as he wrote that those who follow Christ must be prepared to suffer for the sins of others.[1] Leaders of God's people are called to carry his people's burdens. They are to recognize their own shortcomings in the people's sins. The calling of leaders requires them to carry the people's burdens though they did not create them (cf. Gal. 6:2).

From 1998 to 1999, Judy Howard Peterson completed an internship for her degree at North Park Theological Seminary by walking four thousand miles across the United States from Grayland Beach, Washington, to Key Biscayne, Florida. What does one learn theologically by walking four thousand miles? Judy said that she learned two things. The first was, "I am just as loved by God when I am in the middle of a field doing 'nothing' as when I follow the productivity standards of this world"; and the second was, "For all of its beauty, a lot of life also has a lot of South Dakota in it."[2]

She began her walk across America carrying an eighty-pound backpack. She said she was convinced by the end of the second day that she never would make it and wanted to quit. Her legs felt like rubber and her feet were covered with painful blisters. Just when she didn't think she could walk any farther, a woman driving by stopped her van. She offered to carry Peterson's pack to her next stopping point. "She just said, 'I'll take it for you,'" recounted Peterson.

It was a lesson rich with meaning. Physically, the woman in the car took a burden that she did not create. She was not responsible for the burden or the predicament but chose to share the burden for the sake of another's journey. Daniel shows us something very similar. Those who have been spared the burden of sin by the grace of God are responsible to help carry the spiritual burdens of others. Even though we may not have created the burden or caused the predicament, we involve ourselves in the lives and confessions of others to help them on their journey of faith.

This may not be a lesson that we want to learn as we face the responsibility of caring for others. The individualistic spirit of our age trains us to think that we are responsible only for ourselves. But such an exclusive self-focus is not what Christ demonstrated and is not what characterizes those who reflect his grace.

Ordinary Christian teaching enables us to help others learn to deal with *their* guilt, but we do not tend to think of *ourselves* as responsible for their guilt. We tell them to put their burden down at the cross, but rarely do we think that we are responsible to help them carry it there. Yet in a peculiar and ultimately Christlike way, we cannot lead or serve others until we are willing to be responsible for their sin as well as their instruction, sharing in their pain and shouldering the burden of their failures as well as offering them wisdom and direction.

I am not saying that we bear personal culpability for all the sins in our family or community. Looking forward, Jeremiah speaks of the new covenant that now embraces us, saying, "In those days they shall no longer say: 'The fathers have eaten sour grapes, and the children's teeth are set on edge.' But everyone shall die for his own iniquity. Each man who eats sour grapes, his teeth shall be set on edge" (Jer. 31:29–30). We go to Christ to ask forgiveness for our own sin. I do not have to know and confess all the sins of my predecessors to be free of their guilt. But do these words eliminate any consideration of the corporate aspects of evil?

Let us be clear about this. Grace certainly frees individual believers from the guilt of national, familial, and personal sin. The sins of our history and context do not keep us from individually enjoying the benefits of grace. And yet the benefits of grace should not keep individuals from confessing corporate responsibility for the sins of our families and culture. If I am so swept into a culture of materialism that I do not see or fight against the impoverishment of the disadvantaged, then I need to confess my personal sin. In addition, if I see and object to the sin but still live in, and benefit from, the society driven by such aims, then my confession of our corporate sin is appropriate. If I find racism abhorrent but still have advantages from the slave-owning heritage of my family or the oppression-ignoring history of my church, then I should confess the sin of my family and ecclesiastical affiliations. If I personally find the sins of abortion, sex trafficking, and chemical addictions abhorrent but find my life entwined in a culture that promotes such evil, then I have a responsibility to confess *our* sin with the prayer that God would bring his mercy and power to bear upon all of these evils. Grace is great enough to cover all our sin—individual and corporate—but does not free us from responsibilities to confess both.

It is important to recognize that we are not saved merely for individual gain. We are saved to be part of a body for a world-transforming plan of redemption. Salvation is not just about Jesus and me. It is also about being united to Christ, with whom all other believers are corporately bound. And if we believe that we are united with the people of God in the life of faith, we also must believe that we are in some way bound to the people of God in their sin.

What would it mean if we really believed that ministry to others meant shouldering their spiritual burdens with them? My family had to face this question sooner than we expected when I began pastoring a church in our early years of ministry. We accepted the pastoral call with the understanding that, in a previous generation, many people in the region and church had been employed at a notorious printing plant. The plant prospered in that rural area by printing what no one else would print: pornographic magazines. Before we went to the church, we were assured that such printing had ceased. Yet a few weeks after I became pastor we discovered otherwise.

I do not think that people intentionally misled us. The local culture had simply become so immersed in the sin that they no longer perceived it for the horror that it was. But then I had to choose whether to stay to minister amid such sin. The scriptural passage that meant the most to me at that time was the one where Jesus distinguishes between the hireling who runs when wolves come against the flock and the Good Shepherd who gives his life for the sheep (John 10:7–13). I reasoned that someone needed to minister to these people of God, and then realized that I was the somebody who had been called to do it.

We phoned my wife's parents to warn them that we might be coming to live with them if I got fired. Then I began to address the issues—at first in private and then from the pulpit. I know that I made many mistakes, and one of them was that I really thought of the problem as theirs. It was their fault, their sin, their burden. I was happy to condemn it; I am not sure I ever thought of helping them carry it or confessing it as my own. And, in this error, I wonder—although God ultimately delivered us—if I did not prolong the sin and weaken the people by my individualized perception of ministry.

One of the great blessings of that period of my ministry, however, occurred when we began to debate at the regional level of our denomination what we should do regarding this issue. At that time, we discovered that other churches in our area also had members who had participated in this sin for more than a generation. The sin was not just in the actions of the people; it was also in the silence of previous pastors. It was during that debate, in which many were still denying their personal responsibility, that an experienced pastor said, "If Ezra, Nehemiah, and Daniel confessed the sin of their fathers, then I do not know why we cannot confess the sin of those who have come before us." The words became a greater blessing than I ever anticipated when, years later, during the debates over whether our national assembly should repent of the racism of our forefathers, the earlier debate returned to mind, and I was able to quote that wise pastor. Then, with the wise and godly leadership of many pastors older than I, our entire church repented of our present sin and the sin of our forefathers—just as Daniel did.

When we understand that God calls us not merely to condemn but also to carry the sin burden of those to whom he calls us, then we truly have something to say to those who are suffering in sin. If our only perceived task is to condemn them and judge them as worse than we are, then we really have nothing to say to them about the nature of the gospel that humbles us all and by grace alone rescues us all from the sin that we all share.

When we truly perceive our responsibility to bear and confess the sins of others, then cynicism, sarcasm, and ridicule die in the church. Instead of objectifying others as sinners unlike us and standing apart to judge them, we instead get in the boat of need with them, embrace them as brothers and sisters equally in need of the grace we have received without any deserving, and in so doing truly learn about the nature of God's mercy for them and for us. In essence what we begin to learn is that living in grace requires giving ourselves for others—living for them by confessing need with and for them.

Petition Is Not Just about Me

If living for others means confession is not just about me, then it also means that petition is not just about me. When Daniel prays, he also petitions God with two concerns foremost in his mind: the good of others and the glory of God.

The Good of Others

Daniel petitions God to relent from his just judgment against "your city Jerusalem, your holy hill" (v. 16). Daniel seeks God's mercy for the people for whom the prophet is responsible. It is an important step in spiritual maturity to develop this sense of living for the sake of others' good.

When our first child was born, we lived in a rural area and the hospital was about an hour from our home. The day after our son was born, I was so anxious to get back to see Kathy and the baby that my foot unconsciously got heavier and heavier on the gas pedal. At some point, I recognized that I was going about seventy miles per hour on the winding country road. Suddenly it hit me: "I'd better be careful because if something happens to me, my family is really going to suffer." I realized that I was responsible to live for the sake of others. I couldn't be as cavalier or reckless as I had been when my only concern was myself.

Such a realization is also a necessary step in spiritual maturity. Most of us, until we are in spiritual leadership, think of our spiritual lives as only being about ourselves. We start a career, work for our rent, pray for our blessing, and save for our retirement. But at some point we have to move beyond individual concerns and understand that, as members and sometimes leaders of God's people, our lives are not our own. We are bought with a price, and we live and give and suffer for the sake of God's people and their spiritual good.

The Glory of God

Daniel also petitions God to relent from his judgment for the sake of his own name (v. 17—"for your own sake, O Lord, make your face to shine upon your sanctuary, which is desolate"; and v. 19—"Delay not, for your own sake, O my God"). Daniel petitions God to defend and further the glory of his own name. Living for God's glory is also a dramatic change of perspective required for Christian maturity.

One young man who has taught me the most of what it means to live and give oneself for the glory of God has been a church planter in a difficult situation. A few years ago that church plant was near sinking financially. The smart thing to do was for the pastor to cut his losses, close the doors, and move on to greener pastures. Instead, he was willing to consider a remarkable sacrifice for Christ's sake. During the time of the financial crisis for the church, the pastor received a sizable inheritance. With that inheritance he could rescue the church but, of course, he would sacrifice much of his own future. What did he do? As crazy as it sounds by the world's standards—and much of the church's practice—he felt that he was called to live for the sake of the glory and progress of the kingdom of God. He gave his inheritance for the survival of the church and the glory of the advance of the kingdom. That is the true glory of living for the name of the Lord rather than for oneself.

Why should we confess and petition and live for the sake of others? The answer is that not only is confession not just about me, and not only is petition not just about me, ultimately we discern from the prayers and life of Daniel that salvation is not just about me.

Salvation Is Not Just about Me

Daniel looks ahead through his prophetic lens and sees that God promises rescue, not only for the prophet himself but also for his people. The timing of that rescue is, of course, the mysterious part of this portion of the book of Daniel. Through the centuries preachers and commentators have scratched their heads and debated each other about what the seventy weeks of Daniel represent. Several years ago I was asked to add to my earlier book on the life of Daniel by completing a commentary on these final prophetic chapters. I did not take the assignment because I recognized that I was out of my depth in trying to figure out what has caused centuries of debate among our best Bible scholars. What gives me courage to approach the subject now is having read an eminent scholar who, with great humility and charity, wrote that this famous vision has led to such "interminable controversies" that any "interpretation no longer admits of any certainty."[3] If even the best minds struggle to explain this passage, then I am not embarrassed to admit that I cannot with certainty explain all of these mysteries.

What Is Promised?

But saying that there are mysteries is not to imply that there are not obvious truths here that can help us. We know, for example, that Daniel is reading about the seventy years of captivity foretold by Jeremiah when God reveals to this later prophet that a plan of rescue will unfold over seventy weeks ("sevens," see v. 24) of years (i.e., seven times seventy years). It's as though

God is saying that the plan of rescue is immeasurably greater than the trials of the captivity. Something comparable happens when Peter asks if he has to forgive someone seven times, and Jesus's response is that forgiveness should be seventy times seven (Matt. 18:22).

What Is Predicted?

IN GENERAL

While the precise timing of that rescue is the subject of much debate, the nature of the rescue is not. If we will start with trying to understand "what" is predicted before we debate "when" each detail will occur, then we will gain the hope that this passage is really designed to impart. What does Daniel say will happen? The umbrella statements that cover all the details applying to "your [i.e., God's] people and your holy city" are in verse 24. There we are told that the events to come have the following purposes: "to finish the transgression," "to put an end to sin," "to atone for iniquity," "to bring in everlasting righteousness," "to seal [conclude] both vision and prophet," and "to anoint a most holy place [or Holy One]."

While we may not understand precisely what each of these phrases designates, we can easily understand that they are about the ministry of Jesus. Some readers may wince and grin at what appears to be a childish, Sunday-school understanding of a sophisticated prophecy. I can almost hear the chortles now, "Of course, these phrases have something to do with Jesus!"

I will endure the laughs to remind us all that Daniel's chief purpose is to encourage an enslaved people with assurances of the coming and triumph of the Messiah. But Daniel expresses this messianic ministry in terms that his readers probably are not expecting. They are anticipating military and political relief. Instead, Daniel places the priority on spiritual dynamics, saying the Messiah's work will provide for the termination of transgression and sin as well as the commencement of everlasting righteousness for those whose iniquity is atoned for. The Messiah will usher in an era when messianic prophecy is no longer needed and a Holy One (or place, if the intention is to designate our hearts) is anointed for God's people. Surely this last aspect of the prophecy is about the coming of the Holy Spirit to minister Christ's presence among his people.

As plain as these promises are, we sometimes miss them or are afraid to look into them because of the controversies surrounding this passage. My pointing out the obvious meanings is simply meant to remind us not to miss the truths of the gospel in the heat of our debates over the timing of these events.

In Particular

Perhaps I am not right in every detail regarding this general picture, but the particulars that follow confirm the rightness of the general conclusion that Daniel's vision is about Christ's coming to rescue his people. In verse 25, Daniel prophesies that a decree will be issued for the restoration of Jerusalem (which has been ruined by the Babylonians), that the Anointed One will come to the nation, and then a troubled time will follow. These prophecies align with what we know about what happened when Cyrus released the Israelites to rebuild Jerusalem before the time of Christ.

In verse 26, Daniel predicts that the Anointed One would be cut off and have nothing before a later desolation of Jerusalem and its temple by an earthly ruler. This aligns with what we know ultimately happened when Jesus's crucifixion was followed by the destruction of Jerusalem by the future Roman emperor Titus.

Verse 27 is extremely difficult to translate, and it is sad that so many bitter controversies in the church have been based on individuals' confidence in interpretations that should be humbly proffered. In this verse Daniel predicts that "he" (the person is not clearly indicated) will make a covenant with many people and will end the sacrifices and offerings in the temple. Legitimate interpretations allow that the "he" could be Christ, who by his death ended the need for temple sacrifice. However, it is also legitimate to interpret the "he" as Titus, who by his conquest destroyed the place of temple sacrifice.

Verse 27 also predicts, "On the wing of abominations shall come one who makes desolate, until the decreed end is poured out on the desolator." Simply knowing how the words in this phrase should be translated is a task that has stymied scholars for centuries, and interpreting the various translations is even more difficult. Since "wing" is also a term for "extremity" or "apex," and Daniel uses "abominations" to refer to temple defilement (see also Dan. 9:31; 11:27; 12:11; Matt. 24:15), the prophet seems to be predicting that after the temple defilement has reached its apex, one will come who will make things desolate until the end decreed for those who have been devastated. Is this (1) further detailing of Titus's conquest, (2) a prediction of the Holy Spirit's rending of the veil of the temple and removal of divine blessing from Israel until its reclamation, or (3) a distant—and hence foggy—prediction of the rule of the antichrist prior to the end of all things?

The second of these interpretations seems the most likely to me, since the time from a decree for Israel to return to the promised land (see Ezra 7:12–26 for the 458 BC) until the time of Christ's crucifixion (AD 33) was 490 years (remember one year must be subtracted since there was no year 0 for Hebrews), and that is precisely the seventy times seven years Daniel predicted. It may well be that these events are also meant to establish a recognizable pattern of future events that will presage the end-time, but the most natural first reference is to the events surrounding Christ's first coming. Still, there is no need to be dogmatic about this, since the main point of Daniel's vision is not to create eschatology debates but rather to encourage God's people in captivity.

What Does the Prediction Really Mean?

What we know for sure is that Daniel's prophecy is provided in the context of a hurting people who need help. God does not give the vision to vex us with the limitations of our wisdom but to comfort his people with the assurance of his care. How is that care communicated? Consider the simplest and plainest facts that we know about Daniel's vision: it comes in the midst of Daniel's prayer of confession for himself and his people who are in captivity. And in response to Daniel's prayer of confession, God responds in specific ways.

God Responds Swiftly

While Daniel was yet praying, the angel Gabriel comes to him in swift flight (v. 21). The simple message is that God is attentive to the cry of his people and he does not delay his care for those who turn to him, even if there is sin in and about them. This in itself is a wonderful reflection of the grace of God for hurting and sinful people then, as well as for hurting and sinful people now.

God Responds Sacrificially

We should not get so hung up on the puzzles of timing that we miss the clear proclamation of grace in Daniel's vision. God will provide atonement for his people (v. 24) and he will do this through an Anointed One who will suffer on their behalf (v. 26). He will be "cut off" in order to bind up a broken people—he will be broken for our brokenness. And because we now know the Person prophesied, we can grasp the full implications of the grace personified in him: God himself will enter our world of pain and sin in order "to put an end to sin, and to atone for iniquity, to bring in everlasting righteousness" (v. 24). The reason that Daniel is so ready to enter into the sin of his people in order to seek mercy for them is that this is God's own way of dealing with sinners. Daniel simply reflects the gracious character of God in his prayers and petitions, and in doing so teaches us what it means to reflect God's grace in our lives and leadership.

Grace Made Fresh

During a recent Easter season, I experienced the dilemma that I face so often at that time of year. I wanted to sense deep in my heart the reality of the suffering and redeeming Savior. But I have sat through so many Good Friday services and preached so many Easter services; I wondered not only what I could say that was fresh but also how the season could have fresh meaning for my own heart.

The answer I was seeking came during the communion service offered on Good Friday. In that service, we did something unusual for our church. We processed forward in a line to be served the bread and wine by our pastor. My pew filed forward, and I partook and then returned to my seat, still feeling a bit disconnected and empty.

Then something gripped me in a quite unexpected way. I watched as the line before the pastor dwindled to the last few persons. Then a man I had not seen before joined the line. He was the last in the queue, and the reason he waited so long to join it was obvious. He did not want to stand long because he was suffering from Parkinson's disease. His body was bent and he quivered as he walked, seemingly ready to fall with almost every step. He reached for the bread clumsily; his hand shook uncontrollably as he drank the little cup of wine.

The scene suddenly made the grace fresh to me again, as the Lord enabled me to see in the trembling man a spiritual image of myself. I, too, had no basis to stand and no right to be anywhere but last in line for God's mercy. Before the table of God's provision, I knew that I too had stumbled and that my sin was just cause for me to tremble before my Savior. And yet there he was before me in the bread and wine, the symbols of his body broken and blood spilled. He was broken for one broken as I, and took my sin that I might know his mercy.

This is all a mystery past my explanation, and yet my heart deeply knows its meaning. So also the prophecy of Daniel, despite all its mysteries, is meant to speak deeply to our hearts of the mercy of our God. He shared our shame to spare us pain and bore our penalty to free us from guilt. By entering in, he put an end to sin and atoned for iniquity. And now we who know him and reflect him must do the same by witnessing his grace in the way that we face the trials of our world and, in his name, care for others who must face the same.

10

The Three-Touch Gospel

Through the first nine chapters of Daniel we have seen that the prophetic details that sometimes divide devoted Christians are actually small compared to the message of the gospel that is so clearly intertwined within the prophet's visions. Arguments tend to center on the minor matters and miss the major ones. Here in Daniel 10 we are reminded of the major issues. The controversial matters include the identity of the man in white linen and the timing of the wars that he predicts. But there are matters more clear than these that also need attention.

The first six chapters of Daniel provide his biography. Chapters 7 and 8 reveal "conclusions," including the conclusion of Israel's captivity and a message about the conclusion of all things. Daniel 9 is Daniel's confession of sin and the revelation of grand things God is doing of which Daniel knows himself not to be worthy. Now, in Daniel 10, God himself responds to that confession by revealing that good things as well as hard things are ahead. Daniel is so distressed by the hard things that the first verses of this chapter tell us he does not eat for three weeks; he does not anoint or cleanse his body; he is mourning. The explanation begins in verse 4—but there is more than grief unfolding here:

In the third year of Cyrus king of Persia a word was revealed to Daniel, who was named Belteshazzar. And the word was true, and it was a great conflict. And he understood the word and had understanding of the vision.

In those days I, Daniel, was mourning for three weeks. I ate no delicacies, no meat or wine entered my mouth, nor did I anoint myself at all, for the full three weeks. On the twenty-fourth day of the first month, as I was standing on the bank of the great river (that is, the Tigris) I lifted up my eyes and looked, and behold, a man clothed in linen, with a belt of fine gold from Uphaz around his waist. His body was like beryl, his face like the appearance of lightning, his eyes like flaming torches, his arms and legs like the gleam of burnished bronze, and the sound of his words like the sound of a multitude. And I, Daniel, alone saw the vision, for the men who were with me did not see the vision, but a great trembling fell upon them, and they fled to hide themselves. So I was left alone and saw this great vision, and no strength was left in me. My radiant appearance was fearfully changed, and I retained no strength. Then I heard the sound of his words, and as I heard the sound of his words, I fell on my face in deep sleep with my face to the ground.

And behold, a hand touched me and set me trembling on my hands and knees. And he said to me, "O Daniel, man greatly loved, understand the words that I speak to you, and stand upright, for now I have been sent to you." And when he had spoken this word to me, I stood up trembling. Then he said to me, "Fear not, Daniel, for from the first day that you set your heart to understand and humbled yourself before your God, your words have been heard, and I have come because of your words. The prince of the kingdom of Persia withstood me twenty-one days, but Michael, one of the chief princes, came to help me, for I was left there with the kings of Persia, and came to make you understand what is to happen to your people in the latter days. For the vision is for days yet to come."

When he had spoken to me according to these words, I turned my face toward the ground and was mute. And behold, one in the likeness of the children of man touched my lips. Then I opened my mouth and spoke. I said to him who stood before me, "O my lord, by reason of the vision pains have come upon me, and I retain no strength. How can my lord's servant talk with my lord? For now no strength remains in me, and no breath is left in me."

Again one having the appearance of a man touched me and strengthened me. And he said, "O man greatly loved, fear not, peace be with you; be strong and of good courage." And as he spoke to me, I was strengthened and said, "Let my lord speak, for you have strengthened me." Then he said, "Do you know why I have come to you? But now I will return to fight against the prince of Persia; and when I go out, behold, the prince of Greece will come. But I will tell you what is inscribed in the book of truth: there is none who contends by my side against these except Michael, your prince." (Dan. 10:1–21)

A friend of my wife tells of an evening in her childhood made memorable by distress she could not then fully understand. It was in the days before cell phones and before many homes had phone extensions. Telephones were in the central hall or kitchen so that family members could run and catch the phone when it was ringing. This particular evening, the children had gone to bed. Everyone was in their room except her father—he stood in the dark, in the hallway on the phone, talking to her brother long distance in Vietnam.

The brother was scared. He had seen things that had enraged and confused him. Now his dad was half a world away, in the dark of his house, listening to his son's angst. What could he say to his son in the midst of war to bring him comfort and enable him to keep functioning as he must? Our friend says her father would simply wait for his son to pause in the gush of complaint, confusion, and fear, and then he would say, "I love you, David." Another few minutes would pass, and the father would say, "I love you, David." Then another few minutes and another "I love you, David." The father simply affirmed his love for his son during a time of war. Julie says she remembers that night with vivid clarity all these years later not just because she knew that something was very wrong with her brother but also because she learned how powerful and necessary it was to affirm a father's love in a time of crisis.

Something is very wrong here in chapter 10 of Daniel, too. The end of Israel's captivity was near. Jeremiah had prophesied it; Daniel had read about it in Jeremiah, and he knows it is the end. But the end of captivity is not the crisis. Although Daniel knows that end is near, he also has been told that great hardship still lies ahead for the people of God. Generations of war and suffering are ahead, and that message throws Daniel. Things should be getting better, but they are getting worse. How can he keep going? He cannot eat; he mourns for three weeks; he does not take care of his body. Daniel needs some assurance of God's continuing care, but comfort seems distant and impossible.

What happens next is critical for understanding how God comforts Daniel and keeps him able to do as he must. A man, dressed in linen with a gold sash, appears. Who is that? Here the commentators are divided, but a delayed explanation comes in the first chapter of Revelation to help us understand. There, with a very similar description, appears one "like a son of man" who appears among the lampstands representing his churches:

> In the midst of the lampstands one like a son of man, clothed with a long robe and with a golden sash around his chest. The hairs of his head were white, like white wool, like snow. His eyes were like a flame of fire, his feet were like burnished bronze, refined in a furnace, and his voice was like the roar of many waters. In his right hand he held seven stars, from his mouth came a sharp two-edged sword, and his face was like the sun shining in full strength. (Rev. 1:13–16)

Who is being described? Clearly this is the Christ, the anointed Son of Man, who represents the glory and purposes of God. There are many intentional reflections between the chief figures in these chapters of Daniel and Revelation.

The men described in both are clothed in white robes—priestly garb; both have a gold belt—kingly apparel. Both have blazing eyes, both have bronze skin, both have roaring voices—all supernatural traits. In Revelation, the one described holds seven stars in his hand and his face blazes like the sun. Perhaps that explains why the appearance of the man in linen to Daniel makes the prophet faint dead away and causes his friends to run away. The one who comes as a spokesman for God is most readily understood as the Son of God, the Second Person of the Godhead who made the heavens and earth.

The scene might remind us of Dorothy and her friends trembling before the Wizard of Oz, but there are important differences. Though the servants are like the cowardly lion who runs away, the One speaking does not huff and puff and say, "Bow before me." He also does not stay hidden behind the curtain. Instead, he reaches down to the person bowing before him, touches him, and says, "Stand upright." This is the first of three vital touches that communicate three important messages.

The First Touch: Enabling Daniel to Stand

The stage for the unfolding event in this chapter is set in verses 10 and 11: "And behold, a hand touched me and set me trembling on my hands and knees. And he said to me, 'O Daniel, man greatly loved.'" The first thing this glorious heavenly figure says (in our terms) is, "I love you, Daniel." Why is this assurance so important?

Daniel's Distress

LEFT BEHIND

Daniel has to face several sad things as a consequence of the appearance of this heavenly being. First, he's left behind. Daniel, who has received these great visions and who stayed faithful to God, is now writing in the third year of King Cyrus. This is two years after his previous confession and Cyrus's decree allowing the rebuilding of Jerusalem. That means other people are already starting to go back to the Holy Land. This is also the time of Passover, when all faithful Jews would want to be in Jerusalem. But where is Daniel? He is not in Jerusalem. He is still in captivity, and he is ninety years old. He will never get back to his homeland, and he knows it; the man in white linen does not change that reality.

BROKEN BY SIN

Not only does Daniel recognize that his personal plight will not get better, but he also has to confront the radiant purity of this heavenly visage before him. Daniel confessed his own sin and the sin of his people in chapter 9. Now he has to face this awe-invoking presence of the One to whom he has confessed. No wonder he cannot stand!

AWARE OF THE FUTURE

In addition to feeling the weight of sin, Daniel also breaks under the weight of the future distresses revealed to him. Fighting will continue with the king of Persia. Next will come a cruel king from Greece, and Daniel has already been told what will follow him—great devastation for the people of God in Jerusalem. The people who are returning to the city of their forefathers hope to know renewed peace and prosperity, but great heartache lies in their future in that place. Things should be getting better, but they are getting worse. The aged Daniel nearly collapses under the weight of such burdensome knowledge.

Daniel's Comfort

ASSURANCE OF LOVE

Despite the crippling burdens of his situation and knowledge, Daniel finds the strength to stand again in these words from the man in linen: "O Daniel, man greatly loved, understand the words that I speak to you, and stand upright, for now I have been sent to you" (v. 11). The man tells Daniel he is a beloved person. Daniel, who has been down on his knees, stands up. Just the strength of "I love you, Daniel" gets him to his feet.

The assurance of God's care in the midst of our distress is meant to have such an effect, renewing our strength and enabling us to face what we must. And to make sure these are the effects, the messenger's next words are "fear not" (v. 12). These words regularly occur in the Bible with great appearances of God's glory. When God appeared to Abraham, Isaac, and Jacob, he said, "Fear not." When God revealed his glory to the prophets, he said, "Fear not." When messengers announced Jesus's birth to his family and to the shepherds in their fields, they said, "Fear not." When the glory of God is so great that it might obscure the love God has for his people, he always assures them that they need not fear harm from him. The circumstances into which he comes may be frightening, and his own nature requires our awe, but he comes to overcome our fears with the promise of his care.

ASSURANCE OF HEARD PRAYER

The assurance of care for Daniel has evidence. God's messenger says to him, "From the first day that you set your heart to understand and humbled yourself before your God, your words have been heard" (v. 12). Essentially

God says, "I have heard you and I have come to you because you sought me." Such assurance of God's care and presence in response to prayer is always believers' greatest strength in times of trouble. We do not need to have all our questions immediately answered if we know that God hears us. We do not need all of our problems solved immediately if we know that God is with us. When the infinitely powerful and holy God comes to hear and be near to us through our prayers, we can face whatever we must with such assurance of his care.

Assurance of Presence

Daniel does not merely have words to assure him of God's presence. The messenger of God is there with him. Consider the importance of such a presence. Daniel must feel terribly alone. He is alone, knowledgeable of his sin, isolated in his faith (most of his own people no longer honor God), and the few remaining faithful among his people are already starting to leave to go back to Jerusalem. Yet here, in the midst of his isolation and loss, there is this Christlike appearance of God who promises love (v. 11), a hearing (v. 12), and peace (v. 19). Assurance of such presence does not make all our problems vanish, but it does make us able to face them with courage and hope.

A similar thing happened after the resurrection of Jesus Christ. Mary was in the garden, believing that the body of her Redeemer had been stolen away. She knew great loss. Her Master was gone and he was the only One who had received her despite her shame of once having had seven demons inside her. She had known what it was to be in the presence of the One who had freed her from her shame, and now he was gone. She must have felt the shame all over again and feared the future consequences. She also had to feel deep grief. She had seen her Lord crucified.

As she fell to the ground, weeping for all of these losses, someone came near to her. She assumed it was the gardener. She said, "They've taken my Lord away. Do you know where he is?" The One who was standing there simply said, "Mary" (paraphrase of John 20:1–16). Just in that one word everything that needed to be said was expressed. By saying her name, Jesus said, "Mary, I still love you, and I'm here for you." There were still hard things, but knowledge of Jesus's care and presence made it possible to face them with courage and hope. We have no less cause for courage and hope today. Not only did Jesus come to us in bodily form long ago, he also continues to indwell us by his Holy Spirit as evidence of his care and presence. The courage and hope that Daniel and Mary exemplified because of the presence of their God is still ours to claim.

Assurance of Advocacy

But what if we believe that we are not worthy or able to claim the care and presence of our God? Then we still need the testimony of Daniel, even if the words may be strange to us. In verse 13, the man in linen says, "The prince of the kingdom of Persia withstood me twenty-one days, but Michael, one of the chief princes, came to help me, for I was left there with the kings of Persia." What is this about? This angelic representative of God says that he was delayed a few weeks, wrestling with the prince of Persia. This is a reference to a great spiritual battle that is going on behind the scenes of our earthly and material perspectives. We do not see it, but the apostles and the prophets make it plain that parallel to this physical world there is a spiritual world where God's battles are being waged against evil.

Spiritual warfare is real. In our North American, modern, scientific culture, we are encouraged not to think this way. Yet the Bible teaches that the realities of spiritual conflict cannot be ignored if we are to fulfill God's purposes. Abraham Kuyper wrote, "If once the curtain were pulled back and the spiritual world behind it came into view, it would expose to our spiritual vision a struggle so intense, so convulsive, sweeping everything within its range, that the fiercest battle ever fought on earth would seem, by comparison, a mere game."[1]

Recently I spoke with a woman who had been a missionary in Cambodia. She talked about her great frustration in returning to the United States after years on the mission field in a culture where evil spirits are worshiped and where Christianity makes progress only when God's people seek his aid against such demonic powers. She said, "I spent years witnessing the power and reality of spiritual warfare. But I talk to people here in the United States about the need for confronting spiritual powers and their eyes just go vacant or suspicious. It's like the spiritual world doesn't even count or is not real. But I will tell you, it is very real."

The apostle Paul was not joking when he said that we wrestle not against flesh and blood but against powers and principalities and spiritual wickedness in high places (Eph. 6:12). When we are told that Satan goes around like a roaring lion seeking whom he may devour (1 Pet. 5:8) and that there is true spiritual warfare, we may react in various ways. We can become superstitious and see demons around every bush, or we may disregard our spiritual foes and say they represent antiquated thinking.

The healthy alternative is to take the perspective of the apostles, acknowledging for believers, "Yes, you do wrestle against spiritual wickedness, but there is nothing to fear because 'he who is in you is greater than he who is in the world'" (see 1 John 4:4). We have powerful spiritual resources available to us and they are to be employed. The one who appears before Daniel is hinting at these resources when he says that he has responded to Daniel's prayer and, as a consequence, urges the prophet not to fear (v. 12). The words of the man in linen remind us that we have an Advocate in heaven who fights for us. Our foes are not slight, but our God is great and he comes to our aid when we seek him.

Seeking God for aid against unseen foes requires biblical humility. We must come to him and say, "I cannot do what you call me to do in this earthly situation if you do not also help me in the spiritual realm." Daniel teaches us that such prayers are especially important for Christian leaders. There is no one more in the sights of Satan than a Christian who is preparing to minister the gospel to a world that desperately needs it. As I have mentioned earlier, when I graduated from a small seminary, there were only twenty-one in my graduating class. As I looked down that line of friends in their caps and gowns, I recognized with a shiver that every one of us had gone through a major life challenge during seminary. Spiritual warfare is real.

A few years ago, at that same seminary there was a terrible crime—a murder. In a faculty meeting afterward, one of the professors offered an explanation for the yet-unsolved crime. He said that because the seminary had grown rapidly and was being blessed with more influence than we had ever dreamed, Satan was trying to stop us. "But," the professor added, "Satan's reach will exceed his grasp because God's purposes will prevail." Spiritual warfare is real, but so is the power of our Advocate.

Satan's opposition comes not only in times of great crisis. Spiritual battles are everyday occurrences. We may be working on our computer when a terrible internet site pops up. For those who believe the Scriptures, it is not unrealistic to consider this a wile of Satan to distract us and weaken us spiritually. He and his emissaries intend to damage us and to stop us. Such opposition may come through economic deprivation, relational tension, or political opposition as we attempt to pursue the Lord's work. In response to these common challenges, we may react with purely human measures: more money, more work, more networking. But Daniel cautions us to consider the parallel spiritual universe in which Satan is orchestrating his opposition to affect our circumstances, and to call on our heavenly Advocate to help us there.

Satan can bring turmoil into our relationships and circumstances to try to stop us in the pursuit of God's purposes. Maybe that explains why these verses in Daniel let him and us know that this messenger of God fought for three weeks with the prince of Persia. I don't think that we have to believe that "the prince of the kingdom of Persia" is a reference to a specific demon (though that is possible); but it does reflect how the evil forces in the spiritual world who are aligned with a pagan opponent of Israel are doing their best to oppose God's purposes. The same is likely when the man in linen says that the prince of Persia will be followed by the prince of Greece (v. 20). Since we already know from Daniel's earlier prophecies that the pagan Persian empire will be succeeded by the Greek empire, the messenger of God is telling Daniel that these human enemies of God's people have their own evil advocates ("princes") in the spiritual world. Through their influence on human relationships and earthly circumstances, the emissaries of Satan seek to accomplish his will by using the rulers of Persia and Greece. Because these rulers are opposing God's purposes in the physical world, Christ promises to oppose the spiritual forces behind them in the spiritual world—and it is this spiritual influence that will ultimately make such nations the instruments of his purposes.

Daniel's record makes it clear that spiritual warfare is real, while also making it clear that Christ will prevail for those who seek him. Though the man in linen was resisted by the prince of Persia for a few days, he still responded to Daniel's prayers (v. 12), will continue to contend for his people in the spiritual realm (v. 20), will give his angel the mission of continuing protection (v. 21 and 12.1), and will ultimately prevail (12:1).[2] With his first touch, the man in linen communicates these vital gospel messages to Daniel from God: "I love you; I've responded to your prayers; I've come to help you; and I will win."

Assurance for Now

Daniel's assurances of such a powerful advocate were meant to give him powerful assurance in his times of trial, but the God who helped him is still at work. Daniel's words are recorded not simply so that we will observe them as a history lesson but so that we too will call on the same God who loves us as he loved Daniel.

Such present love is demonstrated to me in the life of Gerry Gutierrez, a former General Secretary of the Peruvian Communist youth party known as The Students Revolutionary Front. Gerry is now a missionary pastor and orphanage director in Peru. In recent correspondence about the progress of the gospel in his country and in his heart, he wrote to me: "My former comrades of the Shining Path Terrorists are making a comeback in our area. They used a bazooka to kill five people near us, and the congregation that I pastor is facing a tough discipline problem of adultery in the leadership. A move to split the church hangs like dark clouds over our heads. I am facing apostasy, betrayal, criticism. Discouragement, loneliness, abandonment, and lack of trust surround me like threatening waters; yet I am not alone. Though no one here is beside me, the peace of God that comes from knowing the God of peace indwells my heart."

Some may think that these are empty religious words. But they are the gospel hope claimed by believers in all ages. As Martin Luther said, progress in Christianity is beginning again and again with the gospel.[3] What is that gospel? That a Lord of great glory comes to us in our difficulties and says, "I love you. I hear your prayers. I've come to be with you, and, though we may have to battle physical and spiritual opponents for a while, I will fight for you and will ultimately prevail. So you can be at peace. I am your God and I will take care of you."

The Second Touch: Enabling Daniel to Speak

Enabling Daniel's Speech

To understand the second touch of this chapter we must remember the context. The man in white linen, whose body shines like marble (beryl), whose eyes are like fire, whose legs and arms are like burnished bronze, and whose voice is like that of a multitude (see v. 6), has appeared to Daniel and spoken to him. The man radiates heaven, even though he has "the likeness of the children of man" (v. 16) and the "appearance of a man" (v. 18). These words emphasize the presence of the preincarnate Lord Jesus—a Christophany. Daniel senses the significance and does what all the prophets in all ages do before the glory of God—Daniel turns his face to the ground and shuts his mouth (v. 15).

When the radiance of God's holiness overwhelmed the earlier prophet Isaiah, he said, "Woe is me! . . . I am a man of unclean lips, and I dwell in the midst of a people of unclean lips" (6:5). He acknowledged that he was not worthy to join the "holy, holy, holy" song of the angels that flew about the throne of God. Even a righteous prophet had no right to speak before the holy God. So what did one of the heavenly hosts do? A seraph took a coal from the altar (the place where holiness was made possible through a sacrifice of atonement) and touched the lips of the prophet (Isa. 6:1–8). The message is plain: by the work of God, a man can join the song of heaven. He is made worthy by a divine touch. Only then could Isaiah speak to and for God.

Daniel also gets a touch on the lips (v. 16). This prophet has also been silenced by the radiant splendor of the man in white linen (v. 15). His priestly robes and royal sash well indicate the holiness and power that should silence every voice in his presence. But with a touch on the lips from this same heavenly being, Daniel can also speak. Though the prophet has previously confessed his own sin and the sin of his people, the Lord gives Daniel the right and ability to speak in the presence of holy divinity.

Opening Daniel's Heart

What will Daniel say now that he has the ability to speak? He says, "By reason of the vision pains have come upon me" (v. 16) and I am so weak that I cannot speak (v. 17). The words are incredibly personal. They of course remind us that the prophet's vision has painful content, but most of the content of the vision is yet to be revealed. It will come in following chapters. Daniel's reaction at this point reminds me of when a child of mine had a hidden disobedience exposed. The transgression was too apparent to deny, and his guilt overwhelmed him with shame. Though I wanted nothing more than to help him, my child said, "Please go away. I hurt when you are near because I feel so bad facing you." Daniel confesses pain that is similar. He says, "How can my Lord's servant talk with my Lord?" In the light of the Lord's glory, the prophet recognizes his own inadequacy and confesses that the nearness of his Lord drains him of strength and breath (v. 17).

Daniel recognizes simultaneously that he has permission to speak but has no power to do so. He confesses that he is helpless (v. 16c, "I retain no strength"; v. 17c, "no strength remains in me") and cannot breathe enough to speak (v. 17, "no breath is left in me"). The words sound desperate, but they are precious to our gospel understanding. What they indicate is that the touch of divinity has made Daniel able to open his heart and confess his weakness.

Heaven's touch gives Daniel enough strength to say, "I am weak." The Lord's presence provides him enough awe to say, "I am speechless." The Lord's mercy provides him enough breath to say, "I can't breathe." Each phrase is a confession of utter inadequacy that God both enables and receives.

Before the glory of a holy God, nothing but humility will stand. Our Lord does not want to hear claims of righteousness or protests of adequacy, even from the best of us. True spiritual maturity is on display when someone has the heart to say, "There is nothing in me that merits forgiveness; I deserve whatever judgment is just; I have no right to heaven's blessing; and before the Word of Heaven I can say nothing." Daniel's confession of inadequacy, his utter humility, is the best expression of godliness that can be expressed before the face of God and is precisely what we should expect from Daniel—and what God should expect from us.

Daniel's willingness to confess such helplessness is our great hope. This second touch from God that enables Daniel to open his heart to God without fear of rejection assures us we can confess our helplessness, too. We can confess that we don't have any basis to stand before him, that we don't know what to say, that coming to him brings us pain, and that we can't even find the words to say what we really feel. Not only are these words that we can say, the fact that God enabled Daniel to say them means that they are the words that God wants us to say. God is so merciful and so welcoming that he is willing to come close enough to touch the hearts of those who cannot even find the breath to say how inadequate they are. This is the sweet grace of the gospel, assuring us that we don't need to have our lives cleaned up before God will receive us. He is willing to listen to words from open hearts, even when—and especially when—those hearts confess their utter inadequacy to him.

When I was a young pastor, a friend of mine wrote a song called "The Song without Words." The reason it meant so much to me was that the song so well expressed what I heard from those who were totally broken before God. Such persons usually did not have the right words to articulate their repentance; they rarely had well-formed prayers of contrition. More often they were so empty of confidence and pride that they had no words to say. But in their sense of total inadequacy was the true glimmer of gospel hope that this "Song without Words" captured:

> Tired, yet I can't sleep;
> Wounded, yet I can't weep;
> Sinful, yet I can't pray;
> Father, hear the words I cannot say.

These words, like those of Daniel, are not merely an expression of humility; they are also permission not to have all the right answers and allowance not to have the perfect approach to God. This song harmonizes with Daniel's humility to enable us to say, "I don't know the right answers; I can't find the right words; I know I don't have a right to approach God; but I still believe that he will hear me." If Jesus would bless a man who confessed, "I believe; help my unbelief" (Mark 9:24), then we can still come to him when we are drained of strength and confidence in our righteousness to ask for his help.

We do not have to fear that God will turn from words ill formed, that he will run from emotions wrongly expressed, that he will give up on us because we have given up on ourselves. The cry "God, I am so helpless" was not uttered for the last time from the lips of Daniel. I have heard it more than once from the lips of a frazzled young mother who has raged at her children *again*; from the lips of a teen who has cut herself *again*; from the lips of a teacher struggling with homosexuality who has failed *again*; from my own lips when pride, busyness, and ambition have robbed my family of me *again*. "God, I am so helpless." God has heard it before, and he does not turn away. What does he do? When Daniel has given his Lord every reason to turn away, the Lord touches Daniel again (v. 18).

The Third Touch: Enabling Daniel to Rest

After he had opened his heart about his inadequacy, Daniel records that the man in linen touched him again and strengthened him (v. 18). How did the touch strengthen him? It strengthened him with communication of God's peace. The man of God is not repulsed by Daniel's inadequacy but says, "O man greatly loved, fear not, peace be with you" (v. 19).

Daniel could well have expected other reactions. He has just confessed (in the previous chapter) his sin, before the appearance of this man of radiant power and purity. Here Daniel also trembles before a divine appearance and then acknowledges that it brings him pain and weakness (vv. 16–17). With good reason, the man in white could strike him or reject him or turn from him, but instead the man says to Daniel, "Do not fear because you are loved, I am with you, and I grant you peace."

The promise of peace is no small blessing in this context. Daniel not only has reason to fear the man in linen, but he also has good reason to fear the future. The prophecy that will be related by the man from God is of a great and extended battle that will envelop the world and oppress God's people. Yet the man dressed in linen offers Daniel peace. The result is not merely comfort but also courage.

The man of God says, "peace be with you," and then, "be strong and of good courage" (v. 19a). Daniel continues, "And as he spoke to me, I was strengthened and said, 'Let my lord speak, for you have strengthened me'" (v. 19b). These words, combined with the content of the preceding passage, inform us of an important progression: fear is overcome by assurance of divine love, which leads to personal peace, which provides strength for God's purposes.

Dr. Robert G. Rayburn, the founding president of Covenant Seminary, related how this spiritual progression worked in his first combat experience during the Korean War. He served in the army chaplaincy in World War II, but was recalled from the pastorate for service in Korea. Though he already had military experience, his new assignment filled him with fear. Chaplain Rayburn was assigned to a unit of army paratroopers.

With virtually no training, he was rushed into duty, and Rayburn's first jump was behind enemy lines at night. As the troop plane flew toward the drop site for such a hazardous mission, he noted that men with far more experience began to tremble and break out in a cold sweat. He knew that if he fell apart in fright or showed too much terror, he would not be able to minister to the men. So he began to acknowledge his weakness and fear in prayer to God, asking that God would give him peace so that he would be able to fulfill God's purposes in these men's lives.

Rayburn began his prayer as the plane began its two-hour flight to the drop zone. He started by praying for peace of heart, and the next thing he knew the commander was saying, "Chaplain, wake up. It's four minutes to the jump." God had answered the prayer for peace and provided him with sleep. In the weeks and months of battle that followed, Dr. Rayburn recorded that he had the opportunity to share his faith with virtually all the men in that unit—most of whom said, "I want the God who gave you such peace that you could sleep before your first jump into battle." Before we simply dismiss this account as unlikely to apply to our situations, perhaps we should ask why such peace would be as improbable for Daniel as we may think it is for us.

Daniel Knows What Will Come and What He Has Done

Through his own vision, Daniel knows that great battles are ahead for him and God's people. He has already been informed of these challenges in multiple previous visions (Dan. 2, 7, 8, 9). In addition, more terrifying specifics about those challenges will be revealed in the rest of this vision as it unfolds in chapters 11 and 12. For example, Daniel will soon hear from the man in white how battles with Persian powers will evolve into a war with Greece also (v. 20). Daniel knows what will come, and there is every reason to fear. Daniel also knows (and in previous chapters has confessed) his and his people's failings. He has good reasons to fear heaven's judgment as well as earth's empires. Yet the Lord urges him to be at peace.

Daniel Knows God's Presence and Power

How can peace be possible in light of all that Daniel has to fear? The answer lies in Daniel's knowing not only what will come but also who will be with him. The chapter concludes with what seem to be obscure and odd words. The man of God, who has just alerted Daniel to a coming war of Persia and Greece, now says, "But I will tell you what is inscribed in the book of truth: there is none who contends by my side against these except Michael, your prince" (v. 21). "The book of truth" is the record of history future—that is, what will come. This prophecy from that book is first a precious reminder that things to come are not a surprise to God. He is never caught off guard, never unprepared. His book of truth already records what will come. We need not fear that anything will occur to undo his plan and purpose.

Our fears are also calmed by words the man in white adds to his statement about going to finish his battle with the prince of Persia (see v. 20). The man says that when he is engaged in that fight, the prince of Greece will come (see v. 20, predicting the coming victory of the Greek empires). Only then does the man in linen say, "There is none who contends by my side against these except Michael, your prince" (v. 21).

If we are right that these references to the princes of Persia and Greece are generic references to the spiritual evil that Satan rallies to support pagan rulers, then the promise of Michael's influence is assurance that God will continue actively fighting for his people in the spiritual realm. Again we are reminded that what we see in the material world is not the full picture. At least parallel to, if not above, the temporal, earthly events that unfold before our eyes are spiritual forces vying for eternal destinies. But we are not alone in our battle against powers and principalities and spiritual wickedness in high places (Eph. 6). The man dressed as both a priest and king—Jesus—fights for his people. So also does Michael, whom the man in linen says to Daniel is "your prince."

These last words may be more critical than their brevity indicates. The man in linen says, "None contends by my side against these [the princes of Persia and Greece] except Michael, your prince" (v. 21). If, as indicated earlier, the princes of Persia and Greece are evil spiritual forces supporting the pagan rulers of those empires, then Michael is the spiritual entity identified as Israel's special advocate (i.e., "your prince"). The fact that no other "prince" of any other nation is allied with Christ at this point in redemptive history underscores the special nature of Israel in God's plan. No other nation was fulfilling God's holy purposes for the world. As messed up as Israel was, it was still the nation by which all the nations of the world would be blessed. God was still being faithful to his covenant with Abraham to make his people the path of blessing for the entire world. Despite all of Israel's sins and failures, God would still bring the Messiah through Israel, and Michael will fight to make it so.

Thus, in the great battle of redemptive history where Satan and his forces seek to prevent and destroy the Seed of the woman who will crush the serpent's head, Michael contends alongside our Lord for the sake of Israel's future and ours. The good news is that Michael is a pretty good fighter. He is identified later for Daniel as "the great prince who has charge of your people" (12:1) and who eternally delivers everyone whose name is in God's book. In the New Testament, Jude tells us that Michael even contended for the body of Moses (Jude 9). The apostle John adds in the book of Revelation that Michael is the leader of the heavenly hosts that will cast Satan out of heaven for his final demise (Rev. 12:7). All of this discussion raises many questions in our minds, but the idea meant to stick is that when Michael is on our side, the forces of evil don't stand a chance. The reason this idea is so important to Daniel is made clear in the final two words of the chapter. There the man in linen tells Daniel that Michael is "your prince" (v. 21). This is information Daniel will need if he is to have peace in the face of the world conflicts his vision will reveal in the remaining chapters of this book.

The Lord charges his great warrior angel Michael with the defense of Daniel's people and the protection of Abraham's covenant. Despite the sentiment and superstition we attach to guardian angels, we should not minimize the peace the revelation of this commission to Michael is intended to provide. The psalmist intended for us to take comfort from God's personal promise to "command his angels concerning you to guard you in all your ways" (Ps. 91:11). The angelic promise in Daniel is far broader. It sweeps across empires and eons with the assurance that our God will use his heavenly host to preserve our eternity against the evil more great, powerful, and pervasive than we dare imagine. In the face of coming earthly trials, this is a promise Daniel needed in order to have peace, and it is a revelation we must still treasure to maintain peace in our hearts amid the constant trials of our day.

The three touches that enable Daniel to stand, open his heart, and have peace ultimately grant him the ability to fulfill his prophetic purposes despite the conflicts of body and spirit that weaken him. The revelation of those touches is meant to do the same for us. These touches are precursors of the truths and effects of the gospel meant to grant us peace and strength in this fallen world until the consummation of all things. In this present age, our God does not promise us the absence of trouble, but he does promise his presence, his love, and the fulfillment of his purposes—so we can be at peace and fulfill his purposes.

Such peace and power became lifelines beyond human expectation or expression for the family described at the beginning of this chapter, when they continued to minister to their Vietnam-era warrior. Earlier I described how my friend listened from her bedroom as her father took the phone call of fear, frustration, and rage from his son who was engaged in a war that seemed so futile. The long, listening silence would be broken only as her dad responded with those few words repeated in the pauses his son allowed, "I love you, David. I love you, David. I love you, David."

Those words in the darkness of the night, across thousands of miles to a battlefield in Vietnam, were sent to touch a heart with love so that it might find peace, and through peace find the strength to face another day. My friend, for whom the words were not meant, but who listened, said the words touched her and became the gospel to her own heart for many years to come. She believed in a God who, like her father, would speak to those in a battle-weary world with words as simple as, "Yes, it's true, and it's awful, but I love you, and I will redeem you from it all so that you can have peace to face it today with strength for my purposes."

That touch of the gospel became all the more important to my friend's family when her brother, years after his time in Vietnam and soon after he had come to faith in Jesus Christ, was murdered. The battle for souls was not over. The family experienced things such as Daniel had foreseen—great pain, great heartache, inexplicable sorrow. How would they handle it? My friend said they handled it with the reminder that the God who taught her father to say "I love you" to a hurting son was still loving them, had battled for the soul of her brother, and had saved his soul for eternity. In the midst of great pain, they found peace—and with peace the strength to live for God's purposes. They now pray for the salvation of her brother's murderer.

Those who belong to Christ and want to live for and serve him must know that there are great battles ahead. But we can face them with the reminder of a gospel that allows us to stand before God despite our sin, allows us to open our hearts to confess our inadequacy, and grants us peace in the midst of battles both physical and spiritual so that we will have the strength to fulfill his purposes.

11

An Uncivil War:
North and South

In the first six chapters of Daniel, we saw that accounts often considered to focus on his biography actually reveal a message of God's grace to his people. The latter half of the book contains visions often considered only in terms of their amazing prophetic content. But these passages also reveal a gospel intent that can be obscured by our debates about particular prophetic interpretations. This chapter of Daniel is the middle of three chapters containing one vision. The vision is divided into three chapters because it is long, complex, and the culmination of the book. This one set of predictions covers the developments of human history across empires and eons, from Daniel's time to the final victory of the Messiah long in the future. In their captivity, the Jews longed for this Deliverer. We should long for him, too, because the victory he brings will rescue not only them from their spiritual and earthly oppressors but also us from ours as well. Here Daniel continues the vision begun in chapter 10 with descriptions of a great war between northern and southern empires that will usher in the greater victory of the Messiah:

"And as for me, in the first year of Darius the Mede, I stood up to confirm and strengthen him.

"And now I will show you the truth. Behold, three more kings shall arise in Persia, and a fourth shall be far richer than all of them. And when he has become strong through his riches, he shall stir up all against the kingdom of Greece. Then a mighty king shall arise, who shall rule with great dominion and do as he wills. And as soon as he has arisen, his kingdom shall be broken and divided toward the four winds of heaven, but not to his posterity, nor according to the authority with which he ruled, for his kingdom shall be plucked up and go to others besides these.

"Then the king of the south shall be strong, but one of his princes shall be stronger than he and shall rule, and his authority shall be a great authority. After some years they shall make an alliance, and the daughter of the king of the south shall come to the king of the north to make an agreement. But she shall not retain the strength of her arm, and he and his arm shall not endure, but she shall be given up, and her attendants, he who fathered her, and he who supported her in those times.

"And from a branch from her roots one shall arise in his place. He shall come against the army and enter the fortress of the king of the north, and he shall deal with them and shall prevail. He shall also carry off to Egypt their gods with their metal images and their precious vessels of silver and gold, and for some years he shall refrain from attacking the king of the north. Then the latter shall come into the realm of the king of the south but shall return to his own land.

"His sons shall wage war and assemble a multitude of great forces, which shall keep coming and overflow and pass through, and again shall carry the war as far as his fortress. Then the king of the south, moved with rage, shall come out and fight against the king of the north. And he shall raise a great multitude, but it shall be given into his hand. And when the multitude is taken away, his heart shall be exalted, and he shall cast down tens of thousands, but he shall not prevail. For the king of the north shall again raise a multitude, greater than the first. And after some years he shall come on with a great army and abundant supplies.

"In those times many shall rise against the king of the south, and the violent among your own people shall lift themselves up in order to fulfill the vision, but they shall fail. Then the king of the north shall come and throw up siegeworks and take a well-fortified city. And the forces of the south shall not stand, or even his best troops, for there shall be no strength to stand. But he who comes against him shall do as he wills, and none shall stand before him. And he shall stand in the glorious land, with destruction in his hand. He shall set his face to come with the strength of his whole kingdom, and he shall bring terms of an agreement and perform them. He shall give him the daughter of women to destroy the kingdom, but it shall not stand or be to his advantage. Afterward he shall turn his face to the coastlands and shall capture many of them, but a commander shall put an end to his insolence. Indeed, he shall turn his insolence back upon him. Then he shall turn his face back toward the fortresses of his own land, but he shall stumble and fall, and shall not be found.

"Then shall arise in his place one who shall send an exactor of tribute for the glory of the kingdom. But within a few days he shall be broken, neither in anger nor in battle. In his place shall arise a contemptible person to whom royal majesty has not been given. He shall come in without warning and obtain the kingdom by flatteries. Armies shall be utterly swept away before him and broken, even the prince of the covenant. And from the time that an alliance is made with him he shall act deceitfully, and he shall become strong with a small people. Without warning he shall come into the richest parts of the province, and he shall do what neither his fathers nor his fathers' fathers have done, scattering among them plunder, spoil, and goods. He shall devise plans against strongholds, but only for a time. And he shall stir up his power and his heart against the king of the south with a great army. And the king of the south shall wage war with an exceedingly great and mighty army, but he shall not stand, for plots shall be devised against him. Even those who eat his food shall break him. His army shall be swept away, and many shall fall down slain. And as for the two kings, their hearts shall be bent on doing evil. They shall speak lies at the same table, but to no avail, for the end is yet to be at the time appointed. And he shall return to his land with great wealth, but his heart shall be set against the holy covenant. And he shall work his will and return to his own land.

"At the time appointed he shall return and come into the south, but it shall not be this time as it was before. For ships of Kittim shall come against him, and he shall be afraid and withdraw, and shall turn back and be enraged and take action against the holy covenant. He shall turn back and pay attention to those who forsake the holy covenant. Forces from him shall appear and profane the temple and fortress, and shall take away the regular burnt offering. And they shall set up the abomination that makes desolate. He shall seduce with flattery those who violate the covenant, but the people who know their God shall stand firm and take action. And the wise among the people shall make many understand, though for some days they shall stumble by sword and flame, by captivity and plunder. When they stumble, they shall receive a little help. And many shall join themselves to them with flattery, and some of the wise shall stumble, so that they may be refined, purified, and made white, until the time of the end, for it still awaits the appointed time.

"And the king shall do as he wills. He shall exalt himself and magnify himself above every god, and shall speak astonishing things against the God of gods. He shall prosper till the indignation is accomplished; for what is decreed shall be done. He shall pay no attention to the gods of his fathers, or to the one beloved by women. He shall not pay attention to any other god, for he shall magnify himself above all. He shall honor the god of fortresses instead of these. A god whom his fathers did not know he shall honor with gold and silver, with precious stones and costly gifts. He shall deal with the strongest fortresses with the help of a foreign god. Those who acknowledge him he shall load with honor. He shall make them rulers over many and shall divide the land for a price.

"At the time of the end, the king of the south shall attack him, but the king of the north shall rush upon him like a whirlwind, with chariots and horsemen, and with many ships. And he shall come into countries and shall overflow and pass through. He shall come into the glorious land. And tens of thousands shall fall, but these shall be delivered out of his hand: Edom and Moab and the main part of the Ammonites. He shall stretch out his hand against the countries, and the land of Egypt shall not escape. He shall become ruler of the treasures of gold and of silver, and all the precious things of Egypt, and the Libyans and the Cushites shall follow in his train. But news from the east and the north shall alarm him, and he shall go out with great fury to destroy and devote many to destruction. And he shall pitch his palatial tents between the sea and the glorious holy mountain. Yet he shall come to his end, with none to help him." (Dan. 11:1–45)

A friend of mine once went camping in a rugged and lush area along the Columbia River in Washington State. He arrived after dark and set up his tent, intending to settle in for some welcome sleep after an exhausting drive. But during the night, intense winds and rain developed, whipping his tent and threatening to rip it from its pegs. Yet for a while he feared that was not the worst of his problems. With the wind and rain came the pounding of a deep thunder—not occasional but constant—indeed, too constant to be thunder, but whatever it was seemed no less powerful.

The thunderous pounding had a resonance and force that shook the ground. In the dark, he could not tell what the earthquaking noise was. Earthquakes are not common there, so what was that powerful sound? Mud sliding? Rocks colliding? Buildings collapsing? Trees breaking? What was the storm doing? How close was the danger? In a flimsy tent being pelted by the rain, every new crash was cause for fresh fear. There was no peace of mind and no sleep for the body that night.

Not until daybreak did my friend know the cause of the thundering that had given him such fright. Great trees, many feet in diameter, had broken from the moorings of the lumber company that was floating them down-river to a lumber mill. The trees crashing into one another were making the earthshaking thunder that had caused such fright. All it took was my friend's ability to see by the light of day for him to know that the trees—for all their power and ability to cause terror in the night—were bounded by the shores of the river. Their great power had clear limits, and knowing that enabled him to have some sleep the next night. The thunder that shook the night still came, but knowing its cause and its limits gave my friend the peace he needed to rest.

Chapter 11 is the continuance of a vision that interrupted Daniel's sleep in chapter 10. In the previous chapter a man in white linen comes to Daniel to assure him of God's care before a long night of war comes. As the vision unfolds, the man in white linen (who truly is the Lord Jesus in an early appearance, a Christophany) tells Daniel of thunder that will come in the form of great nations clashing with one another in and around Israel.

Daniel's people are already starting to return to Israel from their exile in Babylon. The great battles Daniel predicts will be so intense and long that the people of God will doubt if God really knows or cares about the trials that thunder upon them. They will wonder in the night of so many swords' loud clashing whether they and the promises of God will survive. So God graciously reveals to Israel, its future generations, and us what will happen before the night of these wars is over, so that all may find peace despite the clashing events about them. God does not promise the absence of thunder nor that the ground will not shake, but he does declare that he knows the cause of the terror in the night and cares enough to establish its limits.

There may not be a more critical message for our age so dominated by the false teaching that God's will for his people is always a life without difficulty or trial or pain. But we should not think that Daniel's correction is merely for prosperity preachers, because in our times of trial we can easily adopt their theology. We too may ask, "If God is for us, then why do we have to go through this difficulty or disappointment or pain?" It is only human to be frightened by thunder in the night and to wonder if God really knows and cares about what we are experiencing. So Christ speaks to us in the light of this vision of Daniel telling some of us before our night comes, and some of us while the night is already upon us, not only of the greatest terrors we can imagine but also of his knowledge and care so that we can find peace.

Knowing That God Knows

Rather than ignoring or minimizing the harsh realities of Israel's future from the time of captivity to the coming of Christ, the Lord reveals to Daniel a great deal of darkness. How does that help? It is somewhat like a child reporting to a parent, "Jimmy's brother says that our school is closing," and having the parent reply, "I know." The parent's knowledge does not remove the child's reasons for concern about loss of friends and familiar surroundings, but it calms the child just to know that the parent, who has greater ability and capacity to handle difficult things, knows. The Lord does not remove the cause for concern Daniel reveals, but the One who has sovereign ability and capacity to handle difficult things says, "I know," and that helps.

God Knows the Big Picture

The Lord demonstrates his knowledge of the big picture in the predictions of what will happen between the major empires of the ancient world. After the king of Persia lets the Israelites return to their homeland, three kings will come, with a fourth rising to prominence (v. 2). That fourth king will stir up his kingdom against Greece. From biblical and secular histories we know this to be Xerxes. Then another king will arise who will be even greater (v. 3), but he will soon be broken and his empire will be divided in four portions, but not among his posterity (v. 4). These predictions (vv. 3 and 4) parallel the life of Alexander the Great, who conquered much, died young, and had his empire divided among his four generals. Daniel then predicts that one of these generals will grow great in power in the south and another ruler will grow strong in the north (vv. 5–6). We know these to be early predictions of the rise to power of the Ptolemy rulers in Egypt (the south) and the Seleucid rulers in Syria (the north). Most of the rest of this chapter (as well as the rest of the book of Daniel) is about various alliances and wars between these ancient superpowers.

The key ideas about these empires are expressed in these early verses, which state that kings shall "arise" (v. 2), "become strong" (v. 2), and "shall be broken" (v. 4). These very words (or some form of them) occur over and over again in this chapter as the Lord establishes a pattern for all earthly kingdoms—they arise, become strong, and shall be broken—a pattern that is quite different from the final kingdom predicted, the kingdom of our Lord.

Of course, if the Lord cares only about the big picture, individuals could fear that they would get lost or used in the grand schemes of empires and kingdoms. So with the sweeping revelations of eons and empires, the Lord also reveals his attention to particulars.

God Knows the Details

One commentator on this passage says plainly, "Nowhere else in the Bible is prediction as specific and detailed as here."[1] The details are so specific that some biblical critics, who recognize that these predictions square with very specific and minute facts also recorded in secular histories, presume that this "prophecy" must have been written after the fact and that there was some convention of fictional authorship accepted in ancient literature (formulating hindsight as foresight). But this assumption would undercut the larger purpose of these prophesies: revelation of God's foreknowledge so that we—knowing that he knows the future—can sleep at night and find rest in days of darkness.[2]

These very specific prophecies include a prediction of an event in which the ruler of Egypt recovers the metal images of gods with their sacred treasures and returns them to the south before agreeing to a peace with the north (v. 8)—just as the secular histories record.[3] Daniel says that a northern king will try to arrange a peace by trying to get his daughter to marry a southern king, but it doesn't work (v. 17). The secular histories tell us that at the same time a Syrian king tried to get his daughter, Cleopatra (not the famous one from Egypt), to seduce the boy king of Egypt (ten years old) so that the north could control the south through her. It did not work (as Daniel predicted) because she fell in love with the boy and turned against her father.

Most importantly, Daniel predicts the culminating ruler of all this north-and-south intrigue (v. 21). He is called "a contemptible person" who shall obtain his kingdom "by flatteries." Predictions of much intrigue and many power plays follow, but the details most important to Israel also follow. This "contemptible person" will "profane the temple," "take away the regular burnt offering," and "set up the abomination that makes desolate" (v. 31). By both timing and action we know who this is. We have seen him before in Daniel 7 and 8. This is Antiochus Epiphanes, who invaded Israel, profaned the temple by putting a statue of Zeus in the holy of holies, took away the regular burnt offerings, put a pig on the altar, and with these abominations made Israel desolate not only by defeating the men in battle but also by killing every circumcised infant—hanging the babies outside their families' homes. This horrible ruler gave himself the name Epiphanes, meaning "God made manifest," and nothing could have been more contemptible to Israel than to so address him.

God Knows the Big, Big Picture

Daniel predicts horror! Generations will subsist and suffer amid dark waves of war between nations that have no concern for the covenant yet envelop the covenant people in their conflicts. But that is not the end of the horror story. Something strange and wonderful seems to start happening around verse 36 with what seems a fairly generic reference: "And the king shall do as he wills." What king is this? The discussion of the contemptible person seems to expand. Antiochus Epiphanes is still in the foreground, but a more distant vision of someone similar begins to enter the prophecy, as though a modern camera lens that has been focused on someone in the foreground begins to zoom to someone in the background. And for a brief moment, as the foreground picture dissolves, we see features of both images until the background picture is in focus.

The sense that we are zooming away from a specific prediction of Antiochus Epiphanes occurs in the remaining part of chapter 11, which describes facts not historically applicable to this original Seleucid ruler. For example, verse 42 seems to say that this future king will defeat Egypt, but in one of the most colorful accounts of ancient history, Antiochus was blocked from his intentions to conquer the land of pyramids. When Antiochus went to invade Egypt, Rome was securing its power and did not want him to gain access to Egypt's resources. A Roman general met Antiochus in the desert, drew a circle around him, and said, "Decide if you are going to go forward or backward before you leave the circle. Because if you go forward into Egypt, then Rome will be your enemy."[4] Antiochus went backward and did not conquer Egypt.

Another reason Antiochus seems not to be the subject of this part of the prophecy is that verse 45 speaks of this future king pitching his palatial tents between the sea and the holy mountain (Jerusalem) where he meets his end. This description of someone meeting his demise in an area between mountain and sea could well be the plain of Armageddon and does not describe the place or nature of Antiochus's death as other historians and the Bible do (cf. 8:25). Apparently Antiochus was east of Israel in Persia or Indian territories when he died of some stomach distress (worms, ulcers, or poison).[5]

If we look forward in the vision to the opening two verses of chapter 12, the matters that most seem to move us away from the era of Antiochus Epiphanes are the descriptions of what happens surrounding this "contemptible" ruler's death. In these verses, we learn that "at that time shall arise Michael" to fight for his people, "everyone whose name shall be found written in the book" shall be delivered (v. 1), and "many of those who sleep in the dust of the earth shall awake" (v. 2). There is going to be a judgment based on whose names are found in a book, and this will be followed by a resurrection. These prophecies definitely do not seem to be about Antiochus Epiphanes anymore!

The culminating prophesies in chapter 12 (which are the continuation of Daniel's vision in chaps. 10 and 11) seem to be describing the rise to power of a "contemptible person" prior to a great tribulation of God's people that is yet future to Antiochus. That is how Jesus also interprets this portion of the book of Daniel when he speaks to his disciples (in the Olivet Discourse just before his crucifixion), saying, "So when you see the abomination of desolation spoken of by the prophet Daniel, standing in the holy place . . . flee to the mountains" (Matt. 24:15–16). In Jesus's only reference to the book of Daniel, he looks forward to the abomination predicted, not backward to Antiochus's profaning of the temple.

From the details that ultimately emerge in Daniel's vision, and from Jesus's use of those details, we come to understand that the evil of Antiochus Epiphanes, though past, models evil to come. Thus Paul speaks of the coming of a contemptible "man of lawlessness . . . proclaiming himself to be God" with echoes of Daniel's description of Antiochus (2 Thess. 2:3–4). Finally, the apostle John in the book of Revelation speaks of the coming beast who will "utter blasphemies against God," "make war on the saints," and seduce "everyone whose name has not been written before the foundation of the world in the book of life of the Lamb" (Rev. 13:5–8)—all occurring before Babylon (rebuilt and repopulated by Antiochus Epiphanes) is destroyed (Rev. 17–18) and the faithful are resurrected to everlasting life (Rev. 20).

What I am suggesting, because of the way these various Bible passages treat these events and persons from Daniel's vision, is that Antiochus Epiphanes is a lens by which we are able to see and understand great evil that persecutes, profanes, and seduces. Antiochus becomes a prototype of all that is "antichrist" to show us the pattern or the "spirit of the antichrist" (cf. 1 John 2:18; 4:3) in every age that will culminate in greatest evil before the end of all ages.

Now the question that must be asked is, why does God reveal such things to Daniel and to us? The answer is in the idea with which we began: it helps to know that God knows. He is not blind to or surprised by the big, big picture; neither is he oblivious to its details. Imagine how this awareness of God's knowledge served the generations in and after Daniel's lifetime. They had to face much heartache before the Son of God would come to rescue them. Isaiah described them as living in "deep darkness" before the light of their salvation would come (Isa. 9:2). Surely in that great darkness they would wonder what all the thunder in the night was about, and not only whether they could make it through but whether God was even aware of their plight. Surely it was of great comfort to them to remember Daniel's specific predictions, when inexplicable things happened such as the ruler of Egypt recovering metal idols from Babylon by marching through Israel. As bad as the event was, it would be of great comfort to consider, "This is just what God said would happen. We still are on the road that God planned."

When my family traveled out west one year, we decided to meet one of my son's friends at the Garden of the Gods in Colorado Springs. It is a big park with lots of amazing stone formations, and we were supposed to meet the friend at the visitors' center. We wondered how to get there. The park ranger at the gate said, "Turn right at the Kissing Camels. You'll know it when you see it." We did not know exactly what we were looking for but started on the way. After a couple of miles, we saw the rocks high on a cliff that were unmistakable. They looked like two camels kissing. Until that moment we were not quite sure what we were looking for or that we were going the right way, but as soon as our experience confirmed the sign that the ranger gave, we knew that he knew what he was talking about, and we knew we were where we should be. We still had a ways to go, but we knew we were on the right path because we could confirm that the ranger knew what we needed to know.

These prophecies in their scope and detail did not take away all of Israel's concerns, but they confirmed that God knew what was happening, and because God's people knew that he knew, they were able to keep going. As they faced all the battles and trials, they must have wondered, "Does God know what's going on here?" And then they would pass one of the kissing camels of history and say to each other, "God knows." These prophecies are meant to work similarly for us. We now know the pattern of what opposes God—the spirit of the antichrist in our age and in the future. At the culmination of all things, the persecution of the just, the profaning of the holy, and the seduction of the weak will occur and should not surprise us. In fact, when we face such things, we know that we are on a path described by God and walked by his people in previous ages. We keep walking because we know from these descriptions that God knows what we are facing.

As a generation we do not talk about eschatology except in the most general terms for two reasons: our biblical literacy is not as great as that of our fathers, and decades of eschatological arguments about minutiae frustrate and repel our sense of how the church should talk and act. But, despite our apprehensions, we should not avoid these subjects entirely. The prophecies of the past and the future are recorded to comfort and strengthen the church in difficult times. When God's people are denied all discussion of eschatology, the church loses its nerve.[6] The prophesies give us confidence that God knows where we are going. If we do not recognize the signs of his prior knowledge, then we will be much less willing to walk the dark and difficult paths that may be necessary for us and for the church.

The missionaries who left for Africa in the nineteenth century with their belongings packed in coffins believed they were being called to hardship and death. Still, they went because they believed that persecution and sacrifice were the marks of the faithful not the faithless. Unlike the prosperity preachers of our day who promise peace and affluence in this age, these men and women who knew the scope of Scripture's promises believed that only the end of the ages promised ultimate reward—and they understood by Daniel's prophesies the nature of the path they were on until that day. They would be challenged by persecution, the profaning of their beliefs, and the seduction of the weak—but this was to be expected on the path to the consummation. The trials marked the correctness of their path, and they were strengthened by the knowledge that God had revealed the path to them.

The same is true of the husband or wife who endures in a troubled marriage with no apparent reward in this life. The same is true of our brothers and sisters who are being martyred in Darfur, and of the pastor who serves unnoticed in a small church while enduring accusation from the immoral, inconsiderate, and ungodly. If we think that today is all that is known to God and that tomorrow is hidden from him, then we cannot go forward with strength and courage and sacrifice. Knowing that God knows is what we need to keep going as he desires. More than once I have endured in ministry by thinking, "God knows," when others have attacked, thought me foolish, or thought my motives ungodly; and, though all the world hate, ridicule, and view me with suspicion, I can walk this path because I know that God knows it. In all the difficulty that Daniel predicts for his people through God's revelation, he provides at least this assurance: God knows what we are facing.

But there is further blessing in Daniel's predictions than the mere fact that God knows what we are facing. God's people also gain peace in the midst of darkness by knowing that he cares.

Knowing That God Cares

What is the evidence that God cares despite all of the horror that awaits Israel—and us?

God Cares Enough to Warn

The prophecies are not only about general events on the world stage; at specific points they also indicate how those events will envelop Israel. Verse 14 tells of a rebellion against Egypt (the king of the south) by militant Jews that will fail. Verse 16 tells of a conquest from Syria (the king of the north) that will succeed against weak Jews. Verses 29–31 tell of Antiochus Epiphanes's rage against Israel when he was turned back from his intention to invade Egypt. In that rage, eighty thousand in Israel were slaughtered. Verses 40–41 tell of armies of the north and south clashing in the "glorious land," with tens of thousands of the covenant people being killed.

These prophetic pictures are horrible, but a clear message also emerges: if God did not care, he would not warn. The warnings help all anticipate and the faithful endure with the understanding that "this is what God said would happen; we are not beyond his knowledge or care."

Daniel's prophecies are like the word of a surgeon before an operation. He does not promise that there will be no pain but rather warns of what we will experience so that we can call upon the resources of heart and mind that we need to endure.

God Cares Enough to Limit

God's care is evident not only in his warning of the horror but also in his limitation of it. Key phrases are threaded through the predictions to remind us that a sovereign hand has never been removed from the events that are unfolding. God is not a passive bystander of what he knows will occur. Instead, we read in verse 27 that two kings shall try to deceive each other but to no avail, for their end will still occur "at the time appointed." In verse 29, "at the time appointed" Antiochus Epiphanes will try to invade Egypt (the south) but will withdraw in fear before coming back to Israel in a rage. Verse 35 records that the persecutions of Antiochus will be so great that even some of the wise will stumble on the path to being purified until "the time of the end, for it [i.e., the end] still awaits the appointed time." Verse 36 describes the king that will prosper despite his blasphemy and arrogance, "for what is decreed shall be done."

Horrible things are prophesied, but they are never beyond God's appointment and ultimate control. The great logs of empires are clashing in the river of human history, but somehow they have been kept within the shores of God's purpose. All may seem chaotic, but things are happening "at the time appointed" and "for what is decreed." Evil forces may appear to be driving world events, but there is a hidden hand yet orchestrating their "end." We have to ask why, and the location of all of these events in redemptive history helps to explain.

It may seem a bit odd or even inappropriate that so much of Daniel's prophecy focuses on Antiochus Epiphanes, who, despite his great cruelty to Israel, was not the greatest of ancient rulers. Alexander the Great of Greece was far more powerful and successful. Antiochus Epiphanes (who is actually Antiochus IV) was not even the greatest of the Antiochuses of Syria. But he was the most cruel and the last great invader of Israel prior to Roman rule. And it is the sequence of events that follows Rome's actions that tell us where we are in redemptive history and why this figure is so important.

In C. S. Lewis's *The Lion, the Witch and the Wardrobe*, there is a scene in which the lion-ruler Aslan gives himself to rescue the people and land of Narnia. The forces of evil gather to mock, cackle, and howl. They believe they have won; they have mustered all their power and intrigue to defeat the only one who can defeat them, and they seem to have succeeded. But something—or rather, Someone—beyond their scheming is at work. Soon Aslan will be on the move again.[7]

To Satan and his warriors, what would it appear had happened through the horrors of Antiochus Epiphanes that Daniel has predicted? The Davidic king long promised to Israel seems to have no chance. The kingdom has been whittled down by its own idolatry and division. Enemy nations repeatedly trample across the covenant land and slaughter its people and their children. There is no power, king, or hope left in Israel. Satan and his minions must howl in glee—except for what is said in the opening words of the next chapter: "At that time [when cruelty has reached its apex and all hopes are dashed] shall arise Michael" (Dan. 12:1).

From the beginning of chapter 11, we have seen how the pattern of the persecutions that come upon Israel (and climax in Antiochus Epiphanes) is repeated: a ruler shall arise, grow strong, and be broken. But as the next chapter begins, we read of this Michael "who has charge of your [Daniel's] people": he shall "arise" and "your people shall be delivered" and shall have "everlasting life" (12:1–2). Michael will arise and grow strong enough to deliver God's people, *but* he is not broken; instead, the power of sin and death is broken. The cycle of rule and destruction is broken by the reign of our Lord.

More attention to these prophecies is given in chapter 12, but the essential message should be clear already: Aslan is on the move again. The darkness has never been complete; evil has never had the final word; hope has never fully vanished. Why? Because God cares enough not only to warn and to limit but also to save.

God Cares Enough to Save

God's intention has always been to save. How do we know? The beginning of chapter 11 in most of our translations begins at a peculiar place. The first verse is actually the second half of a statement of the man in white linen who is speaking in Daniel's vision. At the end of chapter 10 the man in white linen says that no one is willing to contend with him against the forces of evil "except Michael, your prince." Then curious words start the next chapter, and they are the continuation of that same statement that no one has stood by the Lord except Michael, your prince. These are the words that continue: "And as for me, in the first year of Darius the Mede, I stood up to confirm and strengthen him" (Dan. 11:1). These are *not* Daniel's words about his support of Darius but rather are the Lord's words about his support of Michael, Israel's angelic defender who will ultimately fight for the people of God. That great warrior receives his strength and authority from the Lord himself, who is our Savior. From the beginning, the Lord's intention has been to save his people.

Before all the prophecies are given of the horror that could drive all hope away, the Lord has said that he will confirm and strengthen our defender. All is being done according to a plan and a purpose. Why is it this way? We cannot say with certainty why every detail happens as it does. But we can say this: when all other hopes are dashed, then the one hope that remains becomes the Rock to which we will cling. By all the prophecies of the horror to come, God is pointing the covenant people in all ages to the hope that must extend beyond this world—and does. Our Savior, who gives strength to our deliverer, is the hope that does not die.

When we know a God who knows, who cares enough to warn, limit, and save, we can face our darkness, endure, and never lose hope—because we know this world is not the end. Our hope is everlasting because the God who knows and cares limits the evil in this world so that we will have the eternal blessings of the next through the salvation of his Son.

I could not help but think of how these eschatological truths affect our lives when I received an email from a friend recently. The email described the experience of Connie Eller, a Christian mother in urban St. Louis who has given her life to proclaiming the gospel and protecting the unborn. Recently a "stray" bullet came through the window on her front door. Connie writes, "Running and hiding somewhere won't help." Despite the fact that little children are playing outside, up and down the block, "stray bullets happen . . . [here]." But the danger to her own children is not the only darkness she faces with courage.

The email described Connie's zeal for a documentary called *Maafa 21: Black Genocide in the 21st Century*. The video details the decimation of African-American culture through poverty-motivated abortions. When poverty makes people doubt they can care for their children, a sad alternative is to eliminate the children before they are born. Connie is bold enough to speak of this evil consequence of abortion in her own community. In one week, she spoke in five church services, repeating the message that abortion is destroying the future of black America by wiping out its babies—and in that same week a bullet came through her window threatening her own family.

Consider all the darkness and horror that she faces: poverty, racism, the ethnic genocide of the infants of her race, bullets endangering her own family. How does she respond as a Christian to this apparent failure of God to rescue her in these moments? She writes, "I am not afraid. . . . God is good."

> Had I been doing laundry as usual [at the time the bullet came] I would have been in the hallway [where the bullet came] . . . I want to encourage you not to quit, not to give up, not to cower in fear at whatever God has appointed for you to do.
>
> These past few weeks [of fighting for the children of my race] have been great experiences for me. These have been God-awesome days, and so now Satan the loser wants . . . to take it all away.
>
> But God has something good for each of us . . . and we must not get discouraged or frightened.
>
> Do whatever God has given you—appointed for you—to do this day. . . . Don't waste time. Time is short. Get over the anger that you may have at God. This is just a distraction from his love for you. Jesus Christ won the victory on the cross. . . . God is still on this throne. . . . It ain't over until the angels sing.

I do not know if Michael sings well, but I know that he fights very well. Supported with the strength of our Lord, he will prevail and the angels will sing. Thus, even if we face a darkness like Connie's or something worse, we can endure and fulfill God's purposes for our lives.

Though the darkness may come and evil may thunder, God wants us to know that he knows what we face and the trials will not advance beyond their appointed time or limits. Our God still cares and will save. Though Satan's power may arise and strengthen with vicious schemes that drive us to our knees, his reign ultimately will be broken to reveal that there is no hope save in the God who saves eternally. We can endure in the darkness because we know the end of the story and know that the day will dawn when the glory of the Lord shall be revealed, and we will be his forever despite whatever happens now. So though we face persecution, the profaning of what we hold holy, and the seduction of people we considered holy, our hope need not fade because our God will save eternally. That is the end of the story. And because we know the story's end, the charge of Scripture is clear: "Be steadfast, immovable, always abounding in the work of the Lord, knowing that in the Lord your labor is not in vain" (1 Cor. 15:58). The story is not done, but the ending is already written. Our God will save. So we must stand for him.

12

The End(s)

— DANIEL 12 —

At Christmas we sing, "The people living in darkness have seen a great light." Clothed in the sentiment of the season, we may forget how dark that darkness could be for ancient Israel. The book of Daniel reminds us. The prophet's visions caused him to mourn, grow ill, and not eat for weeks. His visions revealed that the nation would live under war for generations, the temple would be defiled, the people would be killed by the thousands, an abomination of desolation would come, and the righteous could only be delivered by supernatural means. But the man in white linen, who began to give this final vision to Daniel in chapter 10, now tells the end of the story in Daniel 12:

"At that time shall arise Michael, the great prince who has charge of your people. And there shall be a time of trouble, such as never has been since there was a nation till that time. But at that time your people shall be delivered, everyone whose name shall be found written in the book. And many of those who sleep in the dust of the earth shall awake, some to everlasting life, and some to shame and everlasting contempt. And those who are wise shall shine like the brightness of the sky above; and those who turn many to righteousness, like the stars forever and ever. But you, Daniel, shut up the words and seal the book, until the time of the end. Many shall run to and fro, and knowledge shall increase."

Then I, Daniel, looked, and behold, two others stood, one on this bank of the stream and one on that bank of the stream. And someone said to the man clothed in linen, who was above the waters of the stream, "How long shall it be till the end of these wonders?" And I heard the man clothed in linen, who was above the waters of the stream; he raised his right hand and his left hand toward heaven and swore by him who lives forever that it would be for a time, times, and half a time, and that when the shattering of the power of the holy people comes to an end all these things would be finished. I heard, but I did not understand. Then I said, "O my lord, what shall be the outcome of these things?" He said, "Go your way, Daniel, for the words are shut up and sealed until the time of the end. Many shall purify themselves and make themselves white and be refined, but the wicked shall act wickedly. And none of the wicked shall understand, but those who are wise shall understand. And from the time that the regular burnt offering is taken away and the abomination that makes desolate is set up, there shall be 1,290 days. Blessed is he who waits and arrives at the 1,335 days. But go your way till the end. And you shall rest and shall stand in your allotted place at the end of the days." (Dan. 12:1–13)

For many years our family gathered for our annual reunion at a recreational village in Hardy, Arkansas. We were always looking for new family activities and one year decided on a canoe trip. My wife and five-year-old daughter were in a canoe with me, and we were about third in a line of canoes going down the river as we approached a set of rapids. Without warning, we watched in horror as the first canoe one hundred yards ahead of us disappeared. It was there on the river, and then suddenly it was not there. It was as though the river had just swallowed it. Then the second canoe ahead of us vanished from sight. We had trouble believing our eyes, but we also had trouble resisting the current that was now pushing us through that same set of rapids toward the same spot where the other canoes had vanished.

It was time for action. I shouted to my canoe mates, "Paddle!" My wife shouted, "Pray!" I shouted back, "Pray hard, but paddle fast!" The one who did not get that message was my five-year-old, who was so panicked by the rough water and the vision of the apparent end of the world ahead of us that she simply closed her eyes and screamed. She was so terrified that she became my bigger worry. I knew that somehow I had to break through her fears. So I shouted to her above the roar of the water that was overwhelming her, "Cori, look at me. Cori, look at me." When she finally did look at me, she stopped screaming because she saw that I was standing in the water, holding the canoe steady. The water was only about a foot deep.

What had caused our panic was a rock shelf that ran the width of the river with a sheer drop of about four feet before connecting to a safe and restful section of river just beyond the rapids. When I stood up in the water, I could see that the family members ahead were drenched from the drop but safe on the other side, and with that knowledge we made it over the drop with a lot less fear, even though we got a little wet, too.

Daniel sees a couple of rivers in his vision. One river is the river of history flowing into the future across many troubled waters. It worries and overwhelms him, because in his vision he sees the river swallow his people in swirls of war and pain. In response, the Lord, envisioned as the man in white linen who has already revealed what will happen at the end of the world, appears again, as if to say, "Look at me." But he does not stand in the water to show it is shallow. Instead, he stands above the waters of the stream to show that he is great—his power and purposes cannot be swept away.

Understanding this powerful image is important if Daniel is to follow the last imperative of this chapter: "Go your way [in life and ministry], Daniel" (v. 9). The image is also important for us who, like him, must navigate the troubled waters of life and ministry, especially when it appears those waters have swallowed friends and peers ahead of us—and when the resulting fear can panic us or turn us from God's way. Like Daniel, we know that there can be darkness ahead. But through Daniel, the Lord provides the vision we need to make it to the other side of life and ministry without the kind of fear that would keep us from either paddling or praying.

The Lord reveals no less future horror in this final chapter than he has in the chapters that have preceded, but he also stands above the river of history to reveal what he will provide in the future to enable us to go our way both enduring and participating in his purposes.

Rescue from Distress

To understand what is ahead, we must remember what we have been told in the previous portions of this vision. Daniel has already prophesied that generations will be enveloped in the wars between the kings of the north and the south, culminating in the rise of one who will mercilessly persecute God's people and profane the temple with an abomination of desolation. Then that evil one, whom we believe is Antiochus Epiphanes, becomes a lens through which we are allowed to glimpse the spirit of the antichrist before the consummation of all things. "At that time," the man in white linen tells Daniel, "shall arise Michael, the great prince who has charge of your people. And there shall be a time of trouble, such as never has been since there was a nation [of Israel]" (v. 1).

We know these first words of this final chapter of Daniel are about the consummation of all things because of the words that follow: "But at that

time [though there has been this time of great trouble] your people shall be
delivered, everyone whose name shall be found written in the book. And many
of those who sleep in the dust of the earth shall awake, some to everlasting
life, and some to shame and everlasting contempt" (vv. 1c and 2).

No passage of Scripture is sweeter for God's people than this. The gospel
truths being revealed were a lifeline of hope to Daniel and are intended to be
the same for us. We should remember that when Daniel receives these words,
he is over ninety years old, being left behind as others are returning to Jerusalem, and now knows that generations will face the cruelties of war. If this
vision contains hope for one in as desperate a condition as he faced, then
all who want to face life's trials without despair will also long to know the
content of this prophecy.

Resurrection

The vision reveals that those who sleep in the dust of the earth shall awake,
and those whose names are written in the book shall awake to everlasting life
(vv. 1c and 2a). This current physical life is not the end. Suffering and death
do not have the final victory. No truth is dearer to God's people than this.

Not too long ago, we spent many hours at home with my wife's dying father.
He died on Christmas day. As awful as that sounds, there were wonderfully
sweet moments leading up to that time. Kathy's family is very musical, and
the children's last days with their father were often spent singing around the
bed. Because it was Christmastime, carols were the frequent choice. We were
surprised at how words about Christ's birth so often rang with fresh poignancy
as our family faced the realities of death:

> From depths of hell thy people save;
> and give them victory over the grave . . .
>
> Disperse the gloomy clouds of night;
> and death's dark shadows put to flight . . .
>
> O come, thou Key of David, come,
> and open wide our heavenly home;
> make safe the way that leads on high;
> and close the path to misery.
>
>   "O Come, O Come, Emmanuel"[1]

The message is simple: Because of Christ's death and resurrection on our behalf, this life and its misery are not our final chapter. "Everyone whose name
shall be found written in the book" (v. 1d) will be saved from the pains of this

life and from death itself. We shall see them again and shall be with them in the presence of the Savior.

Judgment

But though the promise of resurrection is for all, the destiny of all who are resurrected is not the same. Some shall awake to "everlasting life" (the only time this phrase is used in the Old Testament) and others to "shame and everlasting contempt" (v. 2).

We sing in the Christmas hymn "To Us a Child of Hope is Born" these important words: "Justice shall guard his throne above."[2] There will be a differentiation between those who are in the book of life and those who are not. Judgment is real. For those who have suffered at the hands of the wicked, the good news is that God will make things right, vindicate his people, and punish evil. Our God is just and ultimately judges. The scales will be balanced in and for eternity.

Always at Christmastime we are to be sobered with the realization that the glories of the Christmas season are not simply for sentiment and sales. We celebrate the Child in the manger, but we are also declaring the coming of One who will come again to judge the world. For those of us who preach and teach God's Word, this passage is also a sober reminder that we must not trifle. Our efforts are not just about making people feel good now or about avoiding suffering. Heaven and hell hang in the balance for souls. Nothing we can do is more important than making sure that we and others understand the eternal consequences of following or not following the Lord who comes. God has given us a vital and eternally important task in communicating the truth about his coming to others. This is what our carols say:

> Hark, the herald, angels sing,
> "Glory to the newborn king."
> > "Hark! the Herald
> > Angels Sing"[3]

> For the herald's voice is crying
> in the desert far and near,
> Bidding all men to repentance,
> since the kingdom now is here.
> O that warning cry obey!
> Now prepare for God a way.
> > "Comfort, Comfort
> > Ye My People"[4]

Glory

Following this judgment is "everlasting life" (v. 2). Though the concept has appeared earlier, this is the first use of this term in the Bible. The context also makes it clear that the idea is not simply about length of life with our Deliverer but also about our quality of life with him. Those who are raised to everlasting life "shall shine like the brightness of the sky above; and those who turn many to righteousness, like the stars forever and ever" (v. 3).

The book of Revelation, which picks up so many of the images of Daniel, says that the One who comes to deliver us is the bright Morning Star (Rev. 22:16). Since those he saves are also described by Daniel as being like stars, we understand more of what the apostle John means when he says, "When he [i.e., the returning Jesus] appears we shall be like him" (1 John 3:2). We shall be "like the stars forever and ever" (v. 3). Everlasting life is not endless boredom but endless glory.

I recently wrote of the importance of these truths for my developmentally disabled brother, who has the mind of a seven- or eight-year-old. He is imprisoned in mind as a consequence of birth complications beyond his control; he is imprisoned in body as a consequence of crimes he committed before his conversion to Christ. In reflection upon his circumstances, I wrote these words with tears of joy streaming down my face:

> One day Christ will come and renew the earth that he originally made so good (Rom. 8:21–23). All the benefits that humanity originally enjoyed in Eden will be restored: a world full of God's provision and absent of pain (Rev. 21:4). Not only will the creation be restored, we also will be renewed in spirit, body, and mind (1 Cor. 15:52–54). Not only will my imprisoned brother know God's full forgiveness, his body will be pure again, and his mind will be healthy and whole for the first time in his entire existence. My brother will be more glorious than the angels (1 John 3:2–3). He will walk about freely in the new creation with his head up, his eyes bright, and his heart rejoicing in the beauty that surrounds him. My family, those who have already departed and those yet to enter heaven, will have a reunion with him and all those who love Jesus (1 Thess. 4:14–18). We will feast at Christ's table, sing of his goodness, and forever delight in a world made perfect by the grace of our God. The One who came to save sinners provides a salvation so grand that it involves the whole earth, our whole being, and eternity (Rev. 21:1).[5]

Our Christmas carols wonderfully reflect these eternal promises as well:

> He comes to make his blessings flow,
> far as the curse is found.
>
> "Joy to the World"[6]

> Thou comest in the darksome night
> to make us children of the light,
> To make us, in the realms divine,
> like thine own angels round thee shine.
>   "All Praise to Thee, Eternal Lord"[7]

Whatever sadness we are experiencing here is not the end of the story. Glory awaits those whom Daniel describes as "wise," and it is important to note that the term here does not mean "smart." It means "prudent," aligning one's choices, casting one's lot with—or giving one's life in allegiance to—the coming King (cf. 11:33). So much does it please our Lord that his people identify with him that he specifically commends those who "turn many to righteousness" (v. 3c). The words should be both a joy and a challenge to us. Those who cast their lot with Jesus, making him their life's choice, will know glory; and those who turn many to know this glory are the stars of the new heavens. I do not know exactly what that means. I do know it is a good thing. And I know that those who are not facing judgment because of our witness to them will agree.

The Lord tells Daniel to shut up these words he has written and seal the book (v. 4a). The words are not about hiding this vision (after all, the message was written for Israel and passed to us) but indicate that God does not want his revelation to be tampered with, and that he has authorized these words with the testimony of Daniel who will seal the matter. This revelation is of a rescue not complete, but the revelation is sure.

The next words are a bit cryptic: "Many shall run to and fro, and knowledge shall increase" (v. 4b). Are these words set in contrast to Daniel's vision, meaning many will fruitlessly run to and fro seeking to increase knowledge, or does it mean that as people run to and fro, living the story Daniel has envisioned, their knowledge of his meaning will increase? I think it is probably the former, but the clear matter God wants to communicate is that he has authorized what Daniel has written for the ages to come.

Sure Rescue, but Incomplete

One important thing to observe before progressing further into Daniel's vision of the end is this: the rescue is not complete in this life. Our rescue is sure but not complete now.

Daniel will remain in captivity. He will age. He will know pain in the present and grief for the future. He will not see Israel's glory restored. His people will not have a great revival under his ministry. Their enemies will not be conquered in his lifetime. His fondest dreams for this life will go unfulfilled. Glory is not yet, but it is sufficient to keep him faithful in the present.

The implications of glory that is sure but incomplete came to mind while I was meeting with a friend whose best years of ministry (in earthly perspective) are behind him. Despite great acclaim about his potential and despite great opportunities in his youth, he has faced immense opposition in successive ministries without apparent resolution or triumph. He said to me, "All my dreams have died. All that I hoped to accomplish, all I hoped to see, all I hoped to hear—barring some great miracle—will not happen in this life. I have only one dream left: to be faithful to God's calling."

It is possible that God will call us to the service of an Isaiah or a Jeremiah, faithful prophets in a time when the people of God would not listen. What kept them faithful—and keeps this minister friend of mine faithful—is not rescue that is complete in this life but the rescue from all trials and disappointments that is promised to the faithful in eternity. Eternity is meant to outweigh the temporal. As the apostle Paul (who also experienced little rescue here in this life) said, "For I consider that the sufferings of this present time are not worth comparing with the glory that is to be revealed to us" (Rom. 8:18).

Wondrous beyond Understanding

These truths about our ultimate rescue from the brokenness of our world and from ourselves are so wonderful that the man in white linen reappears to confirm them with his presence (v. 5). Then an angel on one side of the river of history asks an obvious question: "How long shall it be till the end of these wonders?" (v. 6). The meaning of the answer is not nearly so obvious. The Lord raises both hands in a magnified sign of an oath (instead of the traditional raising of one hand) and swears by himself—because there is none greater by which to swear (cf. Heb. 6:13). The oath means that the truths revealed are sure, guaranteed by the integrity of God. But what exactly is promised? It is not clear precisely what is asked. Does the question mean how long until these ending wonders occur, or does it mean how long these ending events will last? The commentators vary. But that debate is child's play compared to the debate over the answer the Lord gives.

Perhaps I can help a little in answering these questions. In this book my intention has not been to unravel all the mysteries of the book of Daniel. There are better exegetes than I who have attempted that task and, somehow, the matters still get debated. My intention has not been to further debate but to reveal the indisputable gospel truths in Daniel that unite us and that enable our faithfulness through the events the prophet predicted. Even Daniel did not understand all that the visions meant, and he knew that, in part, their mysteries would be explained only as world events unfolded (e.g., 8:27; 12:8). The Lord is careful not to allow his people to abandon the duties of today by focusing on predictions of the future but rather to strengthen them for today by seeing his promises fulfilled as their trials are endured.

Having explained my intention, let us address the questions. How long will it be till the end of these wonders? The question most naturally relates to what the Lord has just revealed: the time of resurrection, judgment, and everlasting life. Since everlasting life is endless, the question does not relate to how long that period is but rather when it begins. The Lord's answer is "it would be for a time, times, and half a time." Most commentators agree this is probably a reference to one year, years, and half a year (thus, probably three and half years, though there is some conjecture even in this).

Are the three and a half years literal or analogous? The most popular dispensational theologians, believing that they are holding to a "strictly literal" interpretation, will say these three and a half years are literal. Traditional dispensationalists will say that a seven-year tribulation (the last of the seventy weeks of years foreseen in Dan. 9:27) will precede a thousand-year period (Rev. 20:1–6) during which time Christ will reign on the throne of David (Luke 1:32). During this time of tribulation, there will be three and a half years of world peace under an antichrist figure (Dan. 7:8; Rev. 13:1–8), followed by three and a half years of greater suffering (Dan. 12:7; Rev. 6–18). At the end of this period, Christ will return and establish his eternal kingdom (Matt. 24:27–31; Rev. 19:11–21).

Of course, even in this interpretation the weeks are not "literally" weeks but years—and the beasts of Daniel are not "literally" beasts but nations (Dan. 7–8), the horns of the beasts are not "literally" horns but rulers (7:7–8, 11; 8:6–10), and the starry hosts are not "literally" stars but people (8:10; 12:3). Every interpretation must admit that Daniel intends to reveal literal events by speaking in visions that have symbols that we must interpret. I think that is what is also happening with regard to the three and a half weeks.

Wondrous for Understanding

In the book of Daniel, periods of judgment that accomplish God's perfect purposes appear as multiples of seven. For his pride and arrogance, Nebuchadnezzar was made like a beast for "seven periods of time" (4:25). The destitution of the exiles of Israel from the time of their captivity until they have a new prince is seven weeks (or periods of time; 9:25). The total time of Israel's destitution to their consolation will be seventy weeks (or periods of time; 9:24–27). And the period of Israel's exile that Daniel was experiencing and was prophesied by Jeremiah was seventy years (Dan. 9:2; cf. Jer. 25:11).

But now when an angel asks the Lord how long will be the troubled time (cf. 12:1 and 2:6) that leads to the fulfillment of all things, the Lord responds not with seven periods of time but with three and a half periods of time (v. 7b); and that time would only finish "when the shattering of the power of the holy people comes to an end" (v. 7c). The end of the troubled time will come after the shattering of God's people, and the troubled time seems only to be half the story that is completed at the consummation of all things.

If we were to put ourselves in the place of Daniel listening to this conversation, we would think, "Wait, if that distant trouble is only half the judgment, then the other half must come earlier—in the time my people are 'shattered.'" We would have some questions, and indeed Daniel is the next to ask a question. He acknowledges, "I heard, but did not understand," and asks, "O my lord, what shall be the outcome of these things?" (v. 8). This is not quite the same question as the one previously asked by an angel about when all this would happen. The four Hebrew words of Daniel are simply, "Lord, what purpose these?" Lord, why all this?

Wouldn't we ask the same if we had just been told that our people would be caught in wars for generations, that great trouble was ahead, and, though that trouble would be followed by wonderful deliverance, the trouble would shatter our people—and apparently this was just half the story of what would need to be endured? We might ask what could be the purpose of these things, too. And that is what is addressed in the remainder of the chapter. The first seven verses are about rescue from distress by the end of all things, and the last six verses are about the purpose of distress that is the end God intends for Daniel's people.

The Reasons for the Distress

The Wise Refined

The Lord first answers Daniel's question (v. 8) by saying, "Go your way, Daniel, for the words are shut up and sealed until the time of the end" (v. 9). The simple interpretation is, "Just go about your business Daniel. I am not giving more details about this now. The matter is closed and sealed until the end actually occurs."

Though the matter is closed, understanding will be opened. The Lord says that "those who are wise shall understand" (v. 10c) and as a consequence "shall purify themselves and make themselves white and be refined" (v. 10a).

The focus is on the faithful being purified through the fires of suffering, but the wonderful gospel truth is that, as their allegiances are refined, the wise are made white—pure before God.

Two observations can be made from this description of the wise being refined by suffering. First, in their weakness is their rescue. When they are shattered, their Rescuer comes (see vv. 7 and 10). Neither their rescue nor ours is in our own strength. And by suffering, the ends of our strength are known. In suffering, the wise learn the necessity of casting their lot with their Lord, by whom they are made white and refined. Theirs is the faithful identification; his is the cleansing and refining so that they gleam with his righteousness. Brokenness leads to righteousness. As we sing at Christmastime:

> Yea, [our] sins our God will pardon,
> blotting out each dark misdeed;
> All that well deserved his anger,
> he no more will see or heed.
>   "Comfort, Comfort Ye My People"[8]

The second observation regarding the refinement of the wise is this: suffering is not absent from the life of God's covenant people. We live in a real world. But as we endure faithfully, we more and more treasure the wonder and the goodness of the resurrection life our Savior promises. Our claim on that ultimate treasure enables us to live with current deprivations and disappointments. Those without understanding are dismayed by suffering; those that are dishonest deny our suffering; those with wisdom understand that suffering teaches us how wonderful the God who will deliver us eternally from all of this difficulty truly is.

One November I learned this lesson from reading my daughter-in-law's blog after my son had an unexpected and long hospital stay due to complications from chronic Crohn's disease. His wife chronicled throughout his hospital stay and ended with these words, in an entry titled "In All Things Give Thanks":

> Praise God that Jordan is home!
> Praise God that he is feeling (and looking!) much better!
> So much to be thankful for! Considering the past couple weeks. . . .

> At times we can be so far removed from struggle and fall into satisfaction with life as it is now . . . it can take small setbacks (or unexpected surgery) that make us LONG for restoration . . . make us long to be eternally removed from pain and brokenness. Our lives are always broken—our minds know this—but rarely do we FEEL the brokenness. God has been good to us as he has encouraged us

and provided mental and emotional strength to walk through this . . . through life! We are thankful for his provision!

Enjoy your Thanksgiving . . . in all things, give thanks!

Until we are with him, our God does not promise an end to trouble. He says instead, "Those who are wise will understand," and "Many shall purify themselves and be made white and be refined."

The Wicked Defined

In contrast, troubles define the wicked, who "shall act wickedly," and "none . . . shall understand" (v. 10b). We know that in the generations that followed Daniel, many of his own people, who would only live for the moment and not take his visions of eternity into account, would betray their nation, reengage in idolatry, and ultimately turn their Savior over to his enemies to be crucified. Trouble flushes out the wicked, just as surely as it refines the wise.

The temporary gains of the wicked can trouble the wise, who see it happen and wonder why God does not stop the evil sooner. Perhaps it is to further encourage the wise that the Lord gives the final words of prophecy that define the time allotted to the wicked. He says, "And from the time that the regular burnt offering is taken away and the abomination that makes desolate is set up, there shall be 1,290 days." Suddenly we are back in a prophecy Daniel has already given. The abomination of desolation is the reference to Antiochus Epiphanes profaning of the temple prior to the coming of Christ. While Jesus uses the phrase to refer to the activities of the antichrist, Daniel's previous use as it relates to "regular burnt offering" being "taken away" most naturally fits the cruel reign of the Syrian ruler of ancient times. What is this all about?

Again, I am unwilling to be dogmatic about my understanding here. Much is obscure to the best exegetes. That being said, the judgment about which the angel asks and which leads to the end-time is only half of the expected time for judgments (i.e., three and a half years instead of seven). Now we are told that there will be another judgment period that extends from the time that regular sacrifices are taken away until the abomination that causes desolation (such as when Antiochus Epiphanes put a statue of Zeus in the temple).

It seems that when God answered the angel about the end-time, the Lord zoomed to the end of time to describe the tribulation to come, but when Daniel asked, "Why these things?" God returns nearer to Daniel's time and says there will be another 1,290 days (or approximately three and a half years) of tribulation then. There will be great trouble at the end of all things, but there will also be much trouble in the lives of God's people prior to that time. Now in the text the days are not literal but representative of half of God's judgment. It takes both of the times of trouble (i.e., that of Antiochus Epiphanes and that of the antichrist) to fill up the judgment that will fulfill God's purposes.

In essence, the ancient people will have to face tribulation, as will the future people of God, because all live in a world where God's enemies resist his purposes. The Lord raises both hands above the river of history to say that there is judgment past and judgment future. Why? So that the people of God will live for him in all times.

The Faithful Deployed

Ultimately the purposes of the vision are not simply to inform us or to warn the wicked. The visions are to ignite the faithful in God's purposes. There is an additional promise made to God's people through Daniel with this intended effect. The Lord says, "Blessed is he who waits and arrives at the 1,335 days" (v. 12)—that is, just a little longer (forty-five days, a month and a half), after the period of judgment. I have not found a single commentator who will dare to speak with certainty about what this period of time represents. Does this extra promise represent the coming of the Holy Spirit to those who remain faithful after the crucifixion? Or does it somehow symbolize the coming of the church age after Christ's resurrection? Or does it represent the coming of Christ after Antiochus Epiphanes, or the coming of Antiochus's death after the abomination he caused? Many explanations have been offered, but the common thread among them is the understanding that God promises his blessing in his time to those who are faithful through their trials. This has been the ultimate purpose of all of Daniel's revelations. God intends for the prophet's visions to give people confidence in the present through the revelations of God's hand upon the future.

The ultimate meaning is found in the Lord's parting words to Daniel: "Go your way till the end. And you shall rest and shall stand in your allotted place at the end of the days" (v. 13). The Lord has told Daniel "Go your way" earlier (v. 9), but that seemed to be in order to quiet him. The words have a different character this time. Now these are words of encouragement and enabling. It is as if the Lord is saying, "Go on, Daniel. Live your life. Do not worry about the present. Do not let present trial overwhelm your faith or your labor. You shall rest and stand at the allotted place at the end of all things. I have prepared a resting place for you."

Such words from Scripture have strengthened the saints though the ages. Through such promises the Lord makes his intentions plain and powerful: "Though you struggle here, and all the world hate, abandon, or persecute you,

I have prepared for you a resting place. At the last day, you shall stand with all the saints beside your Lord and above the angels to judge the wicked, rule the earth, and rest in the Savior. I have told you what will come in times past and in times to come. Knowing all of this, go your way. Live a life of hope. Labor in the certainty of my love. Work well now for your eternal rest is already won."

> And our eyes at last shall see him,
> through his own redeeming blood;
> For that child so dear and gentle
> is our Lord in heaven above,
> And he leads his children on
> to the place where he has gone.
>   "Once in David's Royal City"[9]

We do not know all that will happen until that final day, but we know that our end is sure, glorious, and blessed. We shall be at rest in the place allotted for us. So certain are we of that day that we can know the beauty of living this day by the seat of our pants. We can glory in faithful, bold, courageous decisions in the face of uncertainty because the end is so certain and good. God has it all mapped. He is never panicked. There are no emergency meetings in heaven. Our God says to us, "Go your way. Live your life in the fullness of my service, because you know that I know the end."

We resonate with Daniel in this generation because we are more like him than we may know. Generations before us here in the United States were a faith majority in a predominantly Christian culture. Politics, social practices, and church emphases were based on the assumption that most people in the culture shared a Christian perspective. We do not have that assumption now. Christians live with the sense of being a minority, needing to make our own way, and needing to make a way for the church in the face of opposition, without respect and without expectation of success. This was Daniel's world, and yet he lived faithfully because he had seen God's design for generations near and far. As a consequence, Daniel knew that God's plan for all time was sufficient reason for faithfulness in his time. So when God said "Go your way" with confidence in heaven's care and an eternal plan for you, Daniel was blessed with boldness for God's purposes though they were beyond what he could see or fully comprehend.

A few years ago, I was listening to one of those radio stations that play all Christmas music all the time during that season. A woman called in to request "Joy to the World" and then told the story behind her choice of that song that includes the phrase "He comes to make his blessings known." She said that when she was a little girl, her family received a monthly magazine written by the children of missionaries. Each told a story about their experiences, and the woman said that the children of her family prayed each month for the child who wrote the story they liked the best.

One month a story in the magazine was accompanied by a picture of the boy who wrote it. The picture showed the boy with a monkey, and because the children reading it thought that it would be neat to have a monkey as a pet, that was their favorite story of the month, and they prayed for the boy. For some reason, the idea of the monkey stuck with them. They kept praying for the boy after that month. In fact, the little girl—now the mature woman on the phone—continued to pray for him for years, whenever the image of the boy with the monkey came to mind.

Years later, when this little girl was a mature woman, her mother died, and the family needed to clean out their old home place. Sorting through boxes, the former children, now adults, came across the missionary magazine with the picture of the boy with the monkey. And the little girl now grown was surprised when her husband of seventeen years said, "Don't throw that out, that's my magazine."

"What are you talking about?" she asked. He replied, "When my parents were missionaries, I wrote a story for that magazine and they put my picture with it—that picture of me with my pet monkey." The little girl, now a mature woman and wife of seventeen years, said that she then screamed and cried and laughed and hugged her husband and gave thanks to God for planning her life so carefully and for making "his blessings known" to her.

We know, of course, that in those seventeen years of the couple's marriage there certainly had been times of pain, trial, and distress. But now this couple has no doubts that God has been orchestrating a perfect plan for their lives because of what he has shown them of his design from the past. Undoubtedly there will be more distress in the future, but we know that they will also boldly "go their way" into the future with confidence, courage, and joy because of the blessed plan God has made known to them. The sign of God's design in the past gives them confidence to live for him and each other in the future—and today.

God has done something even better for us. He has made known to us the blessings of his amazing design of past events and revealed his wondrous provision of future glory so that we can go our way with confidence, courage, and joy. He will rescue his people from distress with resurrection, through judgment, and for glory. His faithfulness through the distress will refine the wise, define the wicked, and deploy the faithful. This is always his way. For though it appeared that evil had won when Daniel's nation was made captive, when the temple was profaned, when the Savior was born in destitution, and when he hung on a cross, nonetheless it was always God's plan to orchestrate these events so that his Son would rescue us and "make his blessings known far as the curse is found."[10] He has come and will come to save, and he has shown us the grand design—past and future—so that we can go our way and live for him today and tomorrow with confidence, courage, and joy.[11]

Notes

Introduction

1. E.g., *English Standard Version Study Bible* (Wheaton: Crossway Bibles, 2008); *New International Version Spirit of the Reformation Study Bible* (Grand Rapids: Zondervan, 2003); for commentary discussions see Joyce G. Baldwin, *Daniel: An Introduction and Commentary*, Tyndale Old Testament Commentary Series (Leicester, UK: Inter-Varsity Press, 1978), 17–46. N.b.: many scholars, including some evangelicals, propose a later date for the book of Daniel. For a helpful overview of varying views see Sinclair B. Ferguson, "Daniel," in *New Bible Commentary*, 21st century ed., ed. D. A. Carson and R. T. France (Downers Grove, IL: InterVarsity Press, 1994), 746–47.

Chapter 3 Faith in the Furnace

1. Samuel Rodigast, "Whatever My God Ordains Is Right," in *The Trinity Hymnal* (Philadelphia: Great Commission Publications, 1990), no. 108.

2. Kay Oliver, ". . . And Why Is She Smiling?," *Moody Monthly*, June 1979, 18.

3. Edith Schaeffer, *Affliction: A Compassionate Look at the Reality of Pain and Suffering* (Grand Rapids: Baker, 1993), 27.

Chapter 4 Me with You

1. "Ozymandias," in *The Complete Poetry of Percy Bysshe Shelley*, ed. Donald H. Reiman, Neil Fraistat, and Nora Crook (Baltimore: The Johns Hopkins University Press, 2012), 3:325.

2. G. Edwards, "The World according to Ben," *St. Louis Business Journal*, December 8, 2008.

3. George Barna, "Evangelicals Are the Most Generous Givers, But Fewer than 10 Percent of Born Again Christians Give 10 Percent to Their Church," news release by Barna Research Group, April 5, 2000, as quoted by Generous Giving, accessed February 1, 2013, http://library.generousgiving.org/page.asp?sec=4&page=161.

4. Rob Moll, "Scrooge Lives," *Christianity Today*, http://www.christianitytoday.com/ct/2008/december/10.24.html?start=2.

5. Ibid.

6. Fanny Crosby, "To God Be the Glory," in *The Trinity Hymnal* (Philadelphia: Great Commission Publications, 1990), no. 55.

Chapter 5 Loving Enough to Warn

1. US Centers for Disease Control, "Sexual Behavior, Sexual Attraction, and Sexual Identity in the United States: Data from the 2006–2008 National Survey of Family Growth," *National Health Statistics Reports*, No. 36 (Hyattsville, MD: National Center for Health Statistics, 2011), 23.

2. The poem, by Alfred Noyes, can be found at http://www.poets.org/viewmedia.php /prmMID/16431.

3. Thomas Kelly, "Stricken, Smitten and Afflicted," in *The Trinity Hymnal* (Philadelphia: Great Commission Publications, 1990), no. 257.

Chapter 6 The Song of a Broom

1. Adapted from Elisabeth Elliot, *On Asking God Why: Reflections on Trusting God* (Grand Rapids: Revell, 2006), 157–58.

2. Eugene Peterson, *A Long Obedience in the Same Direction: Discipleship in an Instant Society* (Downers Grove, IL: InterVarsity, 1980).

3. Martin Luther, "A Mighty Fortress," in *The Trinity Hymnal* (Philadelphia: Great Commission Publications, 1990), no. 92.

4. Larry B. Stammer, "A Prelate of Evangelical Intensity," *Los Angeles Times*, September 5, 2004.

5. As cited by John Woodbridge, "10 Great Truths from Revivals for Preachers Today" (sermon preached at Preaching Before the Face of God Conference, Sydney Missionary and Bible College, Sydney, Australia, 2009). See also Kenneth J. Collins, *A Real Christian: The Life of John Wesley* (Nashville: Abingdon, 1999), 82.

Chapter 7 The Big Picture

1. Dawson Trotman, *The Need of the Hour*, NavClassics (Colorado Springs: NavPress, 2008), 21; available at http://www.navigators.org/us/ministries/college/navfusion/assets /NeedoftheHour.pdf.

Chapter 8 When the Big Rocks Fall

1. Rick Warren, *The Purpose Driven Life* (Grand Rapids: Zondervan, 2002).

2. Peggy Noonan, "Flannery O'Connor Country: The Amazing Story of How Ashley Smith Stopped Brian Nichols's Killing Spree," *The Wall Street Journal*, March 17, 2005, http://online.wsj.com/article/SB122470838006259761.html.

3. Tony Snow, "Cancer's Unexpected Blessings," *Christianity Today*, July 20, 2007, http://www.christianitytoday.com/ct/2007/july/25.30.html?paging=off.

4. Brit Hume, interview with Brian Lamb, *Q & A*, C-SPAN, July 9, 2008, http://www.q -and-a.org/Transcript/?ProgramID=1189.

Chapter 9 Entering Their Pain

1. See Martin Luther, *The Heidelberg Disputation*, nos. 20 and 28, accessed February 27, 2013, http://bookofconcord.org/heidelberg.php; and Robert Kolb, "Luther on the Theology of the Cross," in *The Pastoral Luther: Essays on Martin Luther's Practical Theology*, ed. Timothy J. Wengert (Grand Rapids: Eerdmans, 2009), 50.

2. Judith Howard Peterson, "Biography," Soultosole.cc, accessed February 26, 2013, http://www.soultosole.cc/content/BioPrint.pdf.

3. F. W. Farrar, *The Book of Daniel*, An Exposition of the Bible 4 (Hartford, CT: S. S. Scranton Co., 1907), 417.

Chapter 10 The Three-Touch Gospel

1. Cited in G. C. Berkouwer, "A Half Century of Theology," trans. and ed. Lewis B. Smedes (Grand Rapids: Eerdmans, 1977), 196.

2. Chapters 10–12 of Daniel are sections of a single prophetic vision.

3. "To go forward is nothing else than to start afresh again and again." Martin Luther, *Lectures on Romans*, trans. and ed. Wilhelm Pauck, Library of Christian Classics 15 (Philadelphia: Westminster, 1961), 91.

Chapter 11 An Uncivil War: North and South

1. Joyce G. Baldwin, *Daniel: An Introduction and Commentary*, Tyndale Old Testament Commentary Series (Leicester, UK: Inter-Varsity Press, 1978), 184.

2. For a helpful overview of these issues see Tremper Longman III and Ray Dillard, *Introduction to the Old Testament*, 2nd ed. (Grand Rapids: Zondervan, 2006), 373–75; and Baldwin, *Daniel*, 42–44, 183–85.

3. See Gleason Archer, "Daniel," in *The Expositor's Bible Commentary*, ed. Frank Gaebelein (Grand Rapids: Zondervan, 1985), 7:131; John E. Goldingay, *Daniel*, Word Biblical Commentary 30 (Dallas: Word, 1989), 296; and footnote to 11:7–9 in the *English Standard Version Study Bible* (Wheaton: Crossway, 2008), 1614. For additional insights into these historical references see Archer, "Daniel," 130–48; Goldingay, *Daniel*, 293–319; John J. Collins, *Daniel*, Hermeneia (Minneapolis: Fortress, 1994), 378 (n.b.: Collins has a very different understanding of the relationship of Daniel to history from the position I take here). Josephus (*Against Apion* 2.48) recounts that Ptolemy III Euergetes, king of the Ptolemaic Empire based in Egypt, conquered as far as Syria and then returned to Jerusalem to make sacrifices.

4. H. H. Austin, *The Hellenistic World from Alexander to Roman Conquest* (Cambridge: Cambridge University Press, 1981), 271–72.

5. Doron Mendels, "A Note on the Tradition of Antiochus IV's Death," *Israel Exploration Journal* 31, nos. 1–2 (1981): 53–56.

6. John Polkinghorne and Michael Welker, eds., *The End of the World and the Ends of God: Science and Theology on Eschatology* (Harrisburg, PA: Trinity Press International, 2000), 13.

7. C. S. Lewis, "The Triumph of the Witch," chap. 14 in *The Lion, the Witch and the Wardrobe* (New York: Collier Books, 1978), 142–52.

Chapter 12 The End(s)

1. Latin antiphons, twelfth century, "O Come, O Come, Emmanuel," in *The Trinity Hymnal* (Philadelphia: Great Commission Publications, 1990), no. 194.

2. John Morrison, "To Us a Child of Hope Is Born," in *Trinity Hymnal*, no. 233.

3. Charles Wesley, "Hark! the Herald Angels Sing," in *Trinity Hymnal*, no. 203.

4. Johannes Olearius, "Comfort, Comfort Ye My People," in *Trinity Hymnal*, no. 197.

5. Bryan Chapell, *What Is the Gospel?*, The Gospel Coalition Booklets (Wheaton: Crossway, 2011), 23–24.

6. Isaac Watts, "Joy to the World! The Lord Is Come," in *Trinity Hymnal*, no. 195.

7. Martin Luther, "All Praise to Thee, Eternal Lord," in *Trinity Hymnal*, no. 219.

8. Johannes Olearius, "Comfort, Comfort Ye My People," in *Trinity Hymnal*, no. 197.

9. Cecil Frances Alexander, "Once in Royal David's City," in *Trinity Hymnal*, no. 225.

10. Isaac Watts, "Joy to the World! The Lord Is Come," in *Trinity Hymnal*, no. 195.

11. I am a preacher who must regularly seek the wisdom and scholarship of those who have gone before me. Before concluding this volume, I want to acknowledge my gratitude to those I consulted in general (in addition to the specific citations above) in order that my own thoughts be well informed for the preaching and writing of the material: e.g., Gleason Archer Jr., "Daniel," in *Commentary on the Old Testament*, ed. C. F. Keil and F. Delitzsch, vol. 9, *Ezekiel, Daniel* (repr.; Grand Rapids: Eerdmans, 1976); Edward J. Young, "Daniel," in *The New Bible Commentary Revised*, ed. D. Guthrie and J. A. Motyer (Grand Rapids: Eerdmans, 1970); Rodney Stortz, *Daniel*, Preaching the Word (Wheaton: Crossway, 2004); G. Douglas Young, "Daniel," in *The Biblical Expositor*, ed. Carl F. H. Henry (New York: A. J. Holman, 1973); George G. Hackman, "The Book of Daniel," in *Old Testament Commentary*, ed. Herbert Alleman and Elmer Flack (Philadelphia: Muhlenberg, 1948).